STREETWISE®
BUSINESS PLANS
with CD

Create a Business Plan
to Supercharge Your Profits!

Michele Cagan, C.P.A.

Adams Media
Avon, Massachusetts

Published by Adams Media, an F+W Publications Company
57 Littlefield Street
Avon, MA 02322
www.adamsmedia.com

ISBN 10: 1-59337-620-0
ISBN 13: 978-1-59337-620-8

Printed in United States of America.

J I H G F E D C B A

Library of Congress Cataloging-in-Publication Data

Cagan, Michele.
  Streetwise business plans with CD / Michele Cagan.
    p. cm.
  ISBN 1-59337-620-0
  1. Business planning. I. Title. II. Title: Business plans with CD.

  HD30.28.C32 2006
  658.4'01--dc22

                          2006014733

This book is available at quantity discounts for bulk purchases.
For information, please call 1-800-289-0963.

CONTENTS

Introduction

I've worked with small business clients for over a decade. In some cases I've been along for the whole ride, from the idea stage through success to the eventual dissolution at the end. Most times, though, I've come in to help a floundering company find its legs and finally begin to have sustainable success. The common ingredient in all of the success stories was a business plan. I have never seen a business truly succeed without one, even if it was brought in late in the game.

No matter what industry you are in, no matter how long you've already been in business, your company will be able to reach a higher level of success when you have a solid business plan to follow. Every business runs into obstacles, and every business suffers setbacks. But when you consider these glitches before they happen, your company will be much more likely to weather them and quickly get back on track to being profitable.

That's how this book can help you. A thorough business plan takes you in a logical and analytical manner through all of the big problems your company is likely to face. In that, it helps you come up with solutions—sometimes even preventive measures—that you can implement should the issue arrive. A solid business plan also helps you capitalize on your company's strengths and minimize the impact of weaknesses. Most important, a good business plan maps out your company's success.

To map out your business plan, you won't find a better resource than the CD that accompanies this book. On it you'll find everything you need to create an impressive business plan, one that can help you acquire the necessary funding and start your business on the right foot. The CD will walk you step by step through your business plan, allowing you the flexibility to make changes on the fly. You'll find the forms and templates, and financial statements you need to create your own complete—and successful—business plan.

The business climate is more competitive than it has ever been. Starting and growing a business is hard, and turning a profit is even harder. Having a complete business plan puts your success in your hands, where it belongs. This book gives you all the tools you need to create that plan and to transform your dream into a profitable reality.

About the CD

Requirements: You must have previously purchased Microsoft® Word and Excel® in order to manipulate templates on the CD.

The enclosed CD will walk you step by step through the creation of a business plan. On it, you'll find two full sample business plans (one for a service-based business and one for a product-based business), along with Microsoft® Excel® templates and Microsoft® Word documents to help you create your own plan from scratch. The full sample business plans are presented as PDFs, which will open using Adobe® Reader® (a program that can be downloaded for free from *www.adobe.com*).

To Use the CD:
- **PC Users:** Insert CD into computer; program will launch automatically. If it does not, select the CD icon; then double-click on "index.html" to launch the program.
- **Mac Users:** Insert CD into computer; double-click the CD icon; then double-click on "index.html" to launch the program.

To Open the Downloadable Forms:
- **PC Users:** When you click the "Forms" option during relevant parts of the business plan creation process, you will see a list of the available templates on the left-hand side of your screen. The documents will open automatically when you click on them.
- **Mac Users:** When you click the "Forms" option during relevant parts of the business plan creation process, you will see a list of the available templates on the left-hand side of your screen. When you click on one, you will be directed to a separate window where the document you selected and its icon will be highlighted. Double-click that icon to launch the document.

Troubleshooting

If you receive a message indicating that, "there is no default application specified" to open a document, click "Choose Application," then choose "Enable: All Applications". Select the correct application for the document:

- Microsoft® Word for a document ending in ".doc"
- Microsoft® Excel for a document ending in ".xls"

If you are using a Mac and are directed to "right click", hold down the "control" key on the keyboard and click your mouse button once.

Microsoft® Word and Microsoft® Excel® are registered trademarks of Microsoft Corporation. Macintosh® is a registered trademark of Apple Computer, Inc. Adobe® Reader® is a registered trademark of Adobe Systems Incorporated.

CD created by Boston Logic Technology Partners.

1

The Basics of Business Planning

What Events Trigger the Need for a Plan?

When you think about what a business plan is for, your mind probably goes right to the bank and the process of applying for business financing, as that's the most common use for business plans. But if you're creating this valuable tool only as a part of a required financing packet, you're overlooking its most important function: planning.

Whether you're new to the world of entrepreneurship or a seasoned veteran, a properly crafted business plan can help solidify your vision. And when you're undertaking a new venture, or remaking an old one, a written strategy can help ensure its success. With that in mind, there are particular events (aside from trying to get money) that prompt the need for a full-blown business plan. They include the following:

- You plan to launch a new business.
- Your business has grown substantially.
- You want to expand your existing business into new markets.
- You want to add a new product or product line.
- You're thinking about buying a business.

Any of these circumstances calls for the creation of a business plan, but that doesn't mean you can't prepare one at any other time. If you've already started up a company without the benefit of a plan, for example, you can take a step back and construct one. Yes, business plans take a lot of time and energy to write—but the payoff is well worth the effort.

Planning to Launch a New Business

Launch plans, commonly known as start-up plans, have two main uses: one, to evaluate a new business idea for its success potential; and, two, to define a comprehensive strategy for implementing and running the company. Here you will run through all of the steps you will need to take your new company off paper and onto Main Street. If, after careful research and consideration, you learn that your concept probably won't succeed as is, you still have time to redraft—before you've put even more time and money into the enterprise.

A startup business plan typically starts with a concise narrative about what your company will do and what the main goals of your company will be. You'll talk about the products or services you plan to sell. You'll include information about the expected market for your offerings and why they will want to buy from your company. You'll throw in financial projections to show the plan readers (including yourself) what you believe the company is capable of doing. But the most important thing you will do in this plan is to introduce yourself and what you bring to the table.

▶▶ **Because a start-up business does not have a track record of its own, your experience and personal financial situation are crucial parts of the plan.** Your business plan readers will want to know that you have the requisite skills and knowledge to see your ideas through successfully, as well as adequate resources both to contribute financially to the start-up and to make it through initial lean times. They want to see that you will be shoring up your weak points in demonstrable ways; for example, if you are a chef with no management experience, your business plan might make it clear that you plan to partner up with or hire someone to run the business side of your restaurant.

If you have successfully started and run your own businesses in the past, flaunt that fact. Even if your prior companies are completely unrelated to the one you plan to launch now (for example, you've owned restaurants in the past and now you want to open a clothing store), your entrepreneurial success will be a substantial plus factor.

The Business Expansion Plan

Here, you've hit the ground running. Your existing company has already proven profitable, and now you're ready to take it in new directions. Whether you intend to simply expand to handle sustained market growth, to try to hit new markets to increase your revenue stream, or to introduce a new product (or products) that flow well with your existing line, you'll need a fleshed-out plan to make your company's future as successful as its past.

That upcoming success may depend partly on outside financing, and a full-blown business plan will be part of any deal. You already have a large part of the work done here. You have ongoing financial statements that show profitability and positive cash flow; you have an existing loyal customer base; you have standing relationships with vendors; and, at the very heart of things, you know how to run your business successfully.

The big work here comes in realistic projections, and that takes research. If you plan to move your company in new directions, you must first determine which directions make sense. If an area is already glutted with similar businesses, the chances of yours making a noticeable dent are less—unless you have a unique angle that the others have overlooked. The only way to figure that out is trolling through the data, learning more about the market and its resident customers, and proving (both to yourself and your cash suppliers) that your expansion plans have solid merit.

Buying an Existing Business

When you plan to purchase someone else's business, your plan will have a somewhat different presentation. Acquiring an existing company can be a shortcut to profitability because you're buying a known quantity with an established customer base. The business is already running, and (presumably) the vast majority of kinks have been ironed out.

These advantages can help a brand-new entrepreneur get settled into his role, like flying with a safety net. Those benefits roll over to making business plan creation a little easier. Financial statements already exist, and the current owner probably put together projections to show potential buyers. Though you'll reinvestigate and verify the assumptions behind his projections, it may be easier than starting with a blank page.

▶▶ **If you're new to entrepreneurship, you may want some outside professional advice before jumping into any kind of binding agreement.** The business plan you'll need to develop to get the funding to purchase the company will be part of your due diligence, but it helps to have an accountant or lawyer on your side during negotiations.

When you're putting your plan together, there are some very specific questions you'll need to address. For example, why does the seller want to get rid of a profitable business? You'll also need to prove that you have a thorough understanding of the business and the requisite knowledge and experience (even if it comes from partners or employees) to keep it flowing profitably. If inventory is involved, you'll need to verify its existence and market value. You'll also want to make sure that key employees and important customers will stick with this company, regardless of a change in ownership; if not, you'll need to make some very different assumptions regarding your projections.

A Blueprint Turns Your Idea into Profits

When you dream of opening or growing your own business, a big pile of profits is the light at the end of the hundred-hour-workweek tunnel. To reach that end, you need to know exactly where it is, approximately how long it takes to get there, and what obstacles you may encounter along the way. A business plan provides you with detailed instructions that can turn your inspirations into a moneymaking enterprise.

Whether or not you've put your plan on paper, you still have at least a general plan in mind. This plan, no matter how informal, guides the decisions you make for your business. Maybe you've thought about a price for your product, where you could advertise, or how much time you expect to put into your business. In fact, many entrepreneurs work just that way—keeping track of virtually everything in their heads without the need to write anything down.

When it comes to your business, though, the value of a written plan is unmatched. Its basic structure walks you through every aspect, every question mark, helping to make sure that you've considered every important factor and not overlooked anything significant. Some details may seem insignificant amid the excitement of actually getting started, but considering those seemingly minor points can increase your chances of success.

How, exactly, can a business plan help you to succeed? In the first place, it forces you to take a close look at the viability of your idea—not every great idea makes good business sense. It also sets a loose timeline for operations, and that helps you plan and coordinate more easily. The plan serves as a "what-if" sketch, allowing you to make backup plans should something turn out differently than you've expected. Plus, it gives you a benchmark to measure against, once operations are truly underway. And, finally, a written business plan acts like a résumé for your company, a tool for introducing your business to vendors, financiers, and even potential customers.

Evaluating the Pros and Cons

The most important function of your business plan is to evaluate your business idea—sort of a reality check to see if your dream can be easily translated into a profitable venture. Not only should the plan convince you that your business idea is feasible, but it should be able to assure outsiders—mainly people you want to lend you money or extend you credit—that your company can succeed.

As you follow the steps of developing a comprehensive business plan, you'll be forced to consider dozens of factors that all contribute to your business's profit potential. The effort you spend on creating a thorough plan can actually save you big money in the long run. By testing your assumptions before implementing them, you'll be able to assess which are realistic and which aren't. You'll also recognize potential threats before they strike, allowing you to take a proactive stance. You'll learn how to evaluate your options (different suppliers, credit terms for customers, and advertising opportunities, for example) and make well-informed choices. Most important, though, you'll be taking a realistic look at your chances of success, based on numbers and facts instead of excitement and emotion.

You already believe in your idea—that's what has you thinking about a business plan in the first place. But to translate that great idea into a successful business means looking at it through an impersonal eye. Creating a business plan forces you to take a skeptical look at your core idea. You will have to play your own devil's advocate, and seek those things that could make your plans fail. You'll have to come up with reasonable assumptions and expectations, even if those may point toward business failure. Finally, you'll need to envision every possible worst-case scenario and determine whether there's any real way to turn it around. It sounds like you're looking for ways to kill your dream, but the true goal here is to make sure your dream can work as a business. This is the best time to find out for sure—before you've poured your savings, your time and energy, and your future into something that won't turn a profit.

During this process, you'll learn exactly what it will take for your business to break even, how to realistically forecast profits and losses (keeping in mind that many fledgling companies incur losses before they start making profits), and which way the cash will flow. Yes, there's a lot of

Music Teacher for Hire

Sara Turner was the music teacher at Lincoln High. The kids loved her, she loved the kids . . . but she didn't love the bureaucracy and paperwork involved with the job. She decided to forego the next year's teaching contract and begin giving private lessons out of her home.

Sara figured that many of her existing students would come to her for lessons, and then word would gradually spread. Since she'd be teaching out of her own house, she thought there would be no extra expenses for her to pay. She toted up her monthly expenses and looked at her savings account. Based on those assumptions, she made up a lesson price and started spreading the word.

She opened her doors for business, and several kids signed up right away. She got a few referrals through them, but not enough. Advertising was more expensive than she'd counted on. New sheet music and other supplies were needed sooner than expected. Sara started dipping into her savings. Then another blow came: a music shop opened up in town, offering private lessons for lower fees. Sara couldn't meet that price, and many of her clients switched to the music shop for lessons. By the end of the season, Sara was teaching for the music shop.

Where did Sara go wrong? She counted on talent, friends, and luck to bring in business . . . and she didn't make a comprehensive plan. If she had, she would have realized the costs of advertising. She could have found out about the coming competition, and she would have learned about many business expenses she'd never known existed. Taking the time to develop a business plan could have prepared Sara for bumps, opened her eyes about cash flows, and helped her develop a lasting business.

math involved—but there are relatively simple formulas to fill in and easy worksheets to follow.

Learn What Your Dreams Will Really Cost

Even the simplest business idea comes with a price tag. The old adage is 100-percent true: You do have to spend money to make money. While creating your business plan, you'll discover what types of costs are involved in running your company, figure out how much equipment (or furniture, or vehicles) you will need to purchase, learn about some expenses common to every type of business, and consider your personal expenses (and how you plan to cover them). It will take some time and some research to come up with realistic budget numbers, but the effort you put in now will greatly help you during your start-up days.

Many novice entrepreneurs try to save money by doing everything themselves. While this seems like a good way to cut corners, it's not. In fact, it almost ensures that some tasks will be handled sloppily, while some are skipped and others overlooked; plus, you won't have the time or energy to devote yourself to those areas in which you do excel. The money guys know this, and they expect help to figure into your projected expense budget. It's better to ask for more money at the outset to cover everything you will truly need to get your business up and running smoothly than to underestimate the amount and be out of cash in a couple of months.

As you begin to put together your start-up budget, it helps to think of expenses in two distinct phases: the one-time costs of getting the company rolling, and the ongoing costs associated with the day-to-day running of a business.

Common Startup Costs

Startup costs are incurred before you can officially open your business and start bringing in revenue. These one-time-only expenditures usually include things like the following:

- Security deposits (for rentals or leases)
- Utility deposits (for phone, electricity, and water)
- Formation expenses (to set up your official business structure)
- Professional advising fees (like accounting, legal, and business insurance)
- Licenses and permits (including local, state, and federal, as required)
- Asset purchases (machinery, equipment, office furniture, display cases, computer system, etc.)
- Preopening personnel costs (all expenses associated with payroll)
- Preliminary promotional costs (such as Website setup, brochure design and first printing, "Grand Opening" banners and flags, and signs)

As you can see, your business will incur a lot of costs before the fact, and this is the place to sort them out. Do a little homework as you start listing these expenditures. Call around for printing prices, and shop for your major assets before you commit to buying anything. As you list each expenditure, think about why you need it and jot down an explanation (which you'll have on hand if anyone asks). ▸▸ **Lenders and investors care as much about the reasoning behind the numbers as the numbers themselves—if you can justify your budget, you are more likely to get what you are asking for.**

Standard Ongoing Expenses

Your company's expense budget largely depends on the type of company you have. For example, a bookkeeping firm probably won't have a lot of equipment maintenance expense. Some basic expenditures are common to every type of business, large or small, service or product, brand-new or established.

Virtually every company will have rent, utility bills, office supplies, advertising costs, personnel expenses, and insurance premiums. Product-based companies will also have to account for things like inventory purchases and delivery fees (both from suppliers and to customers). Other common expenses include site maintenance (like landscaping and cleaning services), professional fees (tax preparation, legal advice), license and permit renewals, and credit-card processing fees.

When your company is new, or your existing company is branching out in some way, plan for extra advertising and promotional expenses. Flyers and free giveaways can add up to a lot more than you'd expect. And don't forget business gifts—they can go a long way toward holding onto loyal clients.

Commonly Overlooked Business Expenditures

Especially for those new to the world of entrepreneurship, there are some business costs (both startup and ongoing) that are frequently overlooked. At the top of the list is themselves: They forget to include their own salary in their budget numbers. Include a reasonable paycheck or draw for yourself, and don't forget to include related expenses like payroll taxes and retirement account contributions.

Aside from that, the expenses that tend to slide through budgetary cracks are usually those that don't come regularly and those that seem too small to consider. Examples include magazine subscriptions, business association dues, bank service charges, credit bureau costs (for customer or employee credit checks), seasonal or cyclical employees, continuing education, and coffee. (If you make it at work, it's a business expense.)

Finally, most fledgling entrepreneurs don't consider bad debt expense. With their focus on bringing in sales, they often overextend credit to customers, and unfortunately, not all customers pay their bills. If you plan to offer credit terms to your clientele (this is not the same as accepting credit cards), budget for some percentage (you can start with 1 or 2 percent of estimated credit sales) that will go unpaid.

Getting Personal

You may be wondering what place personal expenses have in a business plan. Your cost of living is a crucial component to this process. If you can't cover your basic expenses, your business can't possibly succeed. This is one of the areas most overlooked by novice entrepreneurs; they simply forget to consider themselves as "business" expenses.

Paying yourself, enough and regularly, must be a factor when you're calculating the true cost of your business. A continuing stream of cash coming in from the outside, such as when you've kept your "day job" until your business takes off, plays a part in your financial planning. The same goes for the opposite. If you've decided to just quit your job and take a stab at going it alone, you'll need to factor that into your business expenses. How much money do you really need? You'll calculate that in exacting detail in Chapter 6; for now, the important point is that it will be more than nothing.

Create a Timetable to Set Your Pace

There are a lot of things you need to do to set up a business. With a complete business plan, you'll create a kind of checklist to make sure you dot every "i" and make sure no essential steps are skipped.

If you're starting or acquiring a new business, you'll have to obtain all the appropriate licenses and permits before you make a single sale.

You'll have to form your company—and that often means filling out and submitting forms to both state and federal governments, and waiting for replies and approvals. These preliminaries need to be factored into your timeline, because you can't open for business without them.

Then comes the business of your business, and the trapeze-artist timing that goes along with it. Dozens of factors will affect your operations, some internal and some from the outside, and all of them need to be accounted for in your timetable. In addition to that, many businesses have cycles, meaning busy times and slow times. With a solid business plan, the pace and flow of your business will be reasonably documented, and that will be the basis for any timing decisions you make.

Timing Factors

As mentioned above, all kinds of issues will impact the flow of your business. With internal factors, you can exercise some control and set the schedule. Items that fall into this category include things like hiring employees, obtaining outside funds, planning special promotions, and placing orders with vendors. When it comes to external factors, you'll usually be in reaction mode, but a little forethought can smooth out crises without your business grinding to a halt. Outside issues involve things like the general state of the economy, development of new technologies, vendor delivery schedules, new competitors cropping up, even the weather.

▸▸ **Your business plan should consider every factor you can think of that could possibly affect the pace of your business and address ways to manage snafus.** Some items may be dependent on others; for example, a vendor may want to see a letter of credit from the bank before he'll allow you to place an order. That impacts the timing of your promotions, as you don't want customers coming in to buy a product you don't have on hand yet. The timeline spells out the order in which activities must take place—and a good timetable allows for flexibility when things don't happen the way you've planned.

The general cycle of your business also plays a role here. It's important to have an understanding of just how that cycle runs so you can plan accordingly. If you're selling swimsuits, late spring and early summer will probably be your busiest season, and you'll likely have some downtime in the colder months. Other retailers may find that the months leading up to the big holiday season see the most business, while the summer months are almost ghostly. The bottom line here? You need to know how your business cycles and adjust your timeline for the peaks and valleys.

Time and Money

"When will I start making money?" is a common question among those undertaking new business ventures. The answer, though, is unique to each business, and it depends on a number of factors. Because small businesses (and even larger ones) live and die on cash flow, having a realistic timeline in place before you jump in with both feet can make or break your company.

For many businesses, the startup period will be a time of negative cash flow, meaning more money will be paid out than brought in. That's another item on your planning cycle, but it's one you have some control over. You can set the credit terms with your customers, you can negotiate payment terms with your vendors, and you can try to schedule loan payments to begin after you expect money to be coming in.

Profits and Cash Are Not the Same

Believe it or not, you can have a profitable company that's going broke. Sounds crazy, but it's absolutely true—and very common among start-ups. Just because you're making lots of sales and earning lots of money doesn't mean that cash is actually coming in. Here's a simplified example. If you buy a clock for $20 and sell it to Joe Customer on account for $50, you've made a $30 profit. But until Joe sends you a check, you have zero cash flowing in. He could pay you in two days, or two months. In the meantime, you have a profitable company with no cash.

Having a realistic picture of your expected cash flow cycle will help you carry your company through lean times. Until your business has an established pattern, assume (at least initially) that more cash will flowing out than in, and plan accordingly to make sure you have some tiding-over money to draw on.

Deal with Changes Before They Occur

To ensure your company's future survival, you need to be prepared for almost anything. Changes occur all the time, and the business that can keep up with them is the one that will survive. But before you can figure out how to deal with upcoming changes, you first have to identify what they could be and where they could come from. This task requires some foresight and imagination, but it also takes experience. If you are completely new to the business world, consider talking to someone more knowledgeable in your chosen field of endeavor, like a mentor.

One practical way to consider potential changes, and what you can do to deal with them more easily, is to perform a SWOT analysis (as you'll learn in Chapter 8). This universal planning tool forces you to identify possible opportunities (the O) that may arise and potential threats (the T) that your company could face. You will complete this type of analysis as a step to developing your business plan.

Investors and lenders want to know that you have an eye to the future and that you are not naively assuming that the status quo will remain unchanged. In your plan, you can lay out the types of risks, obstacles, and opportunities that you expect your business to face. That will be followed up with ways to handle each potential change, good or bad, to keep your business from being negatively impacted—or at least minimize any unavoidable negative impact. And while you are spelling things out for your readers, you'll be solidifying your response plans and increasing your company's ability to negotiate the twists and turns it will inevitably encounter.

A Benchmark to Track Your Progress

Once your business is up and running, you will need to measure its progress against your original expectations. Since your business plan is a complete source of estimates and assumptions, it is the perfect yardstick against which to track your company's development. The bottom line is that your business plan will help you answer the most common questions asked by virtually every business owner on the planet. First, it is how you will know if your business is operating as expected ("How are we doing?"). Second, it provides a quick and easy mechanism to chart your progress ("Is there a simple way I can tell how we're doing?").

For business owners new to the world of business, cash is often the only item looked at when judging success. That is severely limiting, though, and only points to a tiny portion of your company's overall performance. Looking instead at the differences between your original assumptions and your actual experiences can help you track progress and allow you to tweak areas that need fine tuning before they get too far off track. Without this tracking tool, your business could be running widely off course without your knowledge; the only way you can make appropriate adjustments is to be aware of exactly what needs adjusting.

Finding a Business Mentor

Looking for a qualified business mentor? Look no further than SCORE, the Service Corps of Retired Executives. SCORE has been around since 1964, and the organization currently has over 10,000 volunteers in nearly 800 offices around the United States. Since its inception, this nonprofit has helped more than 7 million entrepreneurs start and grow their businesses. The entire focus of SCORE is to further that great American dream of opening your own business. Their group is made up of former executives and entrepreneurs who have been through many of the challenges you are about to face. They offer seminars, workshops, and one-on-one mentoring services. Plus, their Web site (www.score.org) is chock full of helpful business advice, including direct access to mentors online.

What to Monitor

The beauty of using your business plan as your benchmark is that everything is already quantified, in one way or another. For example, you may have set goals calling for sales of $60,000 in your first year or 750 units per quarter. Your goal may have been to obtain thirty clients in your first six months in business or to win five competitive bids. No matter how you projected your goals, you attached some type of numbers to them—and those numbers will be the bases for your comparisons.

Virtually every aspect of your business can be measured in a meaningful numeric way. The success of your sales force can be measured by number of sales, dollar level of sales, frequency of sales, or cumulative sales. Production can be measured by number of units, cost per unit, or labor hours per unit. Overall revenues can be monitored from a strict sales perspective or from a customer viewpoint. How much does the average customer spend? How often does the average customer make purchases?

Which numbers are of the most use to you depends on the type of business you have. When writing your business plan, you turn the most important numbers into goals that you want your company to meet. When your company has some real experience, you can compare the actual success to the goals you set.

How Often Should You Check?

Like weighing yourself every day while dieting, monitoring your business progress too frequently will drive you crazy. It can be disheartening to see very little change from one day to the next; it is better, instead, to have a general idea of what's going through your daily interactions and to do a more formal review over broader periods. If your plan contains monthly estimates, do a comparison at the end of each month. Should you see gaping variations, you may feel more comfortable tracking in two-week increments, until operations fall closer into line.

Along the same lines, do not wait a full year to see how your company is faring. There is no possible way to go back in time and make changes so that your first-year goals can be met. For example, if you set a sales goal of $60,000 for your first year in business, and you find out at year's end that your sales only hit $32,000, it is simply to late to do anything to make up the difference.

When to Make Adjustments

Since predicting the future in painstaking detail is tricky business, expect your projections to be off the mark, at least by a small margin. This is normal, and the only thing you really can predict is that your predictions will not be exactly right. Relatively small deviations do not merit changes to your overall plans, but what is relatively small to one company can be disastrously large to another. Your judgment comes into play here, and that of your business advisors (if you have any).

If your company is striking well below expectations, you must figure out why before you can make appropriate adjustments to your operating strategies. It may be that your projections were considerably overoptimistic and need to be realigned with the existing reality; that calls for adjustments to your business plan. ▸▸ **If it turns out that your plan is sound, but business problems are keeping your company from achieving the goals you have mapped out, that calls for some operational adjustments.**

Your plan can help you ferret out which pieces of your operations puzzle aren't working. It could be that an employee isn't performing as well as you had hoped or that your billing policies don't bring cash in quickly enough. The trouble could be initiated at the vendor stage (maybe they aren't delivering on schedule), or maybe customers are dissatisfied with your customer service follow-up. You will probably find more than one area that could use improvement. The key, though, is to clearly identify the issues so that you can address them effectively.

Other things can bring about change within your enterprise as well. You may consider making operational alterations to take advantage of new opportunities or deal with new threats. Knowing where you stand in relation to your goals and projections can help you figure out your next steps. For example, if you have a much better cash flow position than expected, instead of ignoring it, you could choose to make use of it in several different ways: paying down your debt sooner, thus saving on interest expense; investing in assets that will help grow your business or run it more efficiently; or socking it away for a rainy day in a high-yield but safe investment vehicle.

Your Platform for Future Plans

Once you have a base business plan in place, you can use this valuable tool to help your company grow and branch out in new directions. Even well-established firms should occasionally reevaluate their business plans to dig for innovative ways to increase sales and profitability. In fact, the plan itself can serve as a launching pad for new ideas and help you presell your idea to customers, providing your plans with support before they even begin.

Any time your company will engage in a major undertaking, a new (or at least significantly revised) business plan is called for. Whether it's a physical expansion (opening a second shop), the addition of a new avenue to grab customers (adding Web sales), or an entirely new product line (introducing snow skis into your bike shop), starting with a business plan will help you work through all the ins and outs of your upcoming tasks. Unlike your original launch, though, you now have a solid base of experience on which to base your assumptions and goals. And this time, they have a much better chance of coming close to the eventual reality than they did when your company had yet to begin.

Other Times to Update Your Business Plan

Even if you don't have a big new launch in the works, there are other times when updating your business plan makes a lot of sense, including these:

➲ External factors have changed significantly, like the introduction of new regulations or a major trend shift.

➲ You have made substantial changes to your management team, and you want to provide the newcomers with the most up-to-date information about your company and its goals.

➲ Your company has experienced a landmark event, like crossing the $1 million revenue line or hitting a five-year anniversary of successful operations.

If your current plan doesn't match up with what's going on right now, for any reason, it's time for an update.

Refine Between Revisions

You don't have to wait for a major revision to update your business plan if you see items that bear adjustment. When first created, your business plan covered a fairly far-out time period. As your business moves along, that far-out time gets closer, and you may be better able to predict what is to come, at least with a bit more accuracy than you had at the outset. Now you have actual results to act as a basis for future projections, and you can tweak these numbers to make for more meaningful comparisons.

What's the difference between a refining and a revision? Time and effort. For a revision, you will take into account virtually every goal and factor in your plan and measure the impact of each on the others. A revision is quicker and much less involved—you tweak one or two numbers that you've noticed need minor adjustment. Note the word "minor." This term is relative, as minor tweaks should not have a significant impact on the rest of the numbers—though (of course) others will be affected. A small shift in projected telephone expense impacts only the bottom line. That's a revision. A 15-percent decrease in cash sales will have a much bigger effect on the numbers, and more than just the bottom line will be affected. That kind of "refinement" probably calls for a more significant revision.

▶▶ TEST DRIVE

Before you sit down to begin creating a full-fledged business plan, answer the following questions with regard to your company (existing or potential):

1. What personal dreams and goals will your business help to fulfill?
2. How much money can you afford to lose if your plans flop?
3. How long can this business hold your interest?
4. What is the worst threat you can imagine to your budding business?
5. Is your risk tolerance strong enough to weather downturns without throwing in the towel?
6. With everything that could go wrong, do you still believe your company can succeed?

You Are the Most Important Reader

As you begin to create your business plan, consider who will be reading it and what those people will be looking for. Essentially, there are two main categories of readers—insiders and outsiders—and within those two groups are still more subdivisions. While you're focusing on everyone's needs to create a comprehensive plan, make sure to keep the most important user in mind—you.

This doesn't mean you can't have multiple versions of your plan, each with minor tweaks that differentiate it from the others. In fact, rather than being more difficult, it's actually easier to write when you have a specific focus, and with word-processing programs in common use, it's quite simple to save multiple, and slightly different, versions of your business plan. For example, while you may want key employees to understand your vision, your plans, and the basic finances of the business, you may not want them to see your personal financial information. And while vendors may need a very detailed description of your current and future expected financial picture, you may want to keep the secrets of your marketing plan hidden. But your master plan, the one you'll be working from, will contain everything that everyone else will see and maybe even more.

Virtually everyone else, from bankers to key employees to vendors, will read through the plan thoroughly once. Maybe they'll refer to it from time to time, maybe not. You, on the other hand, will use this business plan as an ongoing tool for running your business. For those reasons, although you want your plan to be informative and appealing to other readers, you should find the style and format comfortable and easy to use.

Business Partners Like to Talk Strategy

Unlike pure equity investors who put up capital and then sit back and wait for profits to roll in, true business partners will be involved in many facets of creating and running your company. After all, they are co-owners with a personal stake in the company similar to yours. So while you may prepare the bulk of the business plan, be prepared for input and edits from potential partners.

In fact, if you plan to both own and run the company together with your partner or partners, it's in your best interests to work on the plan together. That way you can make sure you have common goals (or at least noncompeting ones) and similar ideas of how to achieve those goals. You want to be clear about each person's role in both forming and managing the company, now and five years from now. Plus, it's crucial to your company's success that you and all of your co-owners share the same strategic vision.

Together, you will hammer out the objectives you (as a team) will strive to make your business meet. These will start with when, where, and how your company will launch; you'll move through the directions in which you want your company to grow, in both the near and distant future; possibly, your defined objectives will also include your ultimate goals, like passing the business down to your heirs or selling it outright to enjoy a luxurious early retirement. This is not intended to be an exercise in specifics, like timetables, but rather a general discussion to make sure your goals mesh. If they don't, it's much better to find that out now.

Partners Don't Have to Mean Partnership

Just because you want to have business partners does not mean you have to form your company as a business partnership. In fact, as more options have developed, straight general partnerships are the least recommended business structures for quite a few reasons. The most important is the huge increase in your personal liability. Not only does a general partnership offer no personal liability protection to any partner for any business problems, but each partner is actually held legally responsible for the acts of other partners. For example, if one partner buys a boat in the name of the partnership, the others could end up paying for it—with their personal funds. For this reason alone, it makes sense to consider incorporating or forming a limited liability company (LLC).

Attract (and Keep) Key Employees

High-level employees don't usually come through the want ads, and it may take a lot of convincing to get them to consider working for a company that does not yet technically exist. To attract critical team members, particularly when you need them to supply skills you do not have, you will need to convince them that your company is not only viable but full of money-making potential and staying power. A well-prepared business plan can reassure them that your company will be around for the long haul and that taking a key role in the startup could be one of the best career moves they will ever make.

Once your business begins taking off, you want to make sure that those employees you depend on plan to stick around. While money is a big attractor, high-level employees may be looking for growth opportunities as well. Again, this is where your business plan can come in handy. Show them your ideas for the future, including how you envision their roles expanding.

Start with a narrative description of the positions you intend to fill, each no more than one page long. At this stage, avoid getting bogged down in tiny day-to-day details and lists of tasks. Instead, create an overview of the important role the person filling this position will play, both now and as the company grows. Include broad descriptions of responsibilities and duties and remember: You must offer authority along with responsibility, or you will be setting your key people up to fail.

Introduce Your Company to Vendors

From inventory to office supplies, every business needs something. For a new company, stocking up can cost quite a bit. Sure, you can use the "get it as you need it" method, but then you run the risk of not having the one thing you desperately need at the very moment you need it.

When it comes to retail, the immediate needs are obvious—you need products to sell. That's hardly the end of the list, though. You may need display cases and shelves, maybe a cash register. Before all that, you need a storefront or some sort of space to set up shop. Then come all the things almost every business needs, even those with no physical products to sell, such as the following:

- ➲ Invoices, preferably prenumbered and preprinted with your company name
- ➲ Business cards
- ➲ Office supplies

➲ Office equipment, like phone, fax, and copier
➲ Computer system, plus bookkeeping software

Buying enough to get you going can get pricey. Parting with precious (and probably much needed) cash can put a strain on an already tight cash situation. Enter credit, which managed properly can be the small business owner's best friend. And here's where the Catch-22 comes in. You can't get your business going without credit, and you can't get credit without an established business—unless, that is, you show your vendors and suppliers a detailed business plan that outlines just how soon you'll be up and running and paying them in full.

A Bargaining Chip

The better your business plan looks, the stronger your bargaining position with potential vendors will be. That directly addresses whether they will extend you credit, but it also speaks to your ability to negotiate more favorable terms. Being perceived as a "better" customer can bring a lot of benefits, both over the long run and right in the beginning when your fledgling business needs it most. ▶▶ **Even existing businesses need to prove themselves to new vendors.** In some cases, word of mouth or a good credit report may suffice; at other times, a vendor you plan to do extensive business with may want more of a glimpse into your future plans.

Top-echelon customers can expect better treatment, better prices, and better terms from their vendors. What makes a top customer? The means to pay for all they've bought and the ability to pay up promptly. Buyers that vendors want to keep may get first crack at new merchandise, delivery priority, and superior service. Some vendors offer different pricing tiers, letting their preferred customers buy the same goods for less to keep the relationship running smoothly. For new businesses or existing businesses going through a growth spurt, though, the most crucial bargaining point may be payment terms.

What Vendors Want to Know

As you'd expect, vendors primarily want to get paid. In addition to that, though, most vendors and suppliers look for long-term relationships with their customers. In most cases, they don't really want to make the one-time sale; instead, they want ongoing and standing orders from regular clients. That consistent level of business helps them plan ahead, allows them to search for better deals from their suppliers, and—bottom line—keeps them in business.

As much as your potential vendors want to know that you can pay them if they extend credit, they also want to know how your future plans will affect theirs. Along those lines, your sales projections are essential information to this part of your audience. Of course, your current and future cash flow impacts them as well, and cash flow projections are near the top of the list of most important data.

Show Lenders They'll Get Their Money Back

Whether you're starting a brand-new business or taking your existing company in new and bigger directions, you're going to need some money. These undertakings usually come with a price tag that's bigger than the standard bank account, and that means looking outside for the balance. For most small businesses, the first stop on the cash hunt is the bank. And the very first thing the bank will ask for is your business plan.

Lending institutions, such as banks and credit unions, know a lot about business loans and business failure rates. That makes already conservative bankers overly cautious when it comes to funding a small business, especially one without a proven track record. To ease their minds, and get the backing you need, you may have to jump through a lot of hoops and provide what seems like an endless sea of information. Don't let that intense scrutiny discourage you. The more they grill you, the more likely you are to get your loan.

The message here is to be prepared. When they ask for a number, give it to them. If they want to know how you came up with your figures, show them. Even if all this information is covered in your business plan, they may want to hear it from you, to help them gain confidence in you. After all, what they're really looking for is reassurance that your business will be able to pay them back.

What Lenders Want

Ideally, lenders seek solid-gold loan candidates: people who don't really seem to need the money and who have payback potential coming in very close to 100 percent. Preferred loan applicants (coming in with sound, comprehensive business plans) would include the following:

- The owner of an existing business that already sees enough positive cash flow to make all loan payments promptly
- A new business launched by an owner with a proven track record of profitability and positive cash flow in another independent yet similar business
- A business owner with enough personal assets to cover the business during any lean times

While these borrowing paragons do exist, they are far from the norm when it comes to small business loans. Banks do prefer the near-guarantee, but they also need to stay in business, and the way they do that is by making loans. So they take on less-than-perfect clients as a calculated risk—but the ones they choose to back are the ones who come the closest to their dream clients.

Giving Lenders What They Want

The key word here is assurance. Even if you fit one of the lender's dream-client profiles, your lender will still want proof on paper that your venture can succeed. And if you're not quite there, show them how close you really are. Start with your existing strengths, add sufficient market research, and fill in for any weaknesses (everyone has them).

What kinds of strengths should you include? Number one on the list is your business experience. Having owned a successful business is best, followed by running, managing, or working for a similar successful business. For example, if you've managed a pizzeria on your own for three years and propose to open a sub shop, potential lenders may believe that you're capable of striking out on your own. On the other hand, if you've never managed a business, or have managed an utterly dissimilar business, the confidence level may be somewhat lower. You can resolve that issue proactively by planning to hire people to fill in your experience gaps.

> ### Filling in the Gaps
>
> Joe Coffey managed a very successful bookshop for five years, but his dream was to own an ice cream parlor. As he began putting together his business plan, he took stock of his experience. He had dealt with inventory, hiring and firing employees, analyzing financial statements—most components of business management. However, he had no food service experience at all, and he knew that would be a sticking point for his loan officer. To compensate, Joe began the search for a manager for his almost-existent shop. And though he hadn't yet found the right candidate when he took his first meeting with the bank, he was able to show them that the hunt was on . . . and that was enough to keep them interested.

Your experience and commitment can take you far in this process, but at some point you'll need to show hard facts and figures. Every lender will want to see your marketing plan, existing financial statements, and projected financial statements. Equally important, they want to see that you understand all the numbers in your presentation and know where they came from. Most important, though, bankers want to be convinced that your company will generate positive cash flow, and if not, that it (or you) have enough assets to cover the debt.

Don't fret if your projections show some periods of negative cash flow or loss; bankers know that most new business don't turn a profit overnight. What they want to see is your plan to bounce back from the deficit, how soon you expect to be profitable and in the money, and when they can expect to begin seeing steady payback. Steady—that's a key word here; lenders want the promise of steady, solid growth, and they want to see that clearly outlined in your business plan projections.

Investors Look for Profit Potential

Though both lenders and investors like to see strong numbers, their interests could not lie further apart. As mentioned above, lenders really just want to be paid back, steadily and on time. Investors, on the other hand, want to see growth potential—the bigger and faster, the better. They want to know that profits will hit their pockets sooner rather than later, and that they'll be able to sell for a gain when they want to get out.

These investors are not to be confused with partner-type owners who want to take part in the everyday management and decision-making processes of the company. Consider your investors as venture capitalists or silent partners: people putting up money to get more money back without having to do any of the actual work involved in running a business.

To that end, investors care mainly about the current market opportunities and how much room there is to grow. They want to see, clearly, some convincing data that the market you are entering (whether it be landscaping, résumé writing, or widget sales) will likely grow substantially over the next five years or more. More important, they want comfort that your company can grow with the market, and that you and your management team can easily handle the expanded capacity.

Shaping Your Plan for Investors

When it comes to putting numbers on paper that will attract investors, the primary focus will be marketing and sales information. The current market you're entering will need to be spelled out, as well as why you think your business will succeed there. You'll also need to prove that this market has the potential for quick, solid growth.

Investors will also want to see management plans and financial projections that allow for the impact of rapid growth. For example, this type of reader will be looking for particular expenses to increase along with market share, which could include these:

- Advertising and promotion
- Sales commissions
- Payroll expenses
- Customer service costs
- Delivery-related expenses
- Warehousing or storage facilities

In addition to rising expenses, other areas of your business will also need to be altered to keep up with growth. Your plan will need to show where you expect to get funding to finance that growth, how you expect cash flow to be impacted, a strong and flexible management team, and possibly where and when you expect the next growth spurt will take place.

Looks Are Everything

Check out any big corporation's annual report, and you'll get your first hint at how successfully the company fared during the previous year. Thick, glossy reports printed on heavy paper with lots of photos imply success—whether the numbers back it up or not. The same holds true for your business plan—the first impression it makes is solely based on its appearance. You want to give the impression of success, even if you haven't yet achieved it, to convince investors to give you their money.

That doesn't mean your business plan should look like a magazine, with full color on every page. But it's crucial that your plan look professional. Your plan represents you and your business idea, and it must create the aura of potential. If you can afford it, get your plan professionally printed (at Kinko's, for example). Otherwise, buy high-quality paper and use a laser printer, preferably with color.

Remember, too, that pictures make a bigger impression than columns of numbers. ▸▸ **Use charts and graphs (again, color is preferred here) to demonstrate simply and clearly what your numbers are saying. Graphs make an immediate impact, especially when you're trying to show growth.** Pie charts can work wonders for describing your potential customer base and market shares. But don't go overboard, putting one or two on every page; that can often have the opposite effect, where the most important one gets lost among the rest.

Finally, pay attention to detail. Make sure every word is spelled correctly and that your grammar is impeccable. Double-check the math to ensure that your numbers add up. If your readers find errors and sloppy mistakes running throughout your plan, it can lead them to question whether you'll make similar blunders while running your company.

▶▶ TEST DRIVE

What do you expect to be the most important aspect of your unique business plan to the following readers? Your answers should reflect specific information about your company, which can help you in getting these points on to paper:

- ⮌ Potential business co-owners
- ⮌ Prospective critical employees
- ⮌ Suppliers that you hope will extend credit
- ⮌ Bank loan officers
- ⮌ Investors looking for big, quick profits

Part
one

Part
two

Part
three

Part
four

Part
five

Part
six

A Brief Look at Business Types

Every business type has unique requirements, and understanding those specific differences can help put you on the path to success. Each category calls for different skill sets to run efficiently and profitably. Your business will be best served when you understand which category your company fits into and the particular needs of that business type.

The two main categories are service and product-based, and many businesses combine the two. In addition, there are several subcategories for more specific definition: retail, wholesale, manufacturing, and project/ product development, for example. Knowing the right classification directs the shape of your business plan, helping to give it a clearer focus.

To figure out where your business fits in, consider the following descriptions:

> **Service businesses** involve individuals selling their unique skills, usually in the form of professional advice or task completion, to others.

> **Product-based businesses** sell physical goods, either to individuals (typically retail establishments) or to other companies (usually done by wholesalers or manufacturers).

> **Combination product and service companies** mix the two fields together, offering both a physical product and expert advice or task performance.

Your business type dictates your primary customer base, though you may attract more than one category of customer. Whichever category your company fits into, establishing a steady flow of customers generates sales and (eventually) profits.

Consider Customer Expectations

No matter what kind of business you have, the ultimate success or failure depends largely on your customers. To attract customers, you have to provide something that they need. You can figure out exactly what your customers need by clearly identifying the problem you'll be solving for them with your business. Once you truly understand those needs and problems, you'll be on your way to developing a loyal client base . . . and a successful business.

How can you do this? ▶▶ **Put yourself in your customers' shoes.** Imagine what you would want from the product or service you are offering and what things might make it even more appealing. For example, if your product requires some at-home assembly, will customers need someone (typically an experienced customer service representative) to walk them through the steps? Or would they prefer professional assembly for an additional fee? Walk yourself through the steps your customers will take, from their initial entry to their after-sale satisfaction. This process will help you find weak points, at least from a customer perspective, that you can fix before your launch.

Another matter to consider is the customer motivation process. Again, this is based on the need your customers are interested in satisfying, with more focus on the psychological perspective. What drives the customers to seek out what you are offering in the first place is a key factor in attracting them. If they are driven by the lust for luxury, they won't be lured by blaring bargain-basement announcements. Conversely, if they are budget-conscious shoppers, a focus on top-line product features probably won't grab their attention as much as pricing policies.

The key to understanding customer expectations is to understand, in advance, the market you want to target for your customers. As you narrow in, customer expectations and motivations will become increasingly clear.

Service Businesses Get the Job Done

Service companies perform tasks for their customers. There are a few basic reasons people and other companies will purchase services from someone else:

- They don't know how to do the work themselves.
- They are physically incapable of performing the requisite tasks.

➲ They don't own (or want to own) the necessary tools for the job.

➲ They don't have time to do it themselves.

➲ Paying someone else to perform the task makes them feel more important.

➲ They just don't want to do the work.

The readers of your business plan will want to know which of these reasons best suit the service you're selling and how you plan to convince your customers that you can solve their problems. Once you can get those points across, it will be fairly easy to convince people to supply your endeavors with cash. Here's why. Service businesses typically take less startup cash than product-based businesses, and they offer the potential of much higher margins. Your biggest costs will be people: employees, consultants, you, and your co-owners. Though you will need some assets in place to get going (office furniture, computer equipment, and so on), those costs typically will be substantially lower than the ones associated with product companies. (That's not to say that no service-oriented business requires significant amounts of up-front cash, but the majority of them don't.)

No matter what types of physical assets you will need to get started, your biggest assets will always be your people and your company's good reputation. Focus your plan on grabbing and keeping customer loyalty and on growing your business by growing your standing in the eyes of your target market—plus coming up with additional services you can provide for your clients.

Service Provider or Educator?

Part of attracting clients to your service business is to teach them why they need you. Maybe you are in a tried-and-true profession about which the public has significant awareness, like tax preparation; in that case, the education process will focus more on your company than on the mechanics of the service you provide. However, if the service your company will be offering has not quite yet hit the mainstream, you will have to take a few steps back when it comes to filling people in. You may have to pro-

Overcoming Misconceptions

Sometimes, you will have to deal with potential customers who have little or no information about your service; at other times, the way to attract customers starts with overcoming preconceived notions. Take the story of acupuncturist Sarah Halterberg, for example: Though this ancient Chinese practice is endorsed by the U.S. government for treating several common ailments, it still retains an air of mystery and often conjures up a fear of being stuck with hundreds of needles.

To reach skeptics and needle-phobics, who make up a rather large percentage of the potential market, Sarah gave several "free to the community" talks about this traditional healing art. She explained that often the use of a single tiny needle inserted almost painlessly into a single spot on the body can provide effective treatment. She offered free demonstrations. She took the time to speak to people one on one. She let them know that insurance often covered treatments and how she frequently works with people's primary physicians to come up with a complementary treatment plan.

By directly addressing misconceptions in an educational forum, she was able to overcome any negative perceptions and introduce acupuncture as a most desirable and highly personalized form of treatment. By focusing attention on the uniqueness of each patient, and the tailor-made treatment they would receive, she turned her practice of custom care into a motivating factor.

Slowly but surely, clients came in, often for the treatment of specific acute problems like pain. Once she had them, she continued the education process, explaining how the practice works even better when it's used to maintain health, instead of just fixing something that is wrong right now. Her base of steady use clients began to grow, and they began to act as her educators in the field, as well as her biggest source of new clients.

mote the need for this type of service primarily, and your company as the provider only after potential customers understand what you do—and how it can make their lives better.

Even if your type of business has been around for a while, don't make the mistake of assuming that most people understand it. If there is a good chance that many people don't (and you must be the judge of that), pay some attention to industry education. Let customers understand the basics of what you provide; once they have a grasp of what you do, you have a better shot of convincing them that they need it. For example, the general public understands why dog trainers make sense but not necessarily why they would need a dog psychologist.

When the service you provide is well-known, your educational efforts are free to focus more on the unique benefits of your company. Emphasize special services and whatever else may set your business apart from the others like it. Concentrate that effort on an easy message to pass along—your best source for new clients is old clients.

Product-Based Businesses Require More Planning

When it comes to product-based businesses, there are three ways to go: retail, wholesale, and manufacturing. Each comes with a distinct set of advantages and drawbacks, and each requires some special handling when it comes to preparing your business plan. What they do have in common is physical inventory, and that adds an entirely new dimension into your financial statements and projections, not to mention the way your company will operate.

Crossing Categories

Can a company cross product categories? Absolutely. Think Xerox, for example, which manufactures, wholesales, and retails its products. Or Starbucks, which sells coffee directly to customers in its shops and also from the shelves of the grocery store. To simplify business plan creation for companies that work along different lines, you can separate them into discrete divisions that come with their own financial statements and projections. Then you could add a comprehensive top-level version of each statement that combines the divisions into one company.

As long as all readers of the business plan (including you) understand your distribution strategies in detail, it's fine to have a single business plan that combines every different facet of your company.

Simply put, inventory is the stuff you're going to sell. It takes up space, meaning you'll need to plan for some type of storage facility (even if, at first, that turns out to be your basement or garage). Whether your inventory sells as-is or needs to be created first, you'll need to have it readily available when a customer wants to buy it. Estimating your coming inventory needs gets easier with experience. You don't want to overstock and risk being stuck with products that won't move and that cost you money to maintain; you don't want to understock and risk losing customers to competitors or having to fill in by paying higher prices for "emergency" inventory.

Realistic market research is the only way for a fledgling business to make initial inventory needs estimates. And even the most experienced buyer may need to use the "best guess" approach when starting out in a new market or with a new product. This is another area where a comprehensive business plan will serve you well. It can help you determine reasonable starting inventory levels and help you choose adequate (but not overblown) storage facilities.

Retail Sales

By definition, a retailer buys merchandise from suppliers (usually wholesalers) and sells them right to the end users, a.k.a., the individual consumers. Retailers interact with consumers in a few different forms, including the following:

- Storefront
- Catalog
- Internet
- Telesales

The basic profit mechanics here take the "Buy low, sell high" approach. Retailers purchase bulk goods from wholesalers or directly from manufacturers, then mark up their cost to a profitable retail price (often double or triple what they paid).

Going Wholesale

You'll need to think about big warehouses if your plan is to get into wholesale. These product merchants must stock a wide variety of products, and a sufficient supply of each, to make a go of it. Typically, wholesalers buy in large quantities from manufacturers or merchandise brokers, then resale those products to retail outfits.

Wholesale establishments require a lot of up-front money. Extremely high inventory levels and necessary storage takes a lot of capital. On top of that, to remain competitive, most wholesalers must offer delivery services, which may mean an investment in delivery vehicles.

Wholesalers don't get profit from huge markups like retailers—their margins (the difference between what they paid for products and what they sell them for) usually don't climb higher than the 15- to 30-percent range. Their profitability comes in via volume—they have to sell a lot, and keep the merchandise moving, to make money.

Manufacturers Make Everything

Before products get to either the wholesaler or the retailer, they have to be made. That's the task of a manufacturer: he takes raw materials (like wood and metal) or component parts and turns them into finished goods. This can happen on a small scale, like someone who makes furniture by hand, or on a very large scale, like a car manufacturer, complete with automated assembly lines.

Unlike other types of product-based companies, manufacturers have three types of inventory:

1. Raw materials or components
2. Work in progress
3. Finished goods

The key to success for manufacturers lies in the products they create. They need to make products that are (or will be) desired by the overall market, and they must be able to stimulate long-term sales volume for the enterprise not to flop. In that regard, they almost have to work backward, selling their product before they start making it.

The Numbers

As you read earlier in this chapter, having a product-based business adds a whole new element to your business plan. Your market research is more crucial here than with a strictly service company, mainly due to the need for more initial cash outlay. There's more risk of negative cash flow and for longer periods. Margins will be lower—after all, what you're selling costs you money out-of-pocket—meaning you'll need more sales to turn the same profit levels.

As for putting numbers together (which you'll learn about fully in Part Five), physical products make some of your financial statements longer and somewhat more detailed. Particularly affected will be your income statement, which will require you to complete a whole new section. Projections may also be more complicated, as your business plan readers may want to see how the numbers look at different sales levels.

Selling Products and Services Merits a Combination Plan

Many companies offer their customers some combination of products and services. Take restaurants, for example—they provide products (food and beverages) and services (you don't have to prepare, serve, or clean up after yourself). Because of the dual nature of the business, your plan will necessarily be more complex than if it focused only on one area. Extra issues, like managing the interplay and balance between the product delivery and service performance, need to be examined and spelled out for your plan readers.

With a mixed-bag business, customers will expect the best of both sides: a good product and excellent service. A lack in either area will translate to an eventual lack of customers, and a corresponding lack of revenues. But providing excellence in all areas can put up quite a challenge for novice entrepreneurs. Think about the last time you had a completely satisfying experience in a restaurant—a combination of delicious food prepared to your specifications delivered promptly and politely by a courteous and attentive waitstaff, and you didn't have to ask twice for the check, ask to have your water glass refilled, or fill up on bread because your meal simply did not taste good.

In addition to making sure both your products and your personnel merit top ratings, at least in the minds of customers, here are some other special issues faced by companies selling products and services:

⮕ Pricing must be developed based on both cost of goods and associated labor costs.

⮕ Marketing your company calls for a double dose of unique selling points.

⮕ Each component requires different methods of management and possibly separate management teams.

▶▶ TEST DRIVE

What do you think your customers will expect to get out of doing business with you? Try to come up with a few things that you would want to be a satisfied customer of your company. Start with the initial contact scenario, and jot down things that would keep you (in the role of a customer) from going somewhere else. Next, run through an imaginary sales process, from getting help making your product selection through walking out the door happy. Finally, think about what happens when the sale is complete but you have more questions or concerns. How you would want that after-sale interaction handled to encourage future purchases?

The Front Matter Makes the First Impression

First impressions can mean the difference between the top of the pile and the never looked at when it comes to the external audiences for your business plan. This is especially true of the people you want money from, whether they are lenders or investors. Remember that while you are only writing one business plan, they are wading through stacks of them. If your packet does not stand out, it may not be looked at for quite some time, if ever. So take the time to make your presentation look professional and memorable.

The front matter is composed of five basic items:

1. Cover letter
2. Title page
3. Nondisclosure statement
4. Your strategic vision
5. Table of contents

Depending on the layout of your plan, some of these items may come together on a single page. The following sections provide a quick synopsis of these elements, and in Chapter 11 you'll get step-by-step instructions on how to create them properly.

The Cover Letter

Just like prospective employers may ask for a cover letter along with any résumé, potential lenders and investors often expect the same. Essentially, the cover letter tells them, briefly, why they should bother looking at your business plan when they have twenty others sitting on their desks already. This page is your first sales pitch, convincing your readers to continue on to the inside of your business plan.

Effective cover letters are short and to the point, but they contain enough information to get the readers hooked. Your letter should be printed on company letterhead, preferably on very high-quality paper, even if you are buying or creating only a few sheets of it for now. In it, you'll introduce yourself and your business and explain the exact purpose for your presentation.

Some business plans do come without cover letters, but the cover letter is essential when you are sending the plan out instead of delivering it in person (though it can't hurt to have one either way). In fact, your cover letter can contain one very important element that really does not have any other place in the plan: a recommendation from someone the financier knows and trusts. That can help ensure that your business plan gets read.

Your Title Page

This one sheet of paper sets the tone for your whole plan. It is the first page any reader of your plan will see—and it is, literally, the first impression your business will make on others.

Your title page should look neat and professional. On it, you will include identifying information about you and your business, like the complete name of your company and any "doing business as" (DBA) names, the business address, your name and contact information, the date of plan creation, and the control number (to help you keep track of who has gotten which copy). If you have a company logo, put it on the title page—this helps distinguish your plan from others at a glance.

Nondisclosure Statements

You want particular people to read your business plan: your banker, investors, partners, and potential vendors. But there are others that you absolutely do not want reading it, like competitors. ▸▸ **A nondisclosure statement, or confidentiality agreement, keeps readers from sharing the information within your business plan with any unauthorized people.**

Think about it: Your business plan contains chunks of personal financial information. It includes a detailed strategy for launching and sustaining your business. You do not want this information to fall into the wrong hands. The nondisclosure statement does not guarantee that your plan will not be copied or circulated. But it will inhibit users from openly discussing the contents with other people and encourage them to keep access limited to only those who really need to see your plan (like your loan officer's boss, for example).

Your Strategic Vision

Similar to a mission statement, the strategic vision can be laid out on a separate page for emphasis. If your business plan is very long, you may want to incorporate this section into your executive summary.

▶▶ **Essentially, your strategic vision describes the guiding principles behind your business idea.** It will be clear and concise, no longer than a single short paragraph. Don't confuse this statement with a business description; it should be more like a succinct focus for your overall goals. For example, instead of merely saying that your company will be selling children's books, you could say instead, "Our company will provide incentive for young children to develop a love of reading by offering attention-grabbing books that excite their imagination and desire to learn."

A strategic vision paragraph does more than give your plan readers a brief and enticing glimpse into your dream. It also helps you define your focus and set the stage for how your business will function.

The Table of Contents

A table of contents provides an immediate guide for all of your plan readers. It should let them maneuver through your business plan easily, as well as provide an overview for what they will find inside. A good table of contents will list all of the main sections and important subsections, along with the appropriate page numbers of each. It should also include directions to any appendices or supporting documentation you have included with your core plan.

One thing to keep in mind is length. If your table of contents runs to more than one page, consider editing some of the entries. The lines here should reflect your section headings and subheadings and not include descriptions of each section.

Provide a Quick Focus with Your Summary

The executive summary expands on your strategic vision, incorporating all of your ideas and research into a cohesive abstract. Some small-business experts maintain that this section is the single most important part of your entire business plan, providing readers with a sort of "plan at a glance" feel. This page can be a turning point in the decision-making process, since a captivating summary keeps readers engaged and keeps them reading. In fact, many financiers make their preliminary decision right here.

What should you include in this summary? Hit all the high points of your plan, and emphasize every factor that points to your company's ultimate success. Here you want to generate excitement and enthusiasm, convincing the readers to believe in your dreams . . . without getting too wordy and without using what sounds like hype.

There are some must-haves that plan readers will expect to see in this section. These include who you are and what you plan to do; a definitive statement of what you are looking for from them (for example, exactly how much money you want to borrow, or how much credit you want a vendor to extend); and what results you expect from your endeavors.

In a nutshell, your executive summary will let your readers know exactly what you want, why they should provide it, and how you plan to make it worth their while.

Introduce Your Operations and Management Plans

The operations and management section of your business plan starts the detailed section of your document. You'll begin this part with background information about your company, define the business entity, and revisit the concepts in your mission statement with a little more meat behind them.

This chapter of your business plan will provide an overview of your intended operations, including a brief definition of the products and/or services you intend to offer. It will spell out operational details: where you will set up the base of operations, how you will obtain or create your products or services, how those will be brought to customers, and what type of follow-up you will offer after the sale.

Finally, your operations and management section will introduce the people behind the business. That includes you (and co-owners, if you have them), but this section also speaks to your management team, key employees, and any outside professionals you will engage (like accountants, lawyers, and other advisors or consultants).

What's Your Business Entity?

A business entity is the form your company will take. It defines the basic structure, which dictates both legal and tax aspects. There are four main business entities and some variations within those options. The big four include sole proprietorships, partnerships, limited liability companies (LLCs), and corporations. Then come the subcategories. Partnerships (which must have more than one owner) can be general, limited, or limited liability (either general or limited). Limited liability companies can have either one owner or many, and they can choose their tax treatment based on the number of owners. Corporations come in two major varieties: C (or "regular") and S. Some states also allow very small companies to elect close corporation status, to lighten the paperwork load.

Show You Know the Market

You can have the best idea ever in the history of the business world—but if you can't sell it, you will be out of business before you even get started. To figure out whether your great idea will actually draw paying customers, you have to do plenty of market research. This will take a lot of time and thought, and (maybe) some money, but all that is better done before you launch than after the fact.

Your market research must be comprehensive to be useful. There are many angles to cover and facts to collect. This information will provide support for your intuition and creativity, helping you create the best version of your product or service and ensuring the existence of a customer base.

But your marketing section doesn't stop there; market research is just step one. Next comes analyzing the data to discover what it means to your business and your future profitability.

Start with the Industry Overview

Your business is part of a larger industry, and the more you know about it as a whole, the better chance your company has for success. So before you start focusing on your immediate market, you'll need to come up with a basic industry overview. Industry factors include things like these:

- Its general state, such as whether it's on the upswing or in a downtrend
- How other industry participants are faring, regardless of their size
- The typical sales cycle, and at which point your company will enter
- Standard distribution channels, meaning where your products will come from and how they'll get where they're going
- The industry size, both in dollars and number of companies
- Recent growth patterns, and what's expected in the future
- External factors that affect performance, like oil prices or climate changes
- Government regulations, at all levels, including required licenses and operating permits

Wireless
PDA, Google MSFT Yahoo

Once you've nailed down the industry information, you will turn your efforts toward defining your segment of the market.

Defining Your Target Market

To bring customers in the door, you'll have to figure out what part of the market you want to invite. In most cases, the group of people or businesses who will be interested in buying what you're selling will be fairly narrow. It's up to you to determine exactly who they are and focus your efforts accordingly.

The target market for your business is merely a set of customers with particular traits in common, making them easy to distinguish from the overall population. In this part of your plan, you will list those common traits and explain why they make these your ideal customers. The characteristics could range from the general (men over age fifty) to the highly specific (who also have more than one dog). You will define both qualitative (such as what they like, what they need) and quantitative factors (like their age and income levels), until you come up with a clear picture of your customer type. Once you know precisely whom you'll be selling to, your market research will have a tighter focus.

Your Market Analysis

Your business relies on sales to survive. Analyzing every facet of the market is the only way to tell whether your company has a chance to compete, thrive, and turn a healthy profit. The time and research you put into your market analysis can help ensure that your business idea truly is feasible, with real potential for success.

Once you've defined the market in which your business will compete, you'll have to assess its current environment. That analysis includes things like economic conditions, general buying attitudes, and the physical area (accessibility and parking, for example). Then you'll identify your desired customers, narrowing them to a target audience to whom all your marketing efforts will be directed.

Evaluate Your Competition

Competition is a fact of life and business. The general business environment is highly competitive. For your company simply to survive, you need to know exactly what and whom you are up against.

In this section of your plan, you will describe your competitors for your readers in some detail. Not only will you need to name names, but you also must understand how each of them can compete against you and how you can position your company to stay in the game with them. By knowing their strengths and weaknesses as well as your own, you'll be able to better pinpoint your competitive edge.

To that end, you will need to do some research, especially if you are starting a brand-new company or taking your existing company in a new direction. You will need to start a file on each competitor—or, if your competition can easily be categorized (such as department stores, boutiques, mail-order catalogs), you can create your files by grouping them.

In addition to your direct competitors, you need to take indirect (and sometimes less obvious) competitors into account.

Indirect Competitors

When listing your potential business rivals, be sure to include your indirect competitors. These companies sell the same products and services that yours does, but to a different customer set.

Why do these companies figure in to your competitive analysis if they're not targeting the same market? Because they can easily shift focus toward your customer base. For example, one of your suppliers could begin selling directly to consumers, rather than only through retail outlets.

For service businesses particularly, your fiercest "competition" can come from your customers themselves. For example, suppose you provide bookkeeping services to small businesses. As some of your clients begin to grow, they may decide to hire an in-house dedicated bookkeeper—taking the job away from you.

Keeping tabs on your competition will be an ongoing process, and creating this analysis as part of your overall business plan will initiate you to the ins and outs of market survival. Rivals will continue to crop up, and taking a proactive stance will serve you better than running to catch up after you've lost customers of either the existing or potential variety. Staying ahead of the competition is a must if you want to stay in business.

Describe Your Products and Services

When it comes to what your business will be selling, there are three very important questions the readers of your plan will want answered:

1. How are your products or services different from similar offerings already on the market?

2. How will you capitalize on these differences to capture market share?

3. How do you plan to satisfy your customers' wants and needs?

There are millions of products and services in the market—with thousands more entering every day. The things you plan to sell must have some unique facet or some characteristic that make them more valuable than anything else out there. In this section of your business plan, you'll specify what sets your offering apart from the rest and what gives you the edge over existing competition.

Here you will also describe your products or services in exhaustive detail. The information will include things like how your product will be used, in what ways it will be valued by your customers, and how long you expect it to be saleable as is.

That brings up the product/service life cycle, which will also be addressed in this portion of your business plan. Every product or service generally follows the same progression: introduction, growth, maturity, and decline. Your plan will address each life stage and how it impacts your overall business (as you'll see in detail in Chapter 15). You may also incorporate some of your more distant future ideas, like further development or planned innovations to your existing offerings.

A Look at the Numbers

In business, it's all about the numbers: market share, profitability, break-even, available cash, and advertising budget (just to name a few!). There is a huge amount of math involved with starting and maintaining a business. Luckily, there are also accountants, bookkeepers, investment advisors, and software programs readily available to do most of the calculating. Supplying the right data is the burden that falls squarely on your shoulders.

There are different sets of numbers that you'll include in your financial plan. First will come all your market research statistics, as described earlier in the chapter. Then come formal financial statements. The first to be included will provide existing detailed financial information for your business (if it's ongoing) or for yourself (if you're starting from scratch). After that, you'll prepare projections to illustrate the future expected financial position. A basic set of financial statements includes a balance sheet, an income statement, and a statement of cash flows.

The Balance Sheet

▸▸ **Sometimes referred to as the statement of financial position, the balance sheet tells your business plan readers where you stand, financially, right now.** Essentially, this statement lists everything you or your company has (the assets), along with everything you or your company owes (the liabilities). The difference between the two is called equity, and it represents true ownership.

Even the smallest of service businesses have some assets. The computer you will use to track your appointments, the cell phone you use to contact clients, the cash you use to buy paper clips; these are all assets, and they all belong on your balance sheet. It's entirely possible, though, that a small business (particularly a service business) won't have any existing debt to speak of. When that's the case, the flip side of your assets is all equity.

Product-oriented businesses almost always have bigger balance sheets than their service-based counterparts—not necessarily in terms of dollars but often in the number of assets they have to list. All of your inventory counts as assets, as well as any machinery, equipment, or real property your company owns. Along with that typically comes a pile of debt, whether it's accounts payable due to your suppliers for that inventory or longer-term debt associated with large asset purchases. For these types of companies, especially those of the small startup variety, balance sheet debt will often outweigh equity by a wide margin.

The Income Statement

This financial report goes by more than one name: income statement, statement of profit and loss, or statement of operations. Whatever title you decide to go with, the statement still contains the same information. It offers a summary of revenue earned, expenses incurred, and the difference between them for a particular period of time. When revenue exceeds expenses, you have earned profits, but when your expense tally is greater than your revenue, your company has suffered a loss.

The Statement of Cash Flows

While both the balance sheet and income statement are important clues to your company's overall financial health, the statement of cash flows speaks to its ongoing survival. You can have a picture-perfect balance sheet and loads of predictable profits, but if your business is lacking for actual cash in the bank, your company can tank.

Businesses, especially small businesses, can live or die by their cash flow alone. For that reason, your cash flow statement plays a starring role when readers evaluate your business proposal. At its most basic, this statement spells out how much money you have available right now to help you stay afloat while you bring your company to a profitable level with its own sustainable positive cash flow.

This statement also encompasses the cash flowing out of your company—and you can plan on a lot of that, especially in the beginning. Anything you have to write a check for, also known as a cash disbursement, counts as a drain on your money supply. That doesn't mean you should try to cut down on expenditures while you are trying to rev up your company. It just means that you need to be aware of the cash going out today, tomorrow, and next month, and where you expect that cash to be coming from.

Interpreting the Numbers

Once you have prepared the three critical financial statements, you are ready for the next step: analyzing them to see what they're really saying. To that end, there are some standard ratios that experienced financial professionals will apply to the numbers to see if they make sense and if they speak to future potential and growth. In Chapter 23, you'll learn more about how these ratios are determined and what they can say about your business's health and prospects.

▶▶ TEST DRIVE

Now that you know some of the key components of every business plan, jot down some quick thoughts for each of these components in your own plan. This exercise serves two purposes: It will give you an initial direction to take should you feel overwhelmed, and it can help remind you of the enthusiasm you felt at the outset. This is brainstorming, and it doesn't matter whether every thought is golden. List each part on a sheet of paper, then write the first three words or phrases that come to mind, like so:

"Financials: find CPA, learn QuickBooks, set up bank account."

2

Gathering Information

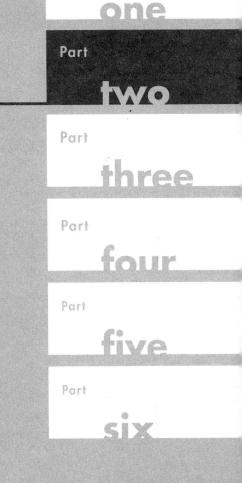

An Established Track Record

When you plan to expand your ongoing business, you will want to focus attention on your past and current success. You will emphasize your strongest points and address any perceived weaknesses, all using the numbers you have compiled over your years in business. Best of all, though, is the fact that your business still exists. This is a statement in itself, which makes it much more likely that someone will offer you financing.

Your existing financial statements hold the key information you will need to make intelligent decisions about the future of your business. When they were prepared, you probably created them for someone else: the Internal Revenue Service, a new supplier, or your bank manager. In fact, you may not even have prepared them yourself; your accountant may have done that while getting your tax returns done. No matter why they exist or who created them, you have a lot to gain from looking over your company's historical financial statements with the perspective gained by time.

While you want your business to shine in the eyes of your external plan readers, reviewing your track record with an eye on past weaknesses provides a prime opportunity to turn those old problems into strengths. Your financial statements give you solid numbers to work with, letting you see exactly what numbers are out of line and which numbers line up with your stated goals.

Historical Financial Statements Show a Pattern

Beneficial or not, your existing financial statements show a clear picture of how your company has been performing over the past few years. If you're looking to expand your business due to its success and growth, your financial statements will provide background for your decision to seek additional business. If, on the other hand, your company has not been doing so well and you want to take it in a new direction with the hope of sparking success, you have a much harder sell on your hands.

Before placing your company's full financial background in other people's hands, take the time to look through it yourself with a new perspective—that of someone on the outside looking in with a critical view.

Especially when you are looking for money, your business plan readers will be looking for flaws. It's better if you see them first, understand why they are there, and come up with possible ways to correct them (if they are not already corrected in later statements). Regardless of your company's level of success, there will be areas that could stand improvement, and you need to spot those before outsiders do.

What Works in Your Favor

When you are trying to expand an existing successful business, you still need to focus your business plan toward fulfilling the ultimate goal of whoever is providing the financing. For lenders, that goal means solid operating cash flow and easily saleable assets. For equity investors, it means demonstrable growth in revenues and, hopefully, profitability.

While you need to include a complete set of financials, you can opt to highlight whatever you want to stand out to your readers. ▶▶ **Chances are that the readers of your business plan are not going to analyze every single number on three years' worth of financial statements for an existing company.** More likely, they will focus on what is important to them or what you direct them to pay attention to.

How can you guide them through your financials? First, you can provide a set of summary statements that "crunch up" the detail numbers into bigger categories. That way, if you have some operating expenses that may seem out of line but your overall expenses look good, you have led your readers to the bigger picture. Second, you can skew your ratios and other analyses to focus on your areas of success. As you'll learn in Chapter 23, these analyses are not typically required to be included in your business plan. However, if they help you present your business in a more positive light, figure them out and put them in. Finally, you can bold any numbers that speak to your company's success. For example, if your company has experienced strong revenue and gross profit growth, print the positive percentage changes in bold, so readers' eyes will be naturally drawn to them.

When It's Less Than Spectacular

Not all new or small businesses hit the ground running. In fact, the overwhelming majority experience significant struggles in the early years. Because of that, many business plan readers consider any company that has been around less than three years to be a start-up. In addition, if your company's historical financial statements leave something to be desired in the profitability department, you have some hurdles to overcome.

Though you can use some of the tips discussed in the previous section to highlight any good points, your readers will know that your company still has a lot to prove. Rather than hiding that fact, embrace it. Show your readers what you have so far and how you plan to either turn things around (if things have not been going as well as you had expected) or to continue improving on your first signs of success.

You still have to include your historical financial statements, and your projections must realistically grow out of what has already occurred. But between the two, there is a lot of room for explanation—and that's where you come in. Talk to the people you are seeking financing from. Tell them what's happened so far and where you plan to take the company from here. Your knowledge, vision, and confidence may just override any perceived negatives in your past financial statements.

Evaluate Your Existing Customer Base

Another item you will have in your arsenal as an existing business is an established customer base. You already know (or should find out right now) the following facts:

- Who is buying from you?
- How often do they purchase?
- How much do they spend each time?
- How well do they pay (especially important for companies that offer customer credit terms)?
- Why do they buy from you in the first place?
- Why do they come back for repeat business?

Each of these points should be covered in your marketing plan; unlike with a brand-new business, you have a lot of information unique to your company to work with.

Once you know the ins and outs of your existing customer base in regard to the products and services your company is offering now, wherever it is already offering them, you can build on that platform to envision your expansion. Whether your plan involves introducing new products, moving to a new or additional locations, or bringing in a new set of customers, it will necessarily feed off of your current customer profile.

Here is one crucial point that your business plan should stress: how you intend to hold on to your current customers while you attempt your expansion. Why does that matter so much? ▶▶ **It is common business knowledge that it can cost ten times more to hook a new customer than to keep an existing one.** Yes, an infusion of new customers can help grow your business, but that should never happen at the expense of the customers you already have, or you could lose more than you will gain. Don't make the (very common) mistake of neglecting your current customers in the thrill of seeking out new ones, and don't oversell new offerings to your current customers, or they may end up taking all of their business elsewhere.

At this stage of the game, your marketing plan should include a clear customer retention strategy. Whether you plan to introduce some kind of loyalty/reward system (like buy ten, get one free), send out special mailings (for special customer-only sale notifications), or some other method of making your existing customer base feel special, spell it out in your business plan. Let your readers know that you are just as serious about (at the very least) maintaining current sales levels as you are about potential growth.

Can Your Suppliers Grow with You?

New small-business owners can develop very close relationships with their suppliers. After all, these are the guys that helped get you up and running. Maybe they offered you lenient credit terms, or they let you slide for a couple of months without cutting off shipments when you went through a temporary rough patch. You may feel extremely loyal to these companies and guilty about even thinking about switching to a bigger outfit. But if your current suppliers cannot keep up with your growing demands, no matter how much you like them and no matter how loyal you feel, you will have to start looking to new companies to keep your shelves stocked.

That's not to say you shouldn't give your existing suppliers first crack at growing with you. If they can truly handle the extra load, and they've always provided crackerjack service in the past, by all means stick with them. At the same time, be wary of small businesses that say they can do it but simply (and obviously) don't have the capacity.

To determine whether or not the suppliers your business is already using can keep up with your plans for growth, consider some of the following questions:

- How have they responded to rush orders in the past?
- Do they have the physical space to deal with expanded inventory?
- Can they offer you better pricing now that you will be purchasing in higher quantities?
- Are their facilities suitable for housing any new types of products you may begin selling?
- Will their existing delivery fleet suffice for your upcoming needs?

Review Your Personnel and Payroll

The team you have developed to get your business where it is today can help you grow your company to even greater heights in the future. By now, you have developed a working knowledge of each team member's strengths and weaknesses, and you have learned how to use each employee's unique skills to your company's best advantage. On the other hand, maybe you have been performing a mainly solo act so far (or counting only on yourself and your co-owners), at least when it comes to running your business every day. Whichever path you've taken up until now, this is the time to review it. A period of expansion typically calls for the addition of some personnel.

Whether you will be adding employees for the first time or merely expanding your roster, there are several points you will need to consider. First, unless your company has grown big enough to warrant its own payroll department, consider outsourcing to a payroll service if you haven't already.

The more people you have working for you, the more time-consuming payroll processing will become, and your efforts may be better spent ensuring the smoothest possible expansion than on the details of deductions.

Second, make sure you are informed on all employee-related legal topics. Some laws kick in when you hire your first employee, while others become relevant when you hit certain quotas. These rules may vary widely from state to state, so talk to your lawyer to figure out what is required of you as an employer.

Third, make sure the additional payroll expense will be justified. Every new employee comes with a price tag, so the benefits they bring must be at least equal to their cost—even if that benefit appears in the future. New employees can be a drain on existing staff. They will necessarily need some help and training to get them to the point of independence; the length of the learning curve is directly related to the difficulty of the tasks to be performed. In addition to payroll costs, benefits, training, and the time drain on other employees, you also incur additional liability risk with every employee you add. So make sure the addition is well worth the cost.

Before you make any final expansion hiring decisions, look closely at your current staff and see how much more they can reasonably handle. Determine how much additional help you really need, based on your most realistic projections, and the best way to fulfill that need. Is temporary help the best way to get the company back on track, or do you need part-time personnel to cover expanded business hours, contractors to perform specific jobs, or full-time long-term employees to grow continually with the business?

Forecasting the Future

While it is somewhat easier to predict growth when you have an existing growth pattern in place, that knowledge will not quite cover the new paths your company will be heading down. Whether your expansion involves bringing in an entirely new group of customers, adding on a location or two, or branching out with fresh product offerings, your forecasts here will involve quite a bit more guesswork on your part.

Turning Things Around

Richard Ross owned a marginally unsuccessful woodworking shop. He seemed to attract enough clients to succeed, but his cash flow was consistently negative, and his bottom line showed small losses for the second year running. When Richard brought his box of receipts, checkbook, and bank statements to Jon, his CPA, at tax time, he asked what he could do to keep his company afloat.

The two men sat down and went over everything. Richard was right; he was attracting enough business. When it came to finances, though, Jon showed Richard several areas that needed attention. The most important involved collecting from customers and paying suppliers. Richard paid his suppliers cash; Jon suggested he ask them to extend thirty-day credit terms. On the flip side, Richard did not bill customers until the end of the month in which their jobs were completed, and he then waited at least thirty days for payment. Jon suggested collecting 25 percent deposits up front, then billing the day work was completed. Implementing these two simple suggestions could easily turn Richard's cash flow problem around.

Jon gave Richard nearly a dozen additional ideas that could help him stay in business. They created some pro forma financial statements that took into account the changes Richard planned to make. The new numbers showed positive cash flow in just three months' time, and steady profits soon after that.

With a small infusion of outside cash, Richard would be able to implement Jon's suggestions. They created a new business plan, included the new pro formas, and talked honestly to the loan officer about how Richard planned to turn things around. Though the loan came with strings—like monthly financial statements for the first three months—the loan did come through, and Richard's business is still going strong.

The methods you will employ, though, are very similar; and you do have some years of running a successful business to bolster your confidence in making assumptions. You know how much money it took to get your business going, and you know how much you currently spend to keep it going. You know what your revenues look like now, and you know the buying patterns of your core customer base. Now imagine what those numbers can look like with the expansion you're planning.

Keep in mind that some of the cash you've previously dedicated to running the business smoothly, and to taking home to your personal accounts, may be redirected to your expansion efforts. Diverting funds will have an impact, at least a temporary one, on your currently well-oiled machine. In addition, you will be diverting other resources as well: your time, the time of your co-owners (where applicable), your employees' time (and some extra cash if you will need to hire more staff or pay overtime), floor space, warehouse space, and advertising time. Those changes could have a negative impact on your current sales level, though the revenues will regain their footing and climb even higher when your new goals start to bear fruit.

To make your job easier, start with forecasts for the business you already have. Once that is complete, factor in the impact of the expansion. Remember to include the effects of a fresh cash infusion (whatever the source of the funding), and any major changes that will be needed to spark the new direction your company will be taking. Finally, tweak the revenue and expense accounts that will be affected on an ongoing basis.

Though you are adding a huge question mark to your pro forma financial statements, these projections should flow naturally from your historical statements. Your sales should not suddenly double in a single quarter if they've been growing steadily at 10 percent for years. It should be clear to your readers how your track record connects to your future plans.

Include Your Perceptions about the Business

No one knows your business better than you. Sure, your accountant may have a better handle on the financial and tax picture, and your warehouse manager may know some items on sight better than you do, but you see the business in ways they never could. Only you know how well your initial vision has been fulfilled. You can see which of your original goals have been met. And only you can clearly see (at least for now) what the future of your company looks like.

In this essay section of your business plan, your readers will have a chance to get to know you more personally, to gauge your passion, and to consider how realistically you can assess both your company and yourself. They know you are already committed to a financially successful enterprise—you have some history under your belt now. Here is where you show them your ongoing commitment to business growth for the longer term.

Present a frank assessment of your business so far, both successes and failures, with focus on failures that you have managed to turn around. Discuss potential changes, but use broad strokes rather than details. Talk about the reasoning behind your expansion plans, and how they can bring your business an even higher level of profitability.

While the way you present these perceptions in your business plan can sway opinion in your favor, focusing on these talking points during your meetings with potential lenders and investors can do even more to help ensure you get the money you are seeking.

▶▶ TEST DRIVE

Take a good look at the people who have made your business successful enough to merit this expansion. Your customers, your suppliers, and your employees have all helped you get to this point, but can they help your company climb to the next level? Answer these questions to find out:

1. How can you get your best customers to increase their annual purchases by 5 percent?
2. How will you ask your two biggest suppliers for increased volume discounts?
3. How can you reward your best employees with something other than money to make them want to stay on?

A Different Approach for New Businesses

A nonexistent business has no track record, no customer base, and no years of success to stand behind. In the absence of this information, your business plan readers will be looking for other things that can support both your potential as an entrepreneur and your company's possible profitability. What you really have to sell here is you and your vision. The more you have that points toward personal experience and successes, the better chance you have to convince lenders and investors that you and your company are a risk worth taking.

Aside from your personal financial situation, which is a crucial part of this plan, the money people will want to know a lot about you. They want to feel certain that you have the requisite experience, educational background, and the desire and drive to succeed in business. You will show them everything you've got going for you in a sort of specialized experience résumé. This document is not like a standard run-of-the-mill résumé that you would send to a prospective employer for a particular job. Instead, your experience résumé highlights your business-related accomplishments, including virtually anything you have done that will help you accomplish your entrepreneurial objectives.

Offset Any Deficiencies

If you know you are lacking in any facet of either the experience or education areas, show your readers how to intend to compensate for that. It's very common for entrepreneurs to outsource some tasks, such as bookkeeping, legal dealings, and daily management. You can use outside professionals (a CPA, a lawyer) or hire in-house staff (a store manager). You may consider taking on a partner who has a background that is complementary to yours. Maybe he has the general business management experience, while you are certified in the service your company will provide.

As long as you have a plan in place—and some specific people, or at least demonstrable attempts to bring in those people—your readers will be reassured.

Focus on Skills and Accomplishments

Even if you have never owned or run a business before, you have skills that are crucial to success. The trick is in how you present your existing talents, accomplishments, and skills to your business plan readers. This is not the place to be self-effacing. You are trying to sell yourself, so use strong language, and play up every valuable attribute you have.

The easiest way to go about this is to first make a list of every job and potentially related extracurricular experience you have ever had. The job list is easy, but what kinds of things can you include in the extracurricular section? Think about things you have done in your life—extensive travel, volunteer work, education, or contests and competitions, for example. Since this is where your readers will get to know you, you can include information about things like your hobbies, family background (especially if any member of your family is well known or has achieved business success), and organizations you belong to (like fraternities or professional associations).

Once you have that list completed, you'll add some details for each item. Start with general information, like what area of the business you worked in at each job (production, sales, or customer service, for example). Follow that up with a description of each thing you achieved while you were doing your job. Now look through your list of achievements, and choose the ones that are most likely to convince your business plan readers that you have what it takes to be successful.

Write a persuasive description of your strongest accomplishments, and try to write in a manner that makes you sound capable, reliable, and innovative without stretching the truth or outright boasting. You want to project an entrepreneurial image but not an unrealistic one. For example, suppose you had a job as a customer-service representative where you answered calls from a variety of customers. Customer interaction is an important building block for any business endeavor, so put a positive spin on the job to show specifically that you know how to deal directly with customers, even difficult ones. Instead of saying just that, put some numbers to it (for example, "I helped an average of 125 customers per day.") Explain how you satisfied those with complaints in a way that lost neither the sale nor the customer's future business. Or maybe you directly increased sales, like when customers called with address changes and you got them to try a new featured product.

Don't Leave Out the Mistakes

Everyone makes mistakes and (hopefully) learns from them. Instead of ignoring any business-related errors you have made in the past, include them and what you did to correct them (if applicable) or what you took away from the experience.

That is not to say you should list every mistake you've ever made. Only include those that have relevance to your business plan. For example, if you flunked out of Marketing 101 the first time you took it in college, leave that off. On the other hand, for example, you can include an explanation of the time you approved a batch of custom-ordered T-shirts that contained a spelling error and how you dealt with the aftermath of the mistake. And if you have any big business mistakes in your past—like a previous enterprise that went belly up—you must include them here. ▶▶ **Full disclosure is a crucial component of trust, and owning up to a mistake can go a long way toward building a solid (and fruitful) relationship with business plan readers.**

The key here is how you present your past mistakes. Admit them, explain why they happened, describe how you handled the fallout, and spell out what you learned—and how that can make you a better business owner going forward. Don't blame other people or take a position you know will be unpopular with your readers (for example, "I had too much credit card debt because the companies kept raising my limit, so it's their fault I had to declare bankruptcy without paying them back."). Accept responsibility, and craft an explanation that will instill confidence in the way you will handle problems in the future ("I got in over my head with credit card debt, and eventually declared bankruptcy. Since then, I have been working hard to restore my good credit rating and stick to a realistic monthly payment schedule.").

Your Personal Financial Situation Is Key

When both your entrepreneurship and your company have yet to be tested, business plan readers will want to know a lot more about you and your finances. Before ponying up any funds, investors and lenders want to know how much you have at stake. To put it another way, they will want to know both how much money you are personally putting into your business and how much money you could be putting into your business. These numbers do not necessarily have to be the same.

To that end, anyone even considering funding your company will want to see a complete and in-depth picture of your financial situation. In addition to looking at your current financial snapshot, investors and lenders also want an idea of how well you handle money. Again, this is not the place to cover up past mistakes. A simple glance at your credit report can tell your business plan readers of any financial mishaps you've endured. If you have had money troubles in the past, explain them and describe what you did to correct them.

Even if your personal financial situation is shaky, don't despair. Investors and lenders know you're looking for money—if you weren't, you would not have come to them in the first place. They just want to see your true financial picture, with its high and low points, and get a sense of how well you will be able to manage their money going forward.

To provide all the information your business plan readers will require, you have to prepare a complete set of personal financial statements for a couple of years, preferably along with some external verification (like corresponding income tax returns). Most lenders will probably conduct a credit check from one of the major credit reporting agencies; if your credit is very good, though, you may wish to include a copy of your credit report here. Other documents that could be helpful include letters of reference from creditors or business associates.

Personal Financial Statements

No start-up business plan would be complete without personal financial statements from the owner (or owners, if there are more than one of you). These serve as an easily verifiable, numeric introduction to your plan readers. It helps them learn how successful you have been at accumulating assets, managing debt, conserving cash, and budgeting within your income, at least up until now. Without an already existing business financial background to recommend you, your personal financial situation will speak for you instead.

Personal financial statements take the same basic form as the ones you would prepare for a business, with some slightly different twists. The balance sheet will contain all of your holdings and debts, resulting in your personal net worth. Your income statement, more typically called a schedule of income and expenses, will list all of the money you have coming in from earnings and all of your living expenses.

Sometimes the financial institution you are working with will have a form they want you to fill out or a preferred format they want you to follow. If that's the case, simply transfer the information you have gathered from your own worksheets on to theirs. Otherwise, you can follow the formats displayed in Appendix 3.

Another point to remember is that these numbers change frequently (especially current outstanding liability balances), so you may need to provide updated statements upon the request of anyone reading your business plan. For that reason, you may want to prepare these listings on a computer, where it will be a lot easier to make quick changes.

Personal Financial Software

The simplest way to create personal financial statements, particularly those that can be updated at a moment's notice, is to use personal financial software like Quicken. Not only will these programs make your business plan creation easier, but they can also simplify your personal life. Most of the programs on the market can now link to your bank accounts online, balance your checkbook, track your investments, create personal budgets, and even make tax time easier by exporting relevant data into your personal tax preparation software.

As for working with your business plan, most personal financial-planning software also exports to Microsoft Word and Excel files, which can easily be integrated into your business plan document.

Taking Inventory of Your Assets and Liabilities

The first step in preparing personal financial statements is figuring out both what you have and what you owe. Start with what you have, your assets. Describe everything substantial you own (even if you do still owe some money against it—you'll get to that part later) and its approximate current value. Here, think of current value as the amount you could get selling that asset today. If you aren't quite sure what something is worth, make a general guess for now. You can fill in a more realistic value later after you have done a little research.

Next you'll take a hard look at everything you owe (that is, your liabilities), from your outstanding student loans to the mortgage on your house. That means absolutely everything, no matter how small (though you can combine several small debts into one miscellaneous category) and no matter the creditor. If you currently owe money to friends or family members, include that here as well. Much of the time, your liabilities will correspond to your assets (like the mortgage on your house), so you can use your assets as a guide to help make sure you don't forget anything.

After you have made a comprehensive listing of both your assets and your liabilities, you add up each separately to come up with group totals. Then you subtract your total liabilities from your total assets to come up with your net worth.

How to Deal with a Negative Net Worth

When your liabilities exceed your assets, you have negative net worth. That means that even if you sold everything you have, there still would not be enough money to pay off all of your current debts. Sounds like an insurmountable obstacle, at least when it comes to attracting lenders and investors, but it's not. Yes, it will be more difficult to get outside funding, but it's not impossible.

There are a few ways to get around this problem. One is to have someone in good financial standing co-sign for a loan. Another is to forego the loan option entirely and look solely for equity investors instead. Or you could go to personal money sources, like family and friends.

Gathering Your Assets

The following list shows some common personal assets that you can include on your personal financial statements. If you own any of the assets jointly with someone else, make sure to indicate that clearly, along with your percentage of ownership:

>
> **Cash includes the balance in every account you have:** checking, savings, credit union, money market, and certificates of deposit plus money you have lying around anywhere else (like in a safe deposit box or vacation jar). Include the account type, number, institution, and balance for each one.

Marketable securities refers to any publicly traded mutual funds, exchange-traded funds, stocks, and bonds that you own. List the name and symbol for each, the number of shares you hold, the current share price (you should be able to find these in a newspaper like the *Wall Street Journal*), and your total current market value (number of shares times current share price).

Life insurance should be included only if you hold whole life policies that come with cash surrender values (typically less than the stated policy value). If you have only term life insurance, don't include anything here. Contact your insurance agent to get the most up-to-date cash value for any policies you hold.

Retirement funds include any monies held in formal retirement plans: individual retirement accounts (IRAs), whether they're traditional or Roth; employer-sponsored plans, like 401(k) or 403(b); and the balance in any accounts related to other businesses you own. Include the institution, account number, and current balance in your listing.

Real estate includes any property you own, whether you live there, vacation there, or hold it for investment purposes. For each property, list the address and type of property (land, residential home, office building, residential rental property) along with its current market value. You can get the approximate value of your home from a local realtor, or you can check the sales prices of comparable homes in your area. Obtaining professional appraisals is your best bet for valuing all other types of real estate.

Personal property refers to basically everything else you own, from your clothing to your car. Include a separate listing for any valuable assets (expensive jewelry, vehicles), and group your other possessions by category (household appliances, artwork). For any significant assets, come up with a verifiable number for the value, like a professional appraisal.

If you have some holdings that don't quite fit into any of these categories, you can create a new heading for them or simply include a section for "other assets." Other assets could include notes you hold (where the debtors are paying you back), annuities, unlisted securities (like stock in a small privately held company), or a family trust. Don't include any income you receive from your assets (like interest on your savings account or rental income from your rental properties); that will appear in the income and expense portion of your financial statements.

Listing Your Liabilities

As with assets, there are some basic personal liabilities that should be included in your individual financial statements. If any of these debts involve cosigners, or if you are a cosigner or guarantor on someone else's debt, be sure to include that information in your listing:

"Credit cards "is used in the broadest sense. Include major credit cards, store accounts, gasoline cards, charge cards, but not direct debit cards. For each one, list the name, account number, current outstanding balance, and credit limit.

Signature loans include any direct debts you have that are not backed by specific collateral. While you can owe these to anyone, including banks, the most common are student loans and loans from friends or family. For each, list the lender, the account number (if applicable), the outstanding balance due, and the loan terms.

Real estate loans are those secured by real property, and they typically come in the form of a mortgage or home equity loan. Include the name of the lender, the address of the property, loan number, remaining principal balance, and the loan terms.

Personal property loans include debts secured by any property that's not considered real estate. Most commonly these include car or boat loans, but they could be backed by almost anything tangible. Again, you will need to list the lender, a description of the property in question, current balance, and loan terms.

What Are Your Loan Terms?

When you list your loans, you need to include the terms of each loan so that the readers of your business plan know the details behind what you owe. Standard loan terms include payment schedules, due dates, interest rates, and any special arrangements (like balloon payments). The very least information you need to include is the interest rate, the date the final payment is due, the current payment, and payment frequency.

If you have an adjustable-rate loan, you will need to add some supplemental information. Include how the interest rate is calculated, how often it adjusts, and any minimums or maximums the rate is subject to.

If you have any other outstanding liabilities, you can lump them together in a catchall category. Other debts you should list include outstanding medical bills, income tax liabilities, loans against life insurance policies or retirement accounts, and even unpaid parking tickets. Don't include ongoing household expenses like your homeowner's insurance or your monthly cable bill; those will show up in the expenses section of your personal budget.

Creating a Personal Budget

Next in your set of personal financial statements comes a schedule of your income and expenses, commonly known as a personal budget. This is similar to a company's statement of profit and loss, with the exception of its resulting bottom line. There is no line for a final net profit or loss, just total income and total expenses.

The first section will cover all of your annual income from every source. Many people confuse this with their assets, since assets often tend to generate income. Here's the difference. Look at a stock that pays quarterly dividends—the stock itself is an asset, the dividends count as income. That includes even dividends that you reinvest, as is common with mutual fund holdings. Make sure that if you show income earned from an asset here that the asset is listed in your asset inventory.

Once you've finished compiling your income, you will turn to your regular annual living expenses. The point of this exercise is to gain a true picture of how much money it takes to live your life the way you live it now. So grab your checkbook, receipts, calendar, printouts from your personal financial software, or anything else you use to keep track of the money you spend. Expenses are the easiest to underestimate or skip, which makes them the area most vulnerable to miscalculation. Make no mistake, though: These figures are among the most important ones that you will prepare *for yourself.* You will not be able to devote yourself to starting a successful business if you are constantly worried about making ends meet. A realistic view of your living expenses will help you figure out how much money you really need to get your company up and running.

Figure Out Your Annual Income

One thing to keep in mind is that potential lenders (particularly) and investors (possibly) may want to see verification of your income figures. They may ask for prior years' tax returns, bank statements, appraisal reports, and other forms of corroboration. So have the following backup documents available for them to see, if requested.

In this section, you will include all the money you receive from every source as of now. That includes income that may stop coming in as you start your business. For example, you should include your current annual salary even if you plan to quit your job to get the company going, and you should include current dividends you receive on stocks that you plan to sell to fund the business. Sources of income include the following:

Annual gross salary should be included for every job you hold. Start with your base salary or wages, then list actual bonuses and overtime separately. Do not include potential income (like an upcoming bonus that is not guaranteed) or expected raises here (but you can mention them in a note, if they are likely to occur).

Other job-based income, such as money earned as an independent contractor, should be added to this list. If you have a long-term contract, include the full amount you will earn this year. If you work on a job-to-job basis, list the income you have already earned separately from the income you expect to earn, and make sure to label the expected income appropriately in a note.

Interest and dividends from any of your holdings also belong on this list. List each account or security and the annual income you expect it to earn. If you reinvest the dividends you earn, list them and include a note about the reinvestment plan. Remember, this income is produced by your assets, and those exact same assets must appear in the asset section.

Rental income comes next, for any real estate or personal property (like a tractor or a boat) that you rent to someone else. Include a brief description of the property (again, it should correspond to something in your asset section) and the annual rental payments you receive. Add in any relevant details about the leases, like when they expire, and be sure to include a note about any upcoming rent increases.

Business income from any other business interests you have can be included here. For example, if you earn moonlighting income (you work for a CPA firm and do taxes for your neighbors on the side), list it here.

Other income covers virtually any other source of incoming funds; if any single source is substantial, list it separately instead of lumping it in here. Other income might include things like alimony and child support, interest payments on money you loaned to someone else, money expected from a court judgment or settlement, and trust fund distributions.

Once you have listed every income source you have, add them all up and list your total annual income on a line at the bottom of the page.

Cover All of Your Expenses

In this segment of your personal financial statements, you will strive to come up with an accurate tally of your current annual living expenses. From the food you eat to the gas you put in your car, everything you spend to get through the day counts here. Many people are surprised once they systematically count up their expenditures; it's almost always more than they expected. Knowing the real deal, even if you are not happy about the number at the end, is crucial to the eventual success of your business.

Remember, list all your expenses by their annual amount, including the following:

Mortgage or rent payments are usually the biggest annual household expense. Write down the name of your landlord or mortgage company, specify whether you're paying mortgage or rent, and include the total annual payment. For your mortgage, this may include interest, insurance, and taxes. Don't worry about the breakdown—just multiply your monthly payment by twelve.

Property taxes, if not included in your mortgage payment, go here. So do any personal property taxes, which are charged by several states. If you know of an upcoming change in your tax payments, due to a reassessment for example, include that information here.

Income taxes need to be accounted for here, federal, state, and local. If you think your total annual income tax bill will be similar to last year's (based on your current income), use the numbers from last year's tax returns. If you think the numbers may be significantly different, ask your accountant to help you come up with a reasonable estimate.

Debt payments for each liability listed in your liability section go here. It helps to copy down the name of each loan and the annual required payment. For credit card debt, use the amount you are currently paying each month, not the minimum payment. (If you pay off your balance every month, put that under living expenses instead of here.)

Insurance premiums for every type of personal policy you carry. That includes life, auto, homeowners, disability, flood, health—even amounts that are directly deducted from your paycheck should be taken into account here. However, don't include any premiums paid by your employer. If your homeowner's insurance is included in your mortgage payment, don't count it again.

Everyday expenses cover a lot of territory, and this is where a look through your checkbook and cash receipts could come in handy. Here's a partial listing to get you started: groceries, utilities, child care, pet care, Internet, cable, gas, auto maintenance and repairs, house cleaning, haircuts, medical co-pays and deductibles, and whatever else you regularly spend money on.

Other expenses can include everything that really doesn't fit anywhere else but still needs to be accounted for. This category can cover things like education costs, alimony and child support, holiday gifts, vacation plans, and emergency funds. This is also a good spot to put any regular savings plans you have in place, including retirement plan contributions.

Just as with your income, you'll add up all of your expenses to come up with a total annual figure. If your expense total exceeds your annual income number, you may want to look for ways to trim your budget before you take on the responsibility of another loan payment.

Estimating Business Income and Expenses

Once you have gotten your personal financial information out of the way, your next task is to figure out how much money your business will need. Although it would seem easier, you cannot just pluck these numbers out of thin air. You need to think through some major issues and make some planning decisions based on realistic estimates of how your company will run and what that means in terms of income and expenses. It sounds tough, but once you get started, you'll see that it's not as bad as you expected.

Chances are that you did not just wake up this morning and decide that you wanted to start your own business. You have probably been thinking about it for a fairly long time, and you may have already considered some of the financial implications. Now you'll have to quantify your ideas, make some basic assumptions (you'll learn how to do that in Chapter 9), and come up with some logical estimates.

There are some basic guidelines to follow when you are starting your financial projections:

1. Take a conservative approach, which in accounting terms means estimate income on the low side and expenses on the high side.
2. Stick with the standards. Follow the normal practices standard for your industry, and use industry averages appropriate to your business size as guideposts in making your estimates.
3. Be consistent. Once you have made an assumption, follow it all the way through.
4. If you need some professional advice, get it—that's what your accountant is there for.

Finally, remember the point of what you are doing. You're really just trying to come up with an accurate idea of the amount of money you need, what that money will be spent on, and how you will be able to repay it.

Estimating Revenue

Trying to come up with an estimated revenue figure can be a very tough job for a novice entrepreneur. While your estimated costs and expenses are typically based on numbers that come from or grow from numbers you can find somewhere else, your revenue estimates come mostly from you. Yes, they will be based on your market research and your ultimate pricing schedule. But you have much less control over how many customers you will eventually have, and how much they will buy, than you have over virtually any other facet of the business.

That said, you have to start somewhere, and that somewhere has to be reasonable. While it's tempting to back into a desired revenue number—one that will help your business show initial projected profits—your business plan readers will demand an explanation as to where your figures came from. The answer they will be expecting contains a nod to industry averages appropriate for the size of your company, the economic state of your market, typical customer buying patterns, and prices that make sense. As long as you have something logical to back up the numbers you use, you will be able to reassure potential lenders and investors that your projected revenue levels are achievable.

Estimated Sales Drive the Cost of Sales

If you are planning for a product-based business, you have to buy every piece of merchandise before you sell it. The money you paid for the item you sold is the cost of sales for that product. For example, you buy a coffee cup for $3 and sell it for $5; $5 is your revenue, and $3 is your cost of sales. Following this example, if you estimate coffee cup sales of $50,000, your cost of sales would be $30,000.

In reality, though, the numbers are not usually quite so simple. You may be selling more than one product, or the one product you sell may have different costs associated with it (for example, depending on the quantity you buy). Don't let yourself get bogged down with minute calculations; instead, go for big-picture numbers and average cost of sales for your projections.

Remember, these are estimates. They are based on facts and reasonable expectations, but they are still estimates, and you can adjust them once you are actually in business and have a better feel for how things really flow.

Calculating Overhead

Overhead refers to the expenses not directly associated with the merchandise your company sells. For service-oriented businesses, virtually all expenses fall into this category. For product-oriented businesses, overhead covers everything but direct product costs (which includes direct labor costs for manufacturing concerns).

Overhead expenses typically include things like these:

 Rent
 Office worker salaries
 Utilities

➲ Insurance
➲ Interest
➲ Office supplies

Here's a good rule of thumb when trying to figure out whether an expense would count as overhead. If you would still incur this cost even if you never had a sale, then it is overhead. A delivery charge, for example, only kicks in when you make a sale; on the other hand, you have to pay rent no matter what.

A Realistic Cash Flow Timetable

When it comes to staying in business, cash is key. Even more important than your revenue and expense projections are your expectations about upcoming cash flow. Should your projections call for more money heading out than coming in, you will need to ask for additional cash to make sure your fledgling company will be able to stay afloat during those initially cash-tight months. Having a realistic picture of the way cash will flow through your company will help you plan for shortfalls well in advance. That kind of forethought holds a lot of weight with potential lenders and investors.

▸▸ **It cannot be stressed enough that new businesses live and die by cash flow.** Even if you predict your business will earn substantial profits right out of the gate, those profits won't carry it through a time of no cash. Especially in the earliest stages, cash is even more important than profits; in the long term, though, profits are what will generate positive cash flow. Positive cash flow means you have more cash coming in than going out; negative cash flow means you have more cash going out than coming in. Negative cash flow is extremely common for brand-new companies, and for that reason, having sufficient cash on hand before you get started will be crucial to your company's continued existence. You can have cash in the bank and negative cash flow; that just means you will need to draw on reserves instead of being able to use only the cash coming in to meet your obligations.

When you set your cash flow timetable, it may not resemble your income and expense projections. That may seem illogical to those new to the ways of business finance, but it's based on the premise that not all income earned generates *immediate* cash, and not all expenses incurred call for *immediate* payment. In addition, loans and capital contributions will bring in cash flow with absolutely no impact on your profit and loss. The opposite holds true for payback of loan principal and owners taking money out of the business for personal use; cash comes out, but no expense is triggered. The trick is to realistically envision how your company's initial operating cash flow (that tied only to items of income and expense) will run, and plan your reserves accordingly.

As you begin to put numbers on paper, your cash budget will take two parts: setup and beginning operations. Initially, part of your cash budget will go toward forming the business and making capital asset purchases. That portion of your plan covers the starting capital investment, or setup. The rest will go toward keeping you afloat during the first few months in business, when operational cash inflow may not be enough to get your company through; that portion will be considered your initial working capital.

Developing a realistic cash flow timetable gives you the basis for coming up with the amount you need to have on hand to use as initial working capital. Based on your income projections, you will develop cash inflow projections, taking into account how quickly you can reasonably expect to see cash realized from your sales. If you will not be making sales on credit, your sales revenue will be the same as your cash inflow; however, if you plan to bill customers, cash inflow will lag behind sales revenue. Next, you will review your expense projections and determine which of those require immediate cash disbursement and which allow for a time lag between purchase and payment. At the end, you will sum the inflows and outflows separately, then subtract outflows from inflows. Do not be distressed if you have negative cash flow initially—expect it, and plan for it.

▶▶ TEST DRIVE

Starting a new business can put a severe (if temporary) cramp in your style of living, not to mention your personal cash situation. To combat any feelings of deprivation during the money- and time-consuming start-up process, you need to find something that makes you feel good and relaxed, away from the business. List three low-cost activities that can help you regenerate positive energy and that force you to spend some time focusing on yourself, your family, and your friends. When things get crazy, make yourself do one of the things on the list.

Start with an Industry Overview

Understanding the bigger picture surrounding your business will provide you with unique insights and a better understanding of the distribution channels your company will be dealing with. The more you know about the industry, the better chance your business has of succeeding. On top of that, investors and lenders want to know that you have a solid grasp of the way your industry works, and here is your chance to prove it. That calls for some homework on your part, in the form of market research.

Lead with a general statement about the current state of the industry as a whole. Follow that up with a nod to existing industry players, which will be addressed in greater detail when you prepare your competitive analysis. Next, include discussion about the overall sales cycle and trends of the industry. Finally, describe the typical distribution channels and how you plan to use them to your company's advantage.

The State of the Industry

To learn what kind of shape your industry is in right now, you first need to identify the industry specifically. The U.S. government comes in very handy here—it created a series of categories and classifications identified by numerical codes called the Standard Industrial Classification (SIC), which was then revised and refined into the North American Industry Classification System (NAICS). You can find these codes at *www.osha.gov*. Once you know the official SIC or NAICS code (both are still widely used) along with the official name for your industry, it makes the numbers search go much more quickly. And while you're at a government Web site, look up any regulations pertinent to your industry.

Next, you will need to look up some key statistics. First, find out the total size of the industry in both revenue dollars and number of participants. You may be able to find this information at *www.fedstats.com* (another U.S. government Web site). You can also check out trade associations, which usually possess a mint of data about their key industries. And don't overlook local libraries as a rich source of information; they often stock trade journals and magazine directories (which can give you an indication of how an industry is faring by how many periodicals it supports).

Give some thought to these numbers. Is the market already huge? Are there hundreds of companies just like yours already out there? Or is the industry mainly made up of very large businesses that cater to very wide audiences? The current size of the market speaks to your company's chances of successfully breaking into it.

Remember, the industry encompasses more than just companies that sell the same things that yours does. It also includes things like common suppliers and companies that sell corresponding products (like lamps and lightbulbs). From the raw materials needed to create the products you carry to the person who hands that final product over to the customer, all of these pieces must be taken into account when you analyze the industry as a whole.

Why Everyone Else Matters

In addition to your competitors, it's important to scope out all of the facets of your industrial chain. The reasoning behind this is simple. If, for example, your suppliers run out of product, so do you. If the delivery truck drivers go on strike, your company will be affected.

Every link in the chain can affect your sales and your profitability directly, sometimes even indirectly. That's why you need a basic understanding of how each part in the chain interacts, what events could be coming up on the horizon, and how you and your competitors can deal with any changes.

Get to Know the Other Industry Participants

Now that you've gotten a handle on the industry as a whole, take some time to learn about the company your company will be keeping. Fully comprehending the ins and outs here means being able to describe the character of the participants.

There is a world of difference between a local farm stand and Del Monte and an equally large difference between vegetable growers and Internet service providers. Understanding the types of companies that dominate your industry will provide guidance as to whether room exists for a new entry.

This is not the same as performing a competitive analysis, though that information often builds on what you've learned from this overview. Don't get bogged down in small details here. Instead, take a big-picture view of the nature and sizes of the companies that make up your industry.

Business Cycles and Industry Trends

Your industry, and therefore your company, exists at the mercy of standard business cycles and market trends. What's the difference between the two? A business cycle follows the same pattern, time after time. It's a predictable, stable, normal part of doing business. An industry trend, on the other hand, comes from the outside—and it can turn on a dime.

▶▶ **Every business has a cycle.** For example, companies that sell Christmas decorations experience predictable peaks and lulls; that's an example of a seasonal, product-driven cycle. If you send out a specials flyer once a month, and sales go up a few days after it hits the mail, you've created an event-driven sales cycle. Essentially, your sales will experience some easily identifiable mountains and valleys, so steady that you can comfortably make plans around them.

Industry trends can signify changes in your overall market. They can be caused by changes in customer demographics; for example, older empty-nest couples move out of the neighborhood, and young families move in. They can be caused by major shifts in consumer tastes, like fads that fall in and out of favor (think bell-bottoms or leg warmers). Or they can be brought on by changes in the basic needs of consumers. For example, if there is another baby boom, diapers and formula sales could hit previously unknown heights. Trends are a little harder to plan around, but knowing where the industry stands right now and understanding how to take advantage of that should be a key part of your plan.

Finding Your Target Market

No matter how great or groundbreaking your product or service may be, it will not appeal to everyone. However, almost every product will be desired by some group of people—and your ability to figure out exactly which group (or groups) those are will have a big influence on the eventual success of your company.

Once you have identified that major subgroup, you can increase your success potential further by narrowing it down into smaller, more distinct groups. These groups are called niches, or segments, and they are the ones most likely to buy your particular product or service. They can be categorized by both demographic and geographic terms, and that will help you reach them in ways that will uniquely impact their buying decisions.

How Target Marketing Helps You

Clearly defining your target customer market benefits your company in a number of ways. First, it helps you focus your promotional efforts. It's simply not possible to convince everyone out there to come in and buy what you're selling. Some people may already have a foot in the door, while others have absolutely no interest at all in buying your offerings. Of the people who are already interested, some are more likely to buy—and buy a lot—than others who need hand-holding and lots of persuasion to finally take out their wallets. Your precious marketing dollars are best spent on the people who are both likely to be interested in your product and ready to buy it.

Then there is the geography feature to consider. Advertising costs money, a lot of it. If you can point your best promotional efforts in the direction of your best potential customers, you will have the funds available to reach them more often instead of wasting your efforts on people out of range. For example, if your shop is in the northwest corner of a relatively large state, advertising in local or county newspapers makes more sense than running a state-wide campaign. It will certainly cost less, as lower circulation typically means lower ad rates. Plus, you will be talking to people in your immediate area. These people are more likely to show up at your shop than those who would have to take a two-hour car trip to get there.

Next comes the impact your market has on your choice of media. With so many options available, it makes sense to frequent those that your target customers are most likely to look at. For example, if your target market consists of people who don't use home computers, putting all of your advertising eggs in an Internet basket probably won't do much to increase your sales traffic.

Develop a Customer Profile

The cornerstone of your marketing efforts is your customer profile. You cannot develop an effective marketing strategy without knowing exactly who you want to buy your product or service. If you don't know who will be buying what your company will be offering and why they're making that purchase, you won't know how to contact them to let them know what you are doing. ▶▶ **Without a narrow picture of your typical customer, your marketing approach will be hit or miss (at best).** Basically, you will end up putting out a generic message and waiting to see who bites. That methodology is inefficient and expensive, even within a target market; your time and resources will be better spent on a more focused campaign.

Developing your key customer profile flows from your target market, focusing more clearly on specific characteristics unique to this group. To get there, you may want to perform a sort of customer character analysis to figure out a representative persona. Speaking to one character, one that you can actually picture in your mind, will make it easier to come up with promotional ideas. If your target market is made up of institutions or other businesses, as opposed to individuals, your task here will be slightly different.

When Your Key Customers Are Individuals

To come up with the best marketing approach, you must have a close, personal view of your target customers. You must get to know them inside and out, from their defining qualities to what they like to eat for dinner to why they prefer dogs to cats. The more clearly you can see this typical target customer, the easier it will be to develop targeted promotions that will draw him or her in.

First, though, you will develop a basic sketch of common characteristics of your potential customers. Not everyone in the target group will necessarily share every single one of these traits, but most target customers will share most of the characteristics. Here are some basic characteristics you can consider when trying to come up with your target customer profile for individual consumers:

➲ Sex
➲ Age group

➥ Education level
➥ Marital status
➥ Neighborhood type
➥ Average household income
➥ Occupation types
➥ Media preferences
➥ Preferred leisure activities

As you begin compiling this information, you may not yet know which particular traits will impact your upcoming business decisions. But be assured that somehow, these common characteristics will flow into virtually all of your marketing decisions, from additional products you will sell to the pricing schedule you set to your primary means of advertising. In marketing, everything will flow back to this target customer.

When Your Customers Are Companies

When your business will be catering to other businesses, the defining characteristics will be very different than those of individuals. Here, instead of looking solely at the personal traits of the people who make up your target market, you will pay more attention to the qualities that define the company. The typical buyer's traits will factor in to your final profile, but the primary focus will be on those elements that define the businesses you are targeting.

When you try to pinpoint your business targets, you will focus mainly on numeric information, such as average annual sales, number of employees, and size of customer base. Next, you can look at descriptive defining characteristics of target customers, such as their general industry, their primary locations, stage of life (whether they're start-ups or firmly established), and who their key customers are.

When companies make purchases, they typically funnel these decisions through a single person. As you try to put together a picture of the primary buying contacts, the traits you come up with will be similar to those of individual consumers, with a business twist. So in addition to their key demographic information (age, marital status, and income level, for example), you will try to put together professional information. This data would include responsibility level (like their relative position within the company), average dollar amount of purchase choices (either monthly or annual, depending on the frequency with which you hope they will buy from you), budget control level (how much spending they can authorize on their own), and preferred contact method (phone, fax, e-mail).

Once you have a distinct view of both your target business customers and of the individuals who will actually be making the buying decisions, you can combine those descriptions into a more focused marketing message.

Know Your Customers' Needs

Now that you know exactly who your key customers are, you will need to alter your focus toward their needs. Why? Because customer needs lead to purchase decisions, and those purchases keep you in business. This area requires minute specificity, both about the needs your customers have and exactly how your product or service will satisfy those needs. Here, you will define exactly the benefits your customers will derive from the products or services you are selling, and those benefits must mesh with the customer needs.

▶▶ **That's the key: your product provides benefits that mirror the solutions to your customers' problems.** The benefits may be direct or indirect. When someone buys a new dresser, for example, they get a place to put their socks, but they also add style to the bedroom. As you consider your customers' needs, consider every possible benefit they could derive from what you are selling, even if it isn't obvious at first glance. It's easy to stop looking with the direct benefits, but experienced marketers know that consumer needs are much more complex than that. That same dresser could be something to boast about (a rare and expensive piece), a story to tell (an antique once owned by someone noteworthy), a contribution to society (made by impoverished tribes in the rainforest). Don't overlook the importance of the indirect customer needs your product can fulfill.

To get your creative juices flowing, start with the obvious. You may be surprised at what other ideas will be triggered, and which may turn out to become key points in your promotional campaigns. Looking at the list from two sides—both what benefits you think your product or service offers and what needs your customer has—may initiate some new ideas as well.

If you can identify a need that your offering can fulfill that can't be satisfied by anyone else out there, your company is in a unique position to succeed—at least until someone else comes along to do what you are doing (and if you succeed, they will). Otherwise, list all the ways those customer needs are already being met, and focus on some complementary needs that your product covers as well. Customer demands are rarely static. When people can get bananas on almost every corner, they start considering other factors in deciding where to get their bananas, such as who has the lowest price, where to find the freshest produce, who offers organic options, or where to find the biggest selection. By identifying and fulfilling more than one need, you have a better chance of attracting customers to your establishment.

What Triggers the Buying Decision?

Customers may not realize they go through a particular thought process every time they buy something. They may not know the reason they choose one product over another that may be almost exactly the same. Even if you ask them directly, you may get only the tip of the decision-making iceberg. You know that customer needs are more complex than first meets the eye, and their motivations can run even deeper.

To truly understand what triggers the purchase decision, you need to use a combination of market research and intuition (which any entrepreneur can develop with time). Market research involves asking a lot of customers a lot of questions, then tabulating those answers to come up with common threads. In this case, you would use that information to come up with the motivating factors behind their purchases. Add to that your own instincts and imagination about what convinces a customer to buy Product A instead of Product B, and you're on your way to understanding how to get them to buy from you.

Two completely separate factors come into play when you are trying to pinpoint those things that will motivate customers to buy products and services from your company. One comes from the customer's perspective, a look at their internal motivators. The other comes from outside influences on the customer's buying behavior. Combined, these will help you identify the conscious and unconscious factors that can set off the purchase process.

Your Customers' Internal Motivators

What gets people to the point of purchase? Different customers are motivated by unique sets of factors. All people have basic physical needs, such as food, clothing, and shelter, to name an obvious few. But at the very core of buying decisions are emotional, human issues. What are some of those internal motivators that drive people to purchase particular products and services? Start with pride and desire, two core drivers that are common to most customers. Pride issues include things like appearance and possession. Typical human desires cover things like acknowledgment, esteem, variety, protection, convenience, and belonging.

Take any one of those core motivators, and you can break it down even further. For example, protection clearly covers physical safety and personal security, but it also includes privacy, health and wellness, and emergency preparedness. The desire for protection could encompass any or all of these issues, perhaps even more. Once you know exactly what could motivate potential customers to purchase your product, you'll be well on your way to tapping in to those motivations and developing a persuasive marketing campaign.

External Triggers

Part of what goes into final purchase decisions has to do with thought processes. There are a basic series of steps that most buyers run through before they buy anything, whether they know it or not. The previous section covered the emotional motivators; here, you instead look at the rational pieces of the decision-making process. The first step is to identify who actually makes the final decision and what external factors can influence his choice.

Here are some questions to consider as you try to figure out the external triggers involved in your customers' purchase decisions when they consider your product or service:

1. Is this typically an impulse purchase or a planned one?

2. Will direct contact (in person, on the phone) usually be a factor in closing the sale?

3. Which is more important, the product itself or the company's reputation?

4. Which product features will be most prone to competitive comparisons?

5. Does the "everyone else has it" idea play more prominently than exclusivity or uniqueness?

6. Can sweeteners and incentives play a part in the decision?

7. Will multiple interactions (more than one follow-up sales call, for example) work well or turn people off?

8. When more than one person is involved in making the purchase, which one makes the final decision?

Finding the answers to these questions can help your eventual marketing strategy in a number of ways. First, it will help you decide how best to interact with your customers. Second, it will help you position your product, both physically and in the marketplace. Finally, it will allow you to focus on the true decision makers.

How to Set Prices

Figuring out the optimum price for your product or service, the price at which your company will make a profit and your customers will not balk, can be tricky. At the very least, your business needs to cover expenses and make some profit; basing your pricing schedule on that is considered cost-based pricing. On the other hand, you cannot really charge more than the market will bear; that approach is called, as you might expect, market-based pricing. In most cases, your costs will set the price floor, or the absolute lowest price you can possibly charge without going broke, while the market will set the price ceiling, the absolute highest price you can charge without scaring away customers. Somewhere in the middle, you will find the optimum price.

▸▸ **Like much else in the marketing game, price is not just a number.** It can symbolize more than merely the amount of cash traded for a product or service—in some cases, for instance, it represents status and worth. In those cases, pricing your product or service too low can make it seem inferior, even if it is exactly the same thing your competitor is offering at a higher price. Customer perceptions enter the picture when the perceived value of a product or service is as important as the intrinsic value. Here, more comes into play than whatever it is you are actually selling—your company's reputation, value-added services, and other intangible triggers all factor into the selling price. And while pricing too low can be a mistake, beware of pricing too high. Crossing that line can also cost you customers.

What kind of information will you need to create an appropriate pricing strategy? You'll need to learn a combination of cost and market factors to come up with the range, then add some judgment to narrow the field. Here is the information you will need to collect:

- The results of your most realistic break-even analysis
- Industry-specific profit margins for companies of similar size to yours
- A sample of the pricing policies of several direct competitors
- The income level of your target customers
- The general spending habits of your target customers

Armed with this data, you will be able to come up with a realistic pricing schedule for your products and services, one that is not too low for your company to realize profits and not so high that it eliminates potential customers.

Scope Out the Competition

For your company to survive and thrive, you need to know who your competitors are and what they are doing. While they should not be your primary focus when you make business decisions, they're still pretty high up on the considerations list. If you're unaware, the competition can squash your company, no matter how great it may be.

There are a lot of solid reasons why knowledge of your competitors matters so much. For example, if the current market you're selling in isn't getting any bigger, the only way you can attract more business and increase your market share is to take customers away from your competitors. Also, you can learn a lot about what works and what doesn't work by simply observing the moves your rivals make and the results they get. At the very least, you need to know how the choices your competitors make affect your business and how you will position your company to attract customers. The first step, though, is to find out just who your competitors are.

How to Identify Your Competition

Just a couple of decades ago, you could simply walk down the street or drive a few miles and see all of your direct competitors up close and in person. Now, competition comes from everywhere, and discovering the identity of your business rivals takes a little more thought and a lot more research.

Instinctually, when you think about your competition, you probably do have a picture in your head of someone local. That company counts as your *known* competition—he's there now, you know who he is, and you know where to find him. Start your competitor list with companies like this, and name everyone you can think of. Include local rivals, companies that are not local but deliver locally, Web sites, catalogs—basically, any type of company that does the same thing your company is doing.

The next group of competitors you need to think about is made up of the companies that could be coming soon. These possible competitors can sneak up on you if you aren't paying attention. This group could include new online suppliers that will offer the same product or service as your company. Also, consider that one of your vendors could cut out the middleman (that's you) and start selling directly to the public. Maybe an existing company is expanding into your area, or a new company is moving in just down the street. Make a list of any company that *could* be a competitor, even if they aren't yet.

Finally, one of the biggest competitive threats can come from alternative products and services. Alternative products provide a different solution to the same problem that your product solves. For example, a hardware store could provide competition for a handyman—if people decide to fix things themselves, that handyman is losing clients. A home water filter is an alternative to bottled water, and a treadmill could replace a gym membership. Getting a handle on this type of competition is tricky, and it requires a lot of imagination on your part. But because these companies can remove the need for your product in customer's minds, it can also be the most important part of your competitive analysis.

What You Want to Know

Now that you have identified all of your competitors (the known, the possible, and the alternatives), you need to uncover information that will help you run your company more effectively. There is a vast amount of data out there, and it could literally take forever to go through it all. Instead, focus your attention on learning specific things about each competitor. The research itself may take a little more time than just searching for general information, but the reading, sorting, and filing phase will go much more quickly without a lot of unusable data to wade through.

The simplest way to handle this is to make a worksheet for each company on your list. Start with the basics: name, address(es), size, and the type of competition they present. Then try to answer some useful questions that can help you when you're creating your marketing plans. You can use the following questions as a jumping-off point, but tailor them to make sense for your unique business situation:

1. Who are the customers of this competitor?
2. How does this company deliver its products and/or services to customers?
3. What types of advertising and promotions does this company use now?
4. How does this company distinguish its product(s) from its competitors' offerings?
5. What are its main advantages and weaknesses compared to your company?
6. How does this company price its products?
7. Does this company have plans to expand? In what way?
8. Does this company have a solid existing capital supply?
9. What is its current market share?
10. How good are its products and services?

Again, these sample questions can help direct you toward the type of information that will be most useful to you. You may also want to find out what their customers think of you and what your customers think of them. Look for answers to any questions that you feel will help you hone your competitive edge.

How to Use the Information

Once you've gotten the inside scoop on your competition, it's time to put that information to good use. Now you know what they have, you know what you have, and you know what differentiates your products from theirs. A good place to focus your marketing efforts is on what makes you better than the competition. Remember, virtually any difference can be turned into an advantageous selling point—and that's what will attract customers to your business.

Your strongest promotional efforts will come from somewhere inside you. But if you're having trouble finding inspiration, the information you uncover in the course of your research can give you a good place to start. For example, you can start by making direct comparisons between your product and your competitor's—"20 percent larger than Brand A." Or you can play up a service you offer that they don't: "Our on-staff home repair experts will help you select the right tool for the job."

You can also use your competitive analysis to come up with a slightly different niche market for your product. Maybe you and your main competitor offer products to new pet owners, but they focus on people who have bought their "babies" from pet stores or breeders, leaving the shelter-adoption crowd free for you to tap.

There are other ways you can develop an edge over your competition. For example, if your main competitor does not have a Web site up yet, get yours up and running—pronto. Or maybe they don't take credit cards, or at least not every credit card, giving you a very simple way to a quick advantage. Every piece of information you have can be transformed to make your company stronger. This is true even if it speaks to something your competitor does better than you that you can't match right now (but maybe you can find an alternative that offers similar customer benefits).

Where to Find All This Information

You are now charged with collecting an awful lot of information. The task can seem overwhelming at first, so try breaking it down into bite-sized chunks. Deal with one type of data at a time, and then move to the next. At the end, you will have a massive pile of research to sift through—that's a good thing. The more information you have at your fingertips, the better able you will be to create a successful marketing strategy.

First things first, though. And first you need to know where to find this vast field of information. The easiest place to start, and the one that offers the most potential, is the Internet. Plan on logging dozens of hours on the information superhighway as you begin to collect your data. When you just can't take sitting by yourself and staring at a screen anymore, hit your local library. Tell the librarian what kinds of information you are looking for, and he will be able to direct you to sources ranging from periodicals to trade journals. When you feel you have amassed enough background information, you can hit the streets and actually talk to people like potential customers, competitors, and suppliers. You want to hear from virtually anyone who can provide you with answers to your outstanding questions.

Going to the Ultimate Sources

Indirect research is wonderful, useful, and helpful, but it does have limits. In the first place, if data is already published (even on the Web), it is already yesterday's news. Some of it may even be hopelessly outdated—for example, U.S. Census information is collected only once every ten years. While you do absolutely need this background data, going straight to the source can provide you with more timely information that just may be more pertinent to your particular business. You can do this primary research on your own, or, if you've got the cash available, you can hire a marketing firm to do it for you. The do-it-yourself method serves two purposes here. It will save you some money, and it will put you in direct contact with your audience, which can be invaluable to your plans. Before you get in people's faces, though, make sure you know what you are trying to find out, and plan your contacts accordingly.

Start with customer research. There are a few ways to go here, including one-on-one interviews (either in person or by phone), focus groups, and written surveys. Choose the method you are the most comfortable with and start with that. ▶▶ **No matter how you approach your contacts, you have to put some time and thought into your questions.** They must be specific, and they must also directly address your concerns about what will draw customers to your business and to your products and services. What kinds of questions might you ask those who make up your target market? Shoot to collect information such as the following:

➲ Demographic information, such as gender, age, occupation, household income, and marital status
➲ Geographic information, such as home zip code, work address, how far they travel to shop for similar products, how far they would go to get them
➲ Media-related information, such as which newspapers they read regularly, whether they use the Internet, what they watch on television

Another important source of primary research is your competition, but here you need to walk a straight and scrupulous line. Studying what your competitors do, such as where they succeed, where they fail, and how they treat customers, can provide you with extremely valuable information. You can learn from their mistakes and from what they are obviously doing well. What you cannot do is steal from them. That counts as industrial espionage (even at the very small business level) and it is 100-percent illegal. Stay away from private or confidential information. On the other hand, reading published material about them, sending yourself in as a "mystery shopper," or calling to get their price list are all practices that are absolutely aboveboard and very useful. One important point to remember is that your competitors may be doing something differently than you do, but that does not mean their way is necessarily the right way. Take your research with a grain of salt.

Putting Together Secondary Research

The amount of secondary source information available to anyone doing basic business research is staggering. To avoid getting bogged down with inefficient sources and unnecessary data, it's best to approach your secondary research with a plan and a list.

First, decide on the specific type of information you are seeking. Going into research mode with only a general idea of what you want to discover will almost guarantee that some of your time will be spent unproductively. Overloading yourself with data that will need to be combed through, much of which will eventually be discarded, wastes your valuable time. A better approach is to know what you want to find, and where you want to look for it, before you get started. If your research results lead you in unexpected directions, follow them through.

Some great sources of market research information include the following:

- Industry and trade publications (magazines, journals, newspapers)
- Your local newspaper (for information about close competitors, for example)
- Industry associations (for an insider's view on the local and national trade)
- National business publications (for economic overviews, for example)
- Government statistical Web sites (federal, state, and local)
- Specific business Web sites (do a search on your business type, and you may be surprised at what comes up)

▶▶ TEST DRIVE

Your company can only succeed if it brings in customers and if those customers buy what you're selling. Before you can convince them to open their wallets, you have to know exactly who they are. You will need to know your ideal customers inside and out, and here you'll start with the outside. Using the list below, identify your target customers' specific characteristics:

- Sex
- Age range
- Minimum household income
- Marital status and number of children
- How frequently they use the Internet
- What types of jobs they hold

Part **one**

Part **two**

Part **three**

Part **four**

Part **five**

Part **six**

What Is a SWOT Analysis?

If you want your business to succeed in this highly competitive world, you need to know what separates it from all the others. That means taking an honest look at good points and bad points and assessing what factors outside your direct control can influence your success. Enter the SWOT analysis, a very commonly used business tool that brings those factors into focus.

The acronym SWOT stands for "strengths, weaknesses, opportunities, and threats." The first two, strengths and weaknesses, describe your company's internal state of affairs. The last two, opportunities and threats, define what's lying right outside your doors.

To perform a successful SWOT analysis, you need to look at your business with a detached, realistic eye. Keep your points brief—use phrases, not paragraphs. You'll need to come up with specifics for each category, so avoid generalities like "We have a great product." A good trick to remember is to couch everything in terms of comparison to the competition ("Our sand pails hold 20 percent more sand than theirs do").

Once you've come up with the key issues for each section of your SWOT, you can use those issues as guideposts to better define your marketing objectives. You'll know where you stand in relation to your competition and how your company can withstand changes in the market environment.

Evaluate Your Business's Strengths

Your company's strong points are made up of the resources and capabilities you will use to give your business a competitive edge. The features you choose depend partly on whether you are starting a brand-new business or whether you have an existing company with history and experience. The key point to remember is that your company's strengths come from within, meaning you have full control over them and over how you will best take advantage of them.

To get you started, here are some examples of items that you could count as strengths of your business:

- Its primary location
- Your innovative product offerings
- A unique talent
- Extensive experience in the field
- Quality assurance procedures
- Long-standing reputation for fair dealing

List as many strengths as you can, and be as specific as possible. For example, if your company's primary location is a strength, state why: "Our coffee shop is located right in the center of a very busy, thriving string of small retail shops and is the only establishment offering sit-down food and beverage service on the block; customers shopping on Main Street must walk past our café en route to other stores."

When you are evaluating your company's strengths, it may help to do so categorically. For example, first tackle the strengths that fall in the marketing category, then move on to the financial area, then the personnel category, and so on. Consider all of your company's balance sheet assets, both tangible and intangible, as everything you have could be considered an advantage.

Once you have a clear understanding of your company's strengths, you will use them to help you figure out your competitive advantage. This understanding can also help gel your strategic plans and ideas. As you review the list, you may notice that some of your strengths are more solid than others, while others could change quite easily. When building your long-term strategies, you may wish to put more focus on those solid items and stress the more variable strengths only in your current plans.

Fixed Strengths

As you look back over the strengths you have listed, mark off those that are virtually written in stone. Examples include things like patents, copyrights, long-term leases in desirable areas, renewable favorable supplier contracts, easy access to additional capital, and exclusive agreements. Each of these items represents a fixed strength, one that will not dematerialize overnight and that your competitors cannot easily take advantage of.

These solid advantages can make up the backbone of your strategic planning as you can count on them for the long haul. They offer you a clear competitive advantage and provide a solid foundation on which you can build your company's success.

Strengths That Could Change

Among your company's strengths are also variable items that you may not be able to count on for the long term. Items on this list may offer up a clear competitive advantage in the here and now, but they should not necessarily be counted on when you look to the more distant future, three or five years out from now.

Examples of variable strengths include things that could change on a dime (and often do without much, if any, warning), such as employees, company reputation, product uniqueness (if it succeeds, it will be copied), and access to uncontracted distribution channels. Though each of these items may be squarely in your company's strength box right now, they are not locked in. While they are working in your favor, they can add to your business's profit potential. However, since any of them could be lost at any time, you may not want to base your entire strategic success platform solely on variable strengths.

Be Realistic about the Weaknesses

Weaknesses include every area in which your company falls short. Just as no person is perfect, no company can do all things perfectly; some areas will definitely call for improvement. ▶▶ **Weaknesses include both problems you may already have and things you actually do not have.** For example, the absence of a particular strength should be listed in the weakness section. In fact, some of your company's strengths might also be viewed as weaknesses if you look at them from a slightly different vantage point.

These are often the hardest items to identify. Right now, you love your business idea, and you want it to work. Picking away at what may be wrong with your plans may seem counterproductive, and as a result, most people choose to focus only on the positives. But a keen awareness of your weaknesses before they have a chance to sabotage your success can help you turn them around, or at least to plan around them. The only antidote for a true weakness is plenty of advance planning. The more accurate and specific you can make your weakness list, the more easily you will be able to address particular areas and maybe even combat them completely.

Examples of common business weaknesses include the following:

- Lack of experience in a crucial business area
- Indistinguishable products or services (everyone is selling the same thing)
- Business location
- Less-than-stellar reputation among customers
- Minimal access to capital
- Bad credit
- Limited access to necessary resources

Once you have pinpointed all of your company's weaknesses, go back and look at your strengths from the opposite view. For example, while a long-term lease may be a strength, it can also lock you in, making it difficult and costly to make a change should circumstances call for one. Similarly, an exclusivity agreement could keep you from switching to a new supplier offering more favorable terms. Not every strength will flip to a weakness, but you should be aware of the ones that may.

Now you know every area where your company does or may fall short. Don't despair! Identifying these weaknesses is the first step toward overcoming them. Compensating for or removing these weaknesses will become part of your overall strategies. And foreknowledge of those weak spots can keep them from overwhelming all the positive strengths your company possesses.

What Opportunities Exist for Your Business?

In the world of the SWOT analysis, opportunities stand for new ways in which your business can profit, prosper, and grow. Opportunities come from outside, and those that allow you to capitalize on your existing strengths are the ones to pursue first. You can, however, also use opportunities to compensate for (even wipe out) your company's inherent weaknesses.

It's important to consider the rapidly changing world around you when you begin building the foundation upon which the future of your company will rest. To do that, you need a basic knowledge of the current business, economic, and political environment in your marketplace and in other markets into which you may want to expand. The key here is basic knowledge. You do not need to become a doctoral candidate in geopolitics or global economic theory to recognize opportunities. What you do need to know is what's going on now, what's coming up in the foreseeable future, and how these things could impact (and by impact, here, we mean increase) your company's profitability.

The number of potential positive influences on your business is great. They can come from virtually anywhere: the government, the marketplace, the scientific community, even societal changes. When you know what may change, you can figure out ways to take advantage of those opportunities rather than get swept up in the tide and watch them wash away. While it's impossible to predict every upcoming opportunity, you can paint some broad categorical strokes that will allow you enough flexibility to take advantage of those that can substantially add to your company's profitability.

Wherever possible, try to apply some time frames to the opportunities you envision. How far into the future might they occur? How long will your company's window of opportunity be open to best take advantage of their potential? Is split-second timing critical to implementation success? Again, the more advance thought you give to any type of opportunity, the better your chances of turning it into an internal strength.

Changes in Technology

Technology advances quite rapidly these days. Think back to just ten years ago, when the number of people with easy Internet access or cell phones was positively miniscule compared to now. In ten years, a now-unknown technology could be completely commonplace.

Being well-versed in the latest computer hardware and software advances can help you take advantage of new technologies before they hit the mainstream, giving you a potential leg up on the competition. Staying informed about advancements in your industry, even those that currently don't have a lot of backing or momentum, can give you an edge over those who stick with the tried and true until it becomes obsolete. New is not the only way that technology opportunities can present themselves, though. Consider these:

- High speed Internet access finally becomes available in your area.
- An up-and-coming technology becomes more easily affordable as it gains popularity.
- Manufacturing processes are perfected that can streamline existing operations.
- Your customers gain technological savvy that makes approaching them, selling to them, and following up with them easier and cheaper.

Due to the amazing pace of technological changes, it is important for new or growing businesses to have the capability of introducing new technologies that prove cost-effective upon analysis. The trick is to implement them quickly and with minimal disruption to current operations. This element, the implementation phase, is what takes planning. Knowing what types of advances are in the pipeline, and which of those could add profitability to your company, will help you decide which to take advantage of and how to do just that.

Legislative Changes

Government rules and regulations change all the time, at every level. Many of these will directly impact small businesses. But laws do not typically change overnight. Instead, legislators tend to go through weeks, months, or even years of debate before they even come to a final vote . . . and the votes don't always turn out as expected. Therefore, while regulatory changes will come, they should not come as a surprise.

Though the business community perceives many legislative changes as threats, many can actually help your business survive and thrive. For example, foreign trade agreements and tariffs could protect U.S. manufacturers. Business tax cuts can help new and growing companies preserve precious cash resources. Changing regulations could make it easier to manufacture, sell, or deliver your products and services. Corporate formality regulations could be reduced, making it easier for small companies to comply.

You can keep abreast of upcoming law changes in a few different ways. First, you can use the Internet to learn about impending legislative votes. Second, you can tap into the resources of industry and trade associations, which often have the inside track when it comes to upcoming regulations that could impact their members. Third, just keeping up with current events can offer valuable insights into the ins and outs of rules and regulations at every level of government.

Social Trends

Consumers can be fickle. Buying trends can swing widely, from boom to bust in no time at all. Major shifts in society and cultures can have a huge impact on the business world, especially when it comes to marketing plans. Over time, society changes in its beliefs, attitudes, and lifestyles. Some changes are technological in nature. Some are influenced by the media, while others can be prompted by demographic shifts, like the impact of the baby boomers on the American marketplace.

Some recent examples of social/cultural issues that have had a huge impact on American businesses include low-carb diets, reality television, and fear of terrorism, just to name a few. New trends can be sparked by the move from cities to suburbia, the introduction of international products, or even changes in the average size of the population. Lifestyle changes necessarily influence purchase decisions. Knowing the current and future states of your main target market can help you adapt your products and services, and keep your business in business even if a trend flows against you.

Know the Threats Your Business Will Face

The world can present an abundance of threats to your business. These threats can come from competitors, changes in government regulations, shifting trends, or even acts of nature. Whatever the source, threats put the continuing profitability of your company in jeopardy. **▸▸ No business exists in a vacuum, and every business involves risks.** While you cannot eliminate these risks—they are, after all, completely beyond your control—you can work to reduce the threats they cause so that they do not put your company's success in jeopardy.

Why are things that have not even happened yet—may not ever happen, in fact—so important to include in your business planning? Because your plan readers, especially those who will be deciding whether or not to lend you large sums of money, want to know that you know the types of threats your business will face. Even more important, they want to know how you plan to deal with these threats for minimal negative impact. Here's where your creative juices will need to flow. You want to specify what those threats are without striking fear in the hearts of your loan officer or investor. Then solve any problems (on paper) that these possible threats may cause, without missing a beat.

Try not to get too far from reality here, and remember to keep the threats you think of within the time frame covered by your business plan. For example, for a small organic farmer, realistic threats would include unexpectedly severe weather conditions (flood or drought) and changes in federal labeling regulations; an unrealistic threat would be a meteor striking the fields and rendering the area fallow. This analysis can help you come up with a range of solutions for the most likely threats that may occur and shore up your company's security in the process.

Putting It All Together

Now that you have identified the strengths and weaknesses of your company, along with the opportunities and threats that it faces, put that knowledge to good use. You can take steps to erase or minimize your weaknesses or even manage to transform them into strengths. You may be able to avoid threats completely, deal with them proactively, or (at worst) react in a manner of your choice rather than struggling to catch up after the fact. With some innovative thought, you can even turn threats into opportunities.

But your analysis should not focus only on the negatives. Clearly identifying strengths and opportunities at the outset helps you use them to your full advantage. In fact, realizing which opportunities play on your company's existing strengths provides a push in a profitable direction.

The typical SWOT analysis is set up as a matrix, allowing you a clear view of the way each factor is interrelated. You see how opportunities may overlap with strengths and weaknesses and how strengths can counterbalance threats and weaknesses. Existing strengths that mesh with potential opportunities set the perfect stage for your business to capitalize on those opportunities. Weaknesses can be overcome to allow your company the chance to grab potentially lucrative opportunities. You can use your SWOT to help you determine ways that your strengths can overcome or counteract threats and also to defend your company's weak spots from impending threats that could wipe it out. You can analyze the state of your SWOT today and then go back to see how it may look different in the future as you gain more experience in your new undertaking.

When your analysis is complete and all crucial issues have been clearly identified, these issues will flow into your planning and marketing objectives. You will match your company's current resources and capabilities to your overall business goals and measure how well they fit into its competitive environment to give your company a solid advantage.

Here's an example of a brief (but thorough) SWOT analysis for an established business:

Meira's Pie Palace

Strengths

Meira's retail and restaurant experience
Excellent chief baker and staff
Easily accessible location
Plenty of tourist traffic April through November
Local seasonal ingredients (cheaper, fresher) add to niche idea

Weaknesses
Dependence on chief baker
Very slow winter sales
Dependence on local farmers
Limited parking available

Opportunities
Ski resort launch planned in two years
Several housing developments underway
Casinos just approved on local ballots
Potential for Internet and catalog sales

Threats
Poor farming and harvest conditions
New strip malls and shopping areas could divert business
Low-carb diet trends
Slower local economy
Rising gas prices could limit tourist travel

▶▶ TEST DRIVE

Now it's time for you to create a SWOT analysis for your company. Grab four sheets of paper, and label each with one initial. It's easiest to start with the strengths—after all, they're the reasons you are confident your business can succeed. After that, list the weaknesses, which are also known quantities. Then work out the potential opportunities and threats. For each facet of the SWOT, try to come up with at least ten items. You don't have to come up with action plans or solutions here, just simple phrases.

What Assumptions Will You Need to Make?

When it comes to writing an effective business plan, you have to think forward. That means making some estimates and educated guesses and taking a few leaps of faith. All of these, when quantified, become your planning assumptions. Though not all of your assumptions will be strictly number based, most of them will be, and most of those will be related in some way to your financial projections.

▸▸ **Your financial assumptions are the backbone upon which all of the numbers in your pro forma financial statements are based.** Those projected numbers have to come from somewhere, and wild guesses simply will not cut it here. Every figure you present has to be founded in something reasonable—in other words, there must be a demonstrable and logical reason why you use each and every number. For example, if you are currently in negotiations to sign a two-year lease for office space—one where the rent will be $1,200 per month each month for the first year, and $1,400 per month each month in year two—you can reasonably project rent expense to be $14,400 for year one and $16,800 in year two. Only the end result numbers (the annual totals, if you use annual statements) will show up on the financial statements themselves, but the way you came up with those numbers will appear in your statement notes. In addition, the discussion in your business plan of the physical space your business will occupy must mesh with your numbers.

Every projected number in your plan is an estimate that is based on an underlying assumption. Before you get to those projected numbers, you have to sit down and develop your planning assumptions. The assumptions you eventually settle on represent decisions you have made. These decisions should be based on experience and research. They should make sense when looked at both individually and in concert, and they should be written out and included with your business plan. When your numbers appear realistic, you will gain credibility with your business plan readers; however, if they seem pulled out of the air, or overly optimistic, your readers may go forward with a much more critical eye.

Basic planning assumptions you will need to make include things like these:

- How many items you expect to sell in any specified time period
- The revenue you expect to bring in for a particular period
- The amount of cash inflow your revenue will generate
- The number of employees you expect to hire
- The average unit cost for each item you plan to stock
- How much you intend to charge customers for your products and services
- Expectations of overhead costs (like utilities)
- Your advertising and promotions budget

None of these items is set in stone, and some numbers may vary widely from what actually happens as your business begins to take shape. No one expects you to be able to predict the future with pinpoint accuracy. However, when you use logical and well-researched assumptions as a base for your projections, you may be surprised by how close to the mark you actually come.

Plan for Flexibility

Your planning assumptions may change as you write your plan. As you learn more about your business (both in general and specifically), your original expectations may alter. That can impact your assumptions—and adapting those will impact all of your pro forma financial statements.

For that reason, the software you use and the way you use it can make a huge difference to your planning process and the amount of time it takes when you make a revision to your numbers. Many prepackaged programs have assumptions sheets that link to every other part of the business plan. When you make a change in the assumptions section, the new figures flow through to every number impacted by that change. If you create the statements yourself using spreadsheet software, take care to set up your worksheets properly from the beginning, linking connected numbers to one another, so a change in one affects a change in any related numbers. A little forethought here can prevent costly mistakes down the road and save you the time of having to track down all of the ripples that spread out from a simple single change.

Most numbers impact all of your financial statements. For example, if you change your assumptions about how many hours per week you will use an employee, it affects your payroll expenses on the statement of profit and loss. That in turn will impact your cash outflows, and the change will also show up on your balance sheet in both the cash and capital accounts.

Where Do These Assumptions Come From?

People new to the business side of business often get bogged down in minute details when they first begin to tackle financials. When it comes to financial assumptions for your business plan, though, focusing on minutiae can make you lose sight of the bigger picture. Your assumptions should not look like a shopping list. Instead, they should hit big items squarely (and with some detail) and group tiny items into categories whenever possible. For example, rather than trying to estimate how many paper clips you will be going through, come up with a general idea of how many office supplies you'll go through. At the same time, when it comes to your office equipment—copier, fax, and so on—you should choose the specific brand and style you want and find an average price for it. Focus the majority of your attention on the numbers that really matter, such as sales projections, profit margins, cash flows (which speak to payback dates, both from customers and to creditors), and major planned expenditures.

Perhaps the most important assumptions you will make will be those regarding your projected revenue streams. Your business plan readers will expect to see those sales figures increasing over time (called an annual growth rate), but they will also want to know how you came up with that increase. For example, do you expect to have growth in your customer base? Or do you expect to increase the average annual sales to each customer? Perhaps some of the growth will come from price increases, or maybe you'll realize some combination of those factors.

Gross profit margins let your readers know how much each sale can be expected to contribute to fixed costs, with something left over for profits. Typically, the projected gross profit margin is expressed as a percentage for each item you will be selling (or, if you will have a vast array of products, for each overall product line). For strictly service companies, gross profit margins equal 100 percent of sales, as there are no product costs associated with sales—that's right, labor does *not* count as product cost here. In the simplest terms, ▶▶ **your gross profit margin (in dollars) equals the difference between the sales price you set and the total amount you paid for the item, including its cost, packing charges, freight charges to get to your location, and any sales tax.** Divide that dollar amount by the sales price, and you have your gross profit margin expressed as a percentage. As you prepare your projections, account for any expected changes in your cost of goods, such as a lower per-unit cost when you have enough sales to justify buying in bulk, that will directly impact your gross profit margin.

Cash inflow assumptions have their roots in your credit policy, built up by your sales projections. If you plan to make only cash sales (and that includes all forms of immediate customer payment, even checks and credit cards), your sales will equal your cash inflows from operations, possibly minus a small percentage for bad checks. Otherwise, your credit terms will partially control when you get your money from customers. The most crucial assumption you will make here, at least to the people who will be funding your business, is the number of days you expect to take to collect. This is an area commonly underestimated by novice entrepreneurs. For example, if your terms are "net 30" (very common terms, which mean that you ask customers to pay within thirty days) you may expect that clients will pay you in thirty days or less. The reality, however, is that you will more likely wait *at least* thirty days between the date of the sale and the day you get the check. If you plan to offer credit terms, have a corollary plan in place to help you collect promptly, and use a realistic eye to estimate how long it will take you to get paid.

Finally, include in your assumptions any key expenditures you expect to incur during the projection period. This category includes things like asset purchases (real estate or equipment, for example), entering into big-ticket, long-term leases, pouring money into product research and development, a large marketing campaign, or any other very large cash outlay you see on the horizon. Related expenses include projected interest payments (if you finance your major purchases), maintenance contracts, and other corollary expenses. Remember, if a loan or lease will be extinguished during your projection period, that needs to be addressed as well—it will free up cash and can improve profitability.

Setting the Time Frame for Your Plan

Whether you are starting a new business completely from scratch or expanding your existing business in new directions, the readers of your business plan will want to see smaller time frames for the initial period, followed up by longer leaps. Typically, for the fluid pro forma statements (cash flows and profit and loss) for any new venture, you will use shorter time spans. Longer time frames are acceptable for the more static balance sheet.

Talking Points Have a Different Span

In the essaylike sections of your plan, you can include a full view of your overall plans for the company, regardless of how many years worth of pro forma statements you have chosen to include. Why is it okay for this to be different? Because you will not be making any detailed numeric assumptions, which are hard to pin down too far out into the future. General goals could include things like "In year five, we will open a second shop" or "Within seven years, we plan to have a staff of 100 professionals."

In most cases, lenders and investors will want to look at financial projections for the upcoming three years. For companies already in operation, plan readers will want to see both current and historical statements (for the past three years or so). Check with specific readers, though, to see if that meets their requirements. In the absence of set guidelines, stick with the times frames listed here.

For your pro forma statement of profit and loss, show monthly projections for the first year, followed by quarterly projections for the next year, and finally annual projections for year three. As to historical statements, include both a year-to-date current statement and full annual statements for the past two years.

Next on the list come your statements of cash flows. For these pro forma statements, use monthly projections for the first year. Follow those up with a year of quarterly statements. An annual statement for year three can be included, but it is not often required. In addition, include historical annual statements for the past two years.

For your balance sheet, typically a much less dynamic statement, you can use quarterly numbers for the first year going forward, then annual figures for the remaining two years. Also include a current balance sheet and those from the last two years.

A Look at the Overall Business Environment

Some of your planning assumptions will be based on the current state of the economy and how it impacts the industry you are in. Some types of businesses boom in successful economies, some boom during economic downturns, and some hold relatively steady no matter what's going on. In addition, your local economy may influence your business more than the state, federal, or global economy. If that's true, the local scenario should be your primary focus, as long as you don't ignore the potential effects on it from the outside world.

The overall business environment has a direct effect on your target customers. When they're flush, they are more likely to spend on everything; when times are tight, they have to pick and choose where they part with their precious pennies. In addition, there will be an impact on marketing trends. For example, during an economic downturn, people may allocate their funds to fixing up their existing homes rather than looking to move into new (bigger, better, more expensive) ones.

Again, no one expects you to be able to predict upcoming economic developments or foresee the future business environment. Knowing where things stand now, though, and what the next steps have been in the past can help you make better predictions about the future of your business. Basic business knowledge—like whether interest rates seem to be heading up or down, or what tax changes are in the pipeline—lends credence to your assumptions.

How Will Your Business Grow and Change?

Included in your assumptions will be your expectations. Where do you envision your company a year from now, or three years from now? Your strategic vision will direct some of your major decisions, and those decisions will influence the ways that your business can grow.

You can avoid a very common mistake made by novice entrepreneurs by expecting your company to grow and making some general plans to accommodate that growth. Many new business owners are so focused on getting started (and with good reason) that they devote virtually no time to what they will do if their companies take off. But even if things go almost exactly as planned, that constitutes a change. After all, you started with no business (or, if this is for an expansion plan, none of *this* business), and now your company has achieved some level of stability and success. That in itself will prompt new goals and effect some change.

Either way, by anticipating success and its byproducts (growth and change), your business will be better prepared to handle them. Believe it or not, rapid success and growth can often kill off a new or small business. When it cannot keep up with changes or expand quickly enough to meet higher demand, a small business runs the risk of being burdened with sudden unplanned (and often very large) costs. Those costs, much higher and more immediate than if they had been anticipated, can quickly suck up existing profits and cash, leaving a growing business that needs seed money without any. Therefore, it's crucial to consider growth scenarios when developing your business plan.

Planning for Unplanned Events

Part of your planning process will include considering "what if" scenarios. These are big deviations from your planning assumptions, in case things do not turn out even remotely like you have expected in particular areas. It can be helpful to look at your SWOT analysis to give you some ideas about where these departures might come from, as well as viable possibilities for dealing with them.

Back to the Drawing Board

Lydia Kohn was a newly graduated fashion designer. She worked in a boutique, selling clothes by day and altering them by night, but she had dreams of opening her own custom dress shop. She started doing some background research, realized she had a decent shot, and put together a rough business plan. She took the plan to her local SCORE office, found a mentor, and turned that rough plan into something more substantial.

When she got to the pro forma profit and loss, Lydia was near tears. Her plans resulted in losses, month after month and year after year. She tried increasing the prices, but that did not turn the tide. She started "reassuming" some of her base assumptions, working the numbers until they showed modest profits. She brought her revisions back to her SCORE mentor, expecting praise, and was instead met with "You can't do that . . . ."

"But here's what you can do . . . ." Lydia and her mentor talked about some changes to her grand startup plans that were feasible. Instead of renting an upscale shop initially, Lydia could rent a much smaller studio off the beaten path. Rather than hiring two seamstresses, she could take on one full-time employee and contract out overflow work when necessary. And, yes, she could increase her prices somewhat; after all, she was offering custom-designed and -sewn clothing to upscale clients.

They ran the numbers again, and now Lydia's dream had a chance of success, even though it would be without the grand splash she envisioned. Now her changes were realistic, based on factual data rather than what she wished might happen. Giving up the fanfare would allow her to strike out on her own, more quietly but with much better odds.

Anticipating the unexpected and working out ways to deal with it is considered contingency planning. Regardless of how well you think out your business plan, no matter how much research you put into your assumptions and projections, and even with years of experience in the business world, things happen. You can't prevent them, and you can't plan for them precisely, but you can think about them and set out some general ideas for dealing with them should they occur.

A solid set of contingency plans clearly identify and assess issues that are *likely* to have an effect on your business. Start by thinking up problems that could occur, and follow the most likely chain of events each problem will set off. For example, let's say you run a interior design firm and your chief decorator leaves with no notice. Jobs will need to be completed; customers who have worked with that designer will have to be matched with someone else; orders in process will have to be reviewed and dealt with; his or her name will have to come off of all promotional materials; and you will have to find a suitable replacement.

Once you have come up with the most likely problems and related fallout, you can set up general response plans. If you have these in place when bad things happen—and when it's hard to think calmly—you will have a logical blueprint to work from to help settle things down as quickly as possible.

Know When to Re-evaluate

After you record your planning assumptions, you will use them to create your pro forma financial statements. But what do you do when those assumptions lead to losses, negative cash flows, and minimal (if any) net worth? Re-evaluate.

That does not mean you should fiddle with your planning assumptions to make the numbers "work out better." Instead, you should revisit your research and talk with your mentor (or advisor or accountant, whomever you turn to for help here) and figure out which assumptions can be reasonably altered. For example, if you have planned to buy a building, see how the numbers work if you lease instead. Some numbers you can't mess around with, as they are completely outside your control. These include things like the minimum wage, the cost of a Yellow Pages ad, and the price of postage, for example. But your suppliers' prices may be negotiable. You can get estimates from different marketing firms, or you could use the U.S. Postal Service instead of FedEx.

Maybe not all of your grand plans are feasible to implement from the outset. Pare down the costs you can, and cut corners where your quality comfort level will not be compromised. Reconsider the number of employees you want to hire; maybe you can use contractors instead until the business starts to take off. Take another look at your pricing structure, too. Maybe you've aimed too low here, in the hopes of making a big splash with customers, and there's some wiggle room to increase prices without sacrificing your competitive edge.

Other areas you can alter include things like your business structure—maybe your company will work better as a partnership than a solo act. In addition to adding complementary skills and talents to your company, it opens up your capital options. You can also change the timing of your launch. Some industries lend themselves to seasonality, and launching at the beginning edge of a natural slump won't work as well as diving in at the outset of busy season. Something as simple as shifting your focus slightly (for example, from tax planning to tax preparation) can shift your projections from loss to profit.

In the end, if nothing you can change will help your projections turn the tide, it's time to put this dream on the shelf and consider other options. Not every business idea turns into a solid gold profit producer. But it is better to find that out before you have invested time, money, effort, and emotion into a project that just won't succeed.

▶▶ TEST DRIVE

To get your planning assumptions going, start with the small easily definable factors that will have a big impact on the rest of the numbers. These may take a little research on your part, and it's important that your inputs are precise. Make sure you know these numbers:

- ⮑ The employer portion of employee income taxes and benefits, as an add-on percentage
- ⮑ The sales tax rate
- ⮑ Standard delivery costs (to get products to customers)
- ⮑ Your credit terms to customers
- ⮑ The current short-term interest rate
- ⮑ The current long-term interest rate

3

Putting Your Business Plan Together

Make Sure Your Plan Gets Looked At

It has probably taken you a good deal of time to pull all of the background information together and set out the framework for your business plan. Combine your time investment with the fact that you may be using the plan as a means to get some funding for your business, and it's imperative that your potential readers become actual readers.

Even when you get your business plan onto the loan officer's or venture capitalist's desk, it is not guaranteed that either one will ever even open it. ▶▶ **Your business plan must make a strong impression to even get read past its first page**—this is definitely a time when the book will absolutely be judged by its cover. The appearance of your business plan sets off the decision-making process, and a professional-looking plan will at least keep your hard work from ending up in the rubbish pile unopened.

In addition to what your plan looks like, the way it gets onto that desk can make a difference as well. Sending an unsolicited, unexpected business plan through regular mail to no specific person can be a death sentence for your proposal. Whenever possible, try to garner a personal introduction to the recipient (through a common business contact, for example) before you submit your plan. In the absence of a connection, at least phone the institution and get a person's name; even better, talk to the person you will be sending your business plan to and let them know you will be sending it. In your cover letter, mention the meeting or the conversation to jog your reader's memory. Your reader is much more likely to take note of your plan if he has heard your name before and is expecting to receive a packet from you.

The Overall Appearance Makes the First Impression

This point cannot be stressed enough: Looks are everything. Your plan must look professional, must feel like it contains sufficient materials, and must conform to each reader's specific guidelines (if applicable). Use a conservative, conventional font on white or cream-colored paper, and make sure any images are crystal clear and not poorly printed or fuzzy.

Even if you will be operating the simplest business on the tiniest budget, your plan should look like a million bucks. While it is okay to make notes for yourself and mark up your own copy of the plan, there should be no visible handwriting on formal versions of your business plan except on pages that require signatures or drawings. Each page should look clean and crisp. Text should not be crammed onto the pages to keep the overall length down.

If you're trying to cut down on costs, you can print the plan yourself using high-quality paper. To hold the pages together, you can use a report binder (easily found in any stationery store); do not hold it together with only clips or staples. If you have the cash to spare, consider getting your document professionally printed and bound.

How Long Should It Be?

When it comes to business plans, the one-size-fits-all approach simply does not apply. There is no single correct length that covers every type of business or every plan purpose. There are some general guidelines and recommendations you can follow. In the end, though, your plan should contain enough information to keep your audience from having to ask for a lot of additional materials; on the other hand, it should not be so voluminous that it looks difficult to get through.

As you begin to put your plan together, you will see which areas could use a little more information and which could stand to be trimmed down. Before you present the plan to lenders, investors, suppliers, or other outsiders with whom you would like to commence business relationships, run your document by a trusted advisor (like your accountant or mentor). They can let you know if there are any sections that call out for enhancement and any long-winded passages that can be cut.

In the end, the final page count is less important than the content and clarity of your business plan. The overall length depends on a lot of factors, including how many tables and charts you've included, whether there are both historical and projected financial statements, and the complexity of the industry you're in, for example.

Some General Guidelines

A typical start-up business plan runs between twenty and sixty pages. Those for service businesses tend to be shorter; retail or wholesale establishment plans fall somewhere in the middle; and manufacturing concerns usually have the longest. Business plans for established companies can be anywhere from fifteen to a hundred pages long. The variation here is mainly due to the purpose of the plan. If you're looking for substantial expansion cash, be prepared to do a lot of persuading, but if the plan's primary purposes are internal, an abbreviated version may be called for.

The underlying nature of your business may also influence the length of your business plan. If your business is part of an easily understandable, common industry, it won't require a lot of explanation. However, if your industry is complex or relatively new, getting your message across may take a good deal of exposition, and that can add a lot of bulk to your page count.

Adding Appendices

Some business plans cry out for appendices. Basically, these add-on sections hold anything that doesn't quite fit into the body of the business plan but that still adds value for your plan readers. As an added bonus, appendices save your readers the task of digging through the whole plan to find clarifying information. Some illuminating appendices include the following:

- Glossaries (when technical terms are involved)
- Blueprints and floor plans
- Upcoming advertising campaign layouts
- Key employee resumes

Follow the Format Required by the User

Before you submit your business plan to anyone, find out if they have any specific guidelines or formatting requirements that all submissions must follow. For example, many banks request particular documentation presented in a precise order to make it easier for their loan officers to compare different plans. All it takes is a quick phone call, and someone in the department can fax you their standard set of requirements. If a certain reader does have a preferred format, and you have not taken the time to find that out and follow it, it won't necessarily derail your plans. However, they may ask you to redo and resubmit the plan, adding some unwanted delay into your funding-finding schedule.

If you plan to shop your plan to mainstream banks and other similar lending institutions, consider what may be their biggest influence: the SBA. Many lenders follow the SBA preferred layout even for unrelated loans just because it's easier for them. Though the format is predetermined, business plans don't follow a cookie-cutter formula. They may be laid out similarly, but their contents—especially in the text portions—must be unique.

The typical SBA general format contains three primary sections: business description, financial data, and supporting documentation. These sections are preceded by a cover sheet, a statement of purpose, and a table of contents. The business description includes all the text of your plan, including your detailed business and product description, marketing strategies, competitive analysis, operational procedures, and personnel background. The financial section includes the obvious historical (for already existing businesses) and pro forma financial statements, but it also covers things like a listing of capital equipment, a break-even analysis, and an actual loan application. The supporting documents section houses everything from personal tax returns and financial statements of the owner(s) to franchise contracts, lease agreements, and business licenses.

To supply your business plan readers with everything they need to make a decision about providing funding for your company, you must know what paperwork will be included in their consideration. When you have taken the time to learn what they require, and provide it in the manner they prefer, you have already taken crucial steps toward locking in a favorable first impression.

Keeping the Plan Professional

While you are putting together the information you will use to prepare your business plan, you may keep informal notes and write in your own shorthand. You may plug in some numbers before you have any backup, just to see how things shape up. And you may store your research and lists any way you like, such as in a big shoebox. That's all fine when you're putting your plan together, but none of it works for the final version. The big factors you want to keep in mind regarding the professionalism of your plan are looks, language, comprehensiveness, and coherence.

When it comes to the look of your plan, focus on what appearance will provide comfort for the readers, regardless of the type of business. Though it may seem okay for creative industries to use a more decorative or colorful format, remember that bankers and investors tend to be conservative. In addition to staying within their comfort zone, a standard appearance will let them focus on the information. To give your plan a polished appearance, consider creating it using business plan software. There are several very good programs out there, with differing levels of help depending on your comfort with business and accounting premises. Most important, though, they help you keep your plans look consistent and professional.

As you write the text sections of your plan, pay attention to your language. You should use standard business language whenever possible and focus on choosing simple, clear words rather than the latest lingo. That does not mean you shouldn't use persuasive language; after all, this is the first place where you will be selling your company and concept to outsiders. Finally, make sure your spelling and grammar are picture perfect.

Though your business plan includes several sections, they should be presented as a whole to every business plan reader. A plan that comes in pieces will likely be ignored, and a plan that is missing standard sections (such as financial projections) may share that same fate. Since you know what most readers will be looking for, make sure that the handout version of your business plan is all-inclusive. That doesn't mean no reader will ask for follow-up information. Some will, and then it is perfectly acceptable to send just what they have asked for, on its own.

The final piece of the presentation puzzle is coherence. Your plan should look and sound the same all the way through. In other words, it should read like one person wrote it from start to finish. Even if the plan is a collaboration, even if you wrote it over the course of three years, even if you wrote the marketing plan ages before you came up with a mission statement, your readers should not be able to discern any gaps in your story or style.

▶▶ TEST DRIVE

Get business plan format guidelines from three or four places. (The SBA is a very good source here.) Once you have them in hand, make notes about what they have in common and where they differ. Then, split a piece of paper into as many columns as you have different guidelines. In each column, make a preliminary table of contents as set out by the rulebooks—this can act as your cheat sheet as you are putting the information together in the different formats. Finally, make a checklist of all the supporting information necessary to meet all of their requirements so you can begin collecting the paperwork you will need (which usually takes quite a bit of time).

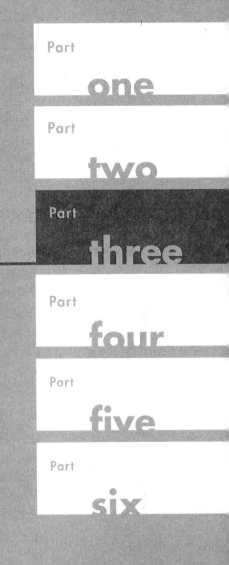

Part
one

Part
two

Part
three

Part
four

Part
five

Part
six

Start with a Cover Letter

A cover letter introduces you and your plan to the reader. While every plan should include one, if only to remind the reader of who you are, business plans that are not presented in person absolutely must be sent with cover letters.

Keep your cover letter brief, no longer than one page, to increase its chances of actually being read. Put it on letterhead printed on high-quality paper to carry an air of professionalism and success. Include only facts in this letter—no sales pitch, and no long descriptive passages.

While you want to keep this letter short and to the point, you also want to include some key information. Tell your reader what type of business you are in. Industry-level information will do in most cases, like so: "Flower Power is in the retail floral business." Then make a concise statement about *why*, not *how*, your business will be successful, with a particular emphasis on what distinguishes your company from the competition: "Flower Power will succeed here because we employ the premier floral designer in the area and we have secured an exclusive contract with three interior design firms."

Next, write a sentence describing the current state of your business. Maybe your company is brand new, or maybe it's been in business for ten years and is looking to expand. Follow that up with a precise statement of what you want in numbers. Bankers and investors, in particular, know you are coming to them for money. If you don't tell them how much you need, they will have to ask you, so you might as well put it right out there from the outset. Use straightforward wording: "We are looking for $50,000 of financing, which will be used to purchase additional warehouse space and delivery vehicles." Finish your cover letter with a specific follow-up plan: "I will call you on Friday to discuss the plan."

Call First

To give your business plan a healthy shot at getting looked at, try to have some form of contact with the reader before you present your plan. This is especially important if you will be sending it instead of delivering it in person. Get an introduction from a colleague or a professional contact, or cold call your reader on the phone. Let them put a face and a name with your business plan to make it seem more personal to them. Once you have successfully made contact, include a reference to that contact in your cover letter. For example, you could write something like "As we discussed when we spoke on the phone last Thursday, I am enclosing the requested copy of my business plan."

Before you send the letter out, proofread it very carefully. Even better, have a few other people look it over for you as well. Pay special attention to the reader's name and contact information, as nothing will put off a potential financier quicker than seeing his name spelled wrong. In addition, make sure that any numbers you've used in the letter (like your financing needs) exactly match information set forth in your business plan. If you are contacting investors, rather than lenders, run the letter past your attorney to make sure you have not inadvertently violated any securities laws.

Include a Nondisclosure Statement

One aspect of a business plan that is commonly overlooked by novice entrepreneurs is the importance of the nondisclosure, or confidentiality, statement. Without it, you have no real legal protection should someone share your plan with others—including those you would not want to see it, like competitors.

Remember, your business plan is just what it sounds like: your plan for your business. It includes detailed financial information, both business and personal. It includes detailed marketing strategies, competitive analyses, even the very customers you plan to target.

A nondisclosure statement spells out the fact that this document is intended only for the person to whom you have presented it. It clearly states that the information within is confidential and not available for public consumption. Most important, it reminds the reader that your business plan cannot be copied or in any way reproduced.

Number Your Plans

You are responsible for keeping track of all the business plans you have in circulation. The best way to accomplish this is by numbering each plan before you hand out any of them. Right on the title page, preferably near the bottom, simply include some wording like this: Copy X of XX. As you distribute copies of your plan, keep a list of which reader has received which copy of the plan. This task has a second, very important benefit to you as well. Should a copy be circulated without your permission, you will easily be able to trace the party responsible for the leak.

Another reason to number your plans has to do with always presenting the latest and greatest information you have available. You may revise your plan, maybe more than once, and your numbering system can help ascertain which version of the plan a reader is holding. In this instance, a coded numbering system may be more useful to you than a straight count. For example, copy number S0603 could indicate that this is the version from September 2006, copy 3. Don't include the word "version" in your numbering system, as that could raise questions in the minds of your readers about which version they might have.

Do You Need a Signed Nondisclosure Agreement?

Although merely having a nondisclosure statement in your plan offers you some protection, in some cases a signed copy of a full nondisclosure agreement (NDA) may be called for. Signed agreements add an extra dimension of protection to the confidentiality of your plan because they are legal contracts, binding the reader to keep the contents strictly private. For your company's utmost protection, do not send out unsolicited copies of your business plan until you have already received a signed copy of your NDA. And if you are going to ask readers to sign an NDA, make sure you have it prepared by a lawyer; if you want legal protection, this is not a do-it-yourself job.

When is a signed NDA called for? When your business involves something highly secret, like a secret formula or a yet-to-be-patented process, you should include an NDA. Yes, all of the information contained in your plan is confidential, but not all of it is necessarily especially confidential in a way that would tempt people to share it. In addition, ▶▶ **it is common practice to ask potential equity investors to sign NDAs.** (Again, get the signed form before you send over the plan.)

However, asking your banker to sign an NDA could be a little more awkward. Bankers and banking institutions pride themselves on their conservatism and honor. While there is a minute chance that a banker would share your confidential information with someone inappropriate, it is highly unlikely. Banking professionals deal with classified and restricted information all the time, and they base part of their reputation on their ability to keep that information private. If you do insist on having your banker sign an NDA, especially if your plan does not contain highly secret information, you run the risk of seeming unprofessional and overly suspicious.

Designing Your Title Page

In the attempt to make your business plan stand out from the masses, it's tempting to design a fancy or decorative title page. Resist that temptation. Unless your company is artistic in nature—a graphic design firm, book illustrators, art gallery—keep your design simple, or you run the risk of looking unprofessional.

Your title page should include some crucial information, but don't make the mistake of loading it up with too much information. Your title page should convey authority and confidence, not desperation. Keep it looking clean and simple while making sure to include these key items:

- The company name
- Your company's logo
- The words "Business Plan"
- Contact information (your name and title, business address, and phone number)
- The plan number (if you use a numbering system)

If your company will be operating with a "doing business as" (DBA) name, include that on your title page as well. Also, if you are not in business on your own and have less than three business partners, you may want to include the names, titles, and contact information for any other owners. If that makes the title page look too unwieldy, though, list just their names and titles here.

Don't Underestimate the Power of a Name

The best business names explicitly state the purpose of the company: Thomas and Johnson, Attorneys at Law; Flowers by Joan; The Pet Primping Palace. As soon as a potential customer learns the name of your company, they clearly understand the basic products and services you offer. Compare that to a name like the Joe Smith Company; no one can figure out what you're selling without asking questions. If at all possible, try to pick a name that can grow with your company. For example, Cella's Children's Clothing is more limiting than Cella's Clothing, which allows Cella to branch out into different age groups without having to change the name of her business.

Before you get anything printed up, though, make sure that your business name is available to be used. Not only do you want to keep from using another company's name for marketing purposes, you also want to avoid potentially sticky legal situations. **You'll need to check on the federal, state, and local levels to make sure your proposed business name is free.**

In addition, some business structures dictate particular words that either must be or cannot be used in your company name. For example, if you form a corporation, the business name must indicate that with words like "Inc.," "Corp.," or "Incorporated," for example. Check with your lawyer to make sure you haven't overlooked any naming requirements—again, before you have anything printed.

You Must Include a Disclaimer

To comply with securities laws, your business plan must have a disclaimer in its front matter, clearly stated and prominently placed. Essentially, this disclaimer will say that the business plan itself does not constitute an offer to sell an interest in the business. The disclaimer should be on every copy of the plan, but it absolutely must be on any copies you present to potential investors.

The wording is pretty important here, as your disclaimer must be explicit. Though you don't need to use these exact words, make sure your meaning is crystal clear: This document is for informational purposes only and does not constitute an offer to sell any securities of the company. The disclaimer helps ensure that your plan has been presented in compliance with this SEC regulation.

In addition to merely having a disclaimer printed on your business plan, you must follow the law in spirit as well. This means that you cannot present your plan to a potential investor, ask him to read through it, and then demand that he give you money based on the information within. Should that potential investor be interested in providing funding for your company, you must go through the proper legal channels to complete that step.

If you have any doubts about this critical language, consult your attorney. He can provide you with solid legal advice and precise wording that will ensure your compliance with both SEC regulations and those of any states in which you will be presenting your business plan.

Organize Your Table of Contents

The table of contents may well be the last page you complete before sending your business plan out to readers, but that does not mean you shouldn't give it as much consideration as the rest of the plan. The table of contents deserves more credit than it typically gets; readers should be able to get a feeling for what's in your business plan just by scanning this page. In addition, they will get a sense of your style, professionalism, and organizational skills.

Your table of contents will look somewhat like an outline. In fact, if you created an outline to help you put the plan together, use that as a basis for your table of contents. You will list all the headings for all the major sections of your plan. Use the same words here that you do in the body so readers can be sure they've gotten to where they expected to go.

You may also include the important subsections, but only if that does not make your contents listing too long.

With a brief glance, readers should be able to easily navigate the body of your business plan. There's one very common mistake that can get your plan booted out of the "read" pile, and that's to forget page numbers. Once your plan has been completed and assembled, number your pages. Then flip back to your table of contents and put the correct page number next to each heading (and subheading, if applicable).

Present Your Strategic Vision

Your strategic vision statement clearly communicates to your business plan readers where you want your business to be in the future. If you can't conceive of what you want your business to look like in three months, six months, five years, or ten years from now, you won't know what steps to take to get it anywhere. Everyone reading your plan wants to know what you want to happen and what you expect to happen—that's your vision of your company's future.

In this section, do not focus on what you have now or what makes your idea or your business a great one. Instead, write about why your company is going to be different from any others, not in specific details but with general concepts. Without going into in-depth descriptions, use some broad brushstrokes to paint a picture of how your company looks to you in the future. Emphasize which attributes make your business unique among its industry peers, but also show how it will grow into something different than it is today.

Here are examples of some points you can include in your strategic vision statement:

- Distinctive features that your company will build on
- Development of industry-leading capabilities
- Instant recognition by target and general populations
- Long-term financial objectives
- Creation of an untapped niche market

▶▶ TEST DRIVE

Creating the title page can be the most fun part of putting together a business plan, but coming up with a good company name can be the toughest. Even if you have already officially named your business, you can always add on a DBA if you want to use something different. You may come up with the perfect name by taking a few minutes now to come up with some creative ideas, like so:

- ➲ Come up with a play on your name
- ➲ Use an unusual or urgent adjective to describe your company
- ➲ Try a twist on your closest competitor's name
- ➲ Describe your product or service in three words

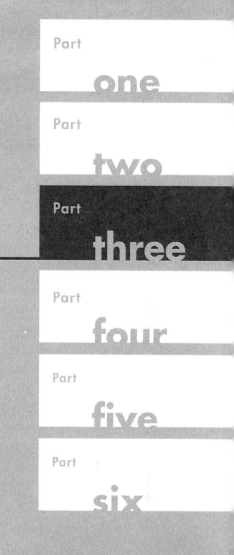

Part **one**

Part **two**

Part **three**

Part **four**

Part **five**

Part **six**

Get Your Plan in the "Read" Pile

Lenders and investors are hit with a virtual onslaught of money requests practically every day. They are going to glance at your executive summary for about sixty seconds, at least initially. That means your write-up has to grab your reader's attention and make him or her want to read more.

With dozens or hundreds of plans hitting their desks every year, bankers and investors don't want to spend a lot of time on plans that just will not pan out. Instead, they want to concentrate on those few businesses that have a real chance of success. Those judgments are made very quickly and are usually based on the executive summary.

Professional appearance and language count here. Plan readers will be looking to see that your presentation appears complete and realistic, and they will base their judgment on the points you have chosen to include in your summary.

Do not treat this crucial first-impression document like a commercial (even though it is your first sales pitch). ▶▶ **Despite your desire to emphasize the positive, your language should not sound like hype.** For example, you can stress your competitive advantage without trashing the competition.

Most important, your executive summary should reflect the essence of your business plan and the enthusiasm you feel for this enterprise. Your excitement can be contagious and convincing. But the bottom line is that you need to show your readers, right up front, what's in it for them. If your summary can get them feeling that they will benefit from your business, they will keep reading.

Summary Style

There are two basic forms of executive summary, the wrap-up and the narrative. The nature of your business and your confidence as a writer will help determine which style you choose, and you should use the style that suits you better. In either case, though, remember to keep it brief and to incite interest.

Wrap-up style summaries are simpler to prepare and are less dependent on the talents of the writer. This straightforward method basically recaps the concluding paragraphs of each major section in your business plan. Each aspect of your business plan is addressed briefly with equal emphasis.

These summaries work well for easy-to-understand businesses that will mainly use common operating procedures. The approach is very professional and businesslike, making it easy for your reader to review it comfortably. Take care to avoid the pitfall of this style, though—a wrap-up style executive summary can sound monotonous if you don't spice it up with a tone of excitement.

Using the narrative style, on the other hand, requires a certain flair for storytelling and the ability to set a scene with words. These summaries can provoke enthusiasm among your readers, especially beneficial for companies that plan to try something innovative or that require a lot of explanation. One or two major themes will dominate here, as opposed to the equal weighting of the wrap-up method. Choose your company's one or two most remarkable attributes, and help your readers understand how these features can make success possible. Make sure to include all of the necessary information listed on page 152–153. Even with a great story, readers still need to know the pertinent facts right up front. Your goal is to generate excitement without turning your summary into a glossy commercial.

Do This Last

Although the executive summary will be the first page in your business plan, and the first thing your readers look at, it should be the last section you write. This single section can be the most important part of your whole business plan. If it doesn't get your plan into the "read" pile, all the rest of your hard work won't be looked at. More than the most profitable point of your business, the executive summary is what will convince people to keep on reading, and only if they continue reading do you stand a chance of getting what you want.

This summary is where everything in your plan comes together. Here, you will include a little bit of everything your business proposal encompasses. But you have to first complete the meaty sections of your plan before you can come back and summarize them in one neat package.

Just Give Them the Highlights

Your executive summary should be just that—a summary. To that end, make sure that it is clear, concise, focused, and (most important) brief.

Your executive summary should not be difficult to follow, awkward, or more than two pages long (and one page is better). The people who will be deciding whether or not they want to read your entire business plan want to look at a single page that hits all the high points but does not get bogged down in any details.

Hitting the high points does not mean you shouldn't include potential challenges that your business may face, especially if they are substantial. In fact, this is not the place to include any technical or in-depth information. You do, however, want to make sure you hit the points that will be important to *this* reader. If this version of your plan is going to a banker, focus your summary on financial information, like cash flow expectations and collateral-type assets. A potential business partner, on the other hand, may want to see what you are bringing to the table and what you will expect from him. As you write the executive summary, put yourself in the place of your audience to solidify your content choice, especially when it starts to run long.

Here are some key points you may want to include:

- What you intend to accomplish with this business
- Specific objectives you plan to meet
- The people responsible for meeting these objectives
- How these objectives will be achieved (including any competitive advantages)
- The amount of money needed to achieve the objectives
- Where that money is coming from
- How your company will repay borrowed funds

Define Your Business Concept

Your executive summary will include a solid description of your business, condensed into just one or two paragraphs. To generate enough excitement, you will create a dramatic picture, using realistic and concise language. Speaking of pictures, if your business will be centered on a single innovative product, include an image of it, such as a sketch or a photo. This will both make part of your point (without the need for long descriptive passages) and help your pitch stand out in the reader's mind.

The business concept section of your summary should contain some very basic ideas that make your company seem real and profitable in the eyes of the reader. Start with the purpose of your business and define what it will actually do. Then you briefly describe your management team (even if, for now, it's just you) and their individual capabilities. Next comes your location(s) and the reasons for your choice. Finally, describe your company's potential for growth.

Business Purpose

Your business purpose is glaringly obvious to you, but the readers of your business plan cannot read your mind, so you need to explain it in clear, simple terms. And while your original idea may seem like a great one today, consider whether it will still make sense a year from now. ▸▸ **Your job here is to convince your readers that your concept has merit and substantial staying power, using as few words as possible.**

Keep in mind that your personal goals are not of paramount importance here. Your own motivations, like building personal wealth, do not speak to the underlying purpose of the business itself. If you can, shift the focus to external parties and discuss things like how your product will improve the lives of your customers or how your company will provide much-needed employment opportunities in the area. At the core, though, this section should succinctly describe the current state of your business (if applicable) and what you hope to accomplish going forward.

If your business plan describes the expansion of an existing company, include a brief statement outlining how long your business has been in existence and a summary of what it has accomplished so far. Be sure to add the purpose of your expansion and what is needed to make it happen. For example, if you are adding a new product line, explain how it complements the items you already sell. If you plan to add a new location, tell your readers how you chose the space and why you think you can fill it with customers.

With a new company, you still want to include the basics, such as product and location, for example. In this circumstance, it is even more critical to convey a sense of reliability and confidence in both yourself and your prospective business. Without stating it explicitly, let your readers know just how thoroughly you have planned and how much research you have done . . . and that all signs point toward real profitability.

Tell Them Who's Who

Business plan readers want to know that the people in charge of running your company are capable of doing so successfully. If you have business ownership or management experience, say so. If you have extensive experience and contacts in the field, indicate briefly how you plan to capitalize on that. Let your readers know what you bring to the table.

For any areas in which you do not excel, explain how you intend to bring in the requisite experience. Choices include taking on business partners with complementary skills, hiring a manager (or management team), or buying professional services (like a CPA) as you need them. List the names of any key personnel and a one-line description of what they add to your business. Show potential investors or lenders that you have a capable, competent team in place, even if that team does turn out to be just you.

Describe the Location

In this portion, tell your readers exactly where and how you plan to interact with customers. Describe your company headquarters (even if it's in your den), and the central locations for the majority of your business transactions.

Let your readers know that you have considered all the physical space requirements of your business, along with any customer convenience issues, and that you have covered all the legal bases necessary to operating in that location. For example, if you plan to start a manufacturing company, tell your readers that you have access to a plant with adequate space for all the necessary machinery and equipment for your projected production capacity. If you plan to offer personal counseling services out of your home, describe the private separate entrance through which clients can enter and the soundproof waiting room in which they can sit until you're ready to see them.

Focus on Success

This section of your plan will set out the steps that must be taken for business to meet the goals you have set. Earlier in your executive summary, you wrote about what, why, where, and who. Now you get to the meat of things, the how. To achieve success, you must have an action plan, and this is the place for it.

Here, you will briefly describe your overall business strategies and current presence in the marketplace. Explain how you plan to take advantage of your competitive edge to attract the customers in your target market. Indeed, this is a good spot to introduce your potential customer base, why they will respond favorably to your products or services, and what additional products or services you plan to offer them in the future.

Though you want to keep this section brief, it should also be written in persuasive, enthusiastic language. ▶▶ **You must convince your audience that profitability is a sure thing by telling them confidently how that can—and will—happen.** Since your entire executive summary will be measured in paragraphs, you must convey an awful lot of information with very few words. To do that, you can include numbers that emphasize your potential for growth: "ABC Company plans to obtain a solid 8 percent share of a market that is growing by 30 percent annually by tapping target customers who make average yearly purchases of $12,500." This kind of short statement is forceful, specific, forward thinking, and (most important) it speaks about success as a given.

Lay Out the Financial Picture

For an existing company, this section will consist of an overview of your current financial position, with a side focus on the growth your company has experienced since inception. For a start-up business, the emphasis will be on what you (and any other owners) are bringing to the financial table and any other means of creative financing you hope to employ.

For a company that has been in business for a while, provide a snapshot that emphasizes the strength of your operations. Here, again, numbers will help demonstrate your point. Include such quick figures as your average annual sales growth, current net profit percentage, and your profit percentage growth. Outline the time frame during which your company has achieved this success, and focus on the fact that you're in the middle of a growth spurt. Give a nod to your balance sheet only if it contains fixed assets and strong receivables on the asset side and a decent debt-to-equity position on the other side. If your company has a proven history of positive operating cash flow, highlight that here.

For companies that don't yet exist, there is no true financial picture to speak of, but that doesn't mean this section will be bare. If you have owned or run other successful companies, you can include a sentence—with numbers—about that. If your personal financial picture is healthy, emphasize that.

Finally, lead into the purpose of this exercise: your company's funding needs. Downplay the hands-out approach a bit by explaining some of your other financing sources. For existing companies, lenders and investors will expect that some of the profits will be plowed back into the company to help fund its expansion. With start-ups, your plan readers will be reassured by the fact that a good chunk of cash is coming from you (and any co-owners).

Identify Your Funding Needs

This is not the place to play coy—you should spell out exactly how much money you want. Your readers will also want to know exactly what you plan to do with that money and how long you think you will need it.

In addition to knowing how much money your company needs, you should have a solid idea about where you expect to find that money. Both lenders and investors will feel more at ease if they know you will be putting up some of the cash yourself, an indication that you are putting your own financial future at stake. The bottom line is that it really does take money to make money, and the expectation is that some of that money will be your own.

Start-up companies especially can eat up a lot of money, from the cash you have to lay out before you open for business on day one to the cash you'll run through once you open the doors. Even existing companies with solid positive cash flow can need a substantial infusion to facilitate their expansion plans. To get the money you need to turn your ideas into a profitable business venture, you have to know exactly what your total cash requirements are, and you have to ask for the money straight out. You will have to detail your company's needs openly in your business plan, making sure to cover each of the following points:

1. The full amount of money it will take to start your company

2. A comprehensive account of how that money will be used

Third Time's the Charm

Jared Huntley and Marissa Parker were going into business together to form a small advertising agency. Each had years of experience working in the ad business as employees of various firms. Now they both wanted more independence and control, so together they ventured into the world of entrepreneurship.

They put together a thorough and very promising business plan and began shopping it around to banks in the area. Of their first round of five targets, two politely turned them down and three simply ignored them. Marissa's brother-in-law, who played tennis with one of those loan officers, found out that he hadn't even bothered to read the whole plan because he had barely gotten through their dry three-page summary.

Marissa and Jared redrafted the executive summary, using the bolder language and imagery that was typical for their client presentations. They got rid of the numbers, threw in lots of power verbs and adjectives, and added color photos—but kept it under two full pages. Then they resubmitted the plan to three other banks. This time, they got no responses at all. Jared called each of the loan officers and asked what he'd found lacking; all three mentioned that the hype-like tone of the summary had turned them off from the overall plan.

The partners revised their summary yet again, falling somewhere between the first two versions. Punchier language describing key points stopped short of hype, a glance at the numbers added weight, and a couple of color photos showed their talent. This time, their summary came in at just over two pages. And this time, it got them two slots on the "in" pile . . . and eventually a loan.

3. From what sources you plan to obtain the necessary funding (including yourself)

4. Exactly how you plan to pay back any loans or reward any investors (discussed further in the next section)

Again, brevity is your friend here, but so is specificity. Hit the highlights, like big-ticket asset purchases or large-scale promotional campaigns, but remember that this is not the place to get into budget details. "To expand our manufacturing capabilities, we seek $78,000 for the purchase of state-of-the-art production machinery and a secondary warehouse in which to store additional finished goods."

Specify Your Payback Plan

Whether you hope to get a business loan or attract investors, the people reading your plan want to know when they will be getting their money back. In this section, you will cover the specifics of your payback plan. Without getting into excessive detail, include information about the number and frequency of payments, the dollar amount of each payment, and when you expect payments to start.

More important than the payment particulars, though, is where that money will be coming from. Hopefully, you will be able to generate sufficient profitability and positive cash flow to pay your backers from your regular customer transactions. In the event that does not happen, though (especially in the case of lenders), include a backup plan to cover your obligations from alternative means—even if that means an additional loan or equity investment.

In the case of a loan, you may want to include any security you have for the loan, whether it takes the form of collateral or a potential cosigner. For collateral, you should include a very short description and a current appraisal of the assets' worth. You may also specify how easily you should be able to sell off this asset in the event of an emergency cash crunch.

▶▶ TEST DRIVE

The goal of your executive summary is to inspire a "Wow!" reaction from your plan readers. To make sure it does the job, see if your readers can answer these questions from your summary alone:

- How big (in dollars) is your company's marketplace?
- What percentage of that market will it acquire?
- What is the name of your most important team member?
- When will your company begin to turn a profit?
- How much funding do you need?

Writing a Business Background Section

In the business background section of your plan, you will basically describe your product or service idea and explain how it satisfies a need for your target market. You will detail what your company will be selling and why customers, whether individuals or institutions, will buy it. This will necessarily include what makes your offering different from anything similar that someone else is offering—that is, what makes your product or service unique. If your product or service is so innovative that no one else is yet selling it, this is the place to explain why your revolutionary idea will generate its own market and the sales that go along with that.

While this may sound like a section where you can let loose with all the wonderful ideas you have and how great you think this company could be, it really isn't. Business professionals will be reading this plan, and they want only information that will help them in their decision-making process. Keep focused on what your plan readers need to know to understand what it is about your company that will launch its success.

This section may also include a history of the industry in which you are entering. Other information highlights you may add include things like how your company will be organized, any funding sources you have already secured, and a descriptive history of your existing company (if this is a business expansion plan). As most of these items will be discussed in detail later in the plan, here they should be mentioned briefly only to give the readers an overall sense of the company.

Focus Your Mission Statement

This is one area of your plan where less is more. In just a few brief sentences, you will convey the primary reason for your company's existence. Don't let the few words used here fool you, though. This tiny paragraph forms the cornerstone of your entire business philosophy and will even guide your plans. All of your business goals and actions will point back to this mission statement, as it's the link that keeps them united.

The mission statement may appear small, but its idea is big. It basically states what your business does and for whom. For example, a mission statement for a children's bookstore might read like so: "To offer fun and educational reading materials and activity-based learning resources to children aged zero to eighteen years at reasonable prices, in a fun purchasing environment that appeals to parents and caregivers as well as children. Within two years, to be the market leader in the Main County area with three retail shops, each designed to encourage families with children to visit, play, and purchase."

This statement remains concise, but it includes the main purpose and direction of the company. At the same time, it imposes limits on the scope of the company. For example, adding bestselling novels for adults to the mix would be contrary to the mission statement. However, adding a playroom with educational children's toys would fit in cohesively.

It may take several days to write those few sentences, but going through this process will help you focus both your business ideas and your business plan. Your mission statement provides definition to virtually everything else that will appear in your plan, so clarifying your business mission is well worth the time you put into it. To make your task a little easier, think about how to answer the following questions:

- What product or service do you plan to offer?
- How will your offering benefit customers?
- To whom do you plan to offer it?
- How will you draw your primary customers?
- What time frame is covered by your current plans?
- Which factors will most contribute to your company's success?
- What makes your company different from all the rest?

Describe Your Business Entity

The business entity in which you choose to house your company can have an enormous impact on everything from paperwork to tax returns to insurance coverage to everyday management. The business entity, quite simply, is the legal structure of your company. There are four main forms, and some come with additional variations.

The four basic business structures are as follows:

1. Sole proprietorship
2. Partnership
3. Corporation
4. Limited liability company (LLC)

Each business structure comes with its own unique advantages and drawbacks. There is no one right entity for every business, not even for every business within the same industry. The right structure for your company depends on your individual personal and professional circumstances. If you have any questions about which business structure is right for your company, talk with an experienced small business professional (such as your accountant, your attorney, or a SCORE mentor) to help you decide. In some instances, it's easy to start out in one form and switch to another. In others, it's virtually impossible to change without getting hit with some pretty big consequences (usually involving money). Play it safe. Do some research and get some advice *before* you set up your company.

Sole Proprietorship

Sole proprietorships are the most commonly used start-up business entities. They take no planning and very little (if any) set-up paperwork. In reality, you could wake up tomorrow morning and decide to go into business for yourself—and that would make you a sole proprietor. There is no business entity that is simpler to form or dissolve. For these reasons, most single-owner companies are originally set up as sole proprietorships. If they are not "set up" at all, they use this entity by default. Sole proprietorships make good trial entities if you are just getting your feet wet and are not sure you want to take more formal steps.

But—and there are some big buts here—simple is not always the best option in business. Sole proprietorships come with some fairly big drawbacks. In the first place, you will be completely personally liable for every penny of business debt and for the settlement of any lawsuit.

Second, you and your business will be considered as one and the same for tax purposes, and that can lead to a fairly hefty income tax bill. Third, the business is easy to dissolve, but it's hard to sell or otherwise transfer. Finally, you are limited to debt financing when your business is a sole proprietorship; selling equity interests requires changing the entity.

Partnerships

Partnerships come in three main flavors: general, limited, and limited liability. All partnerships have at least two partners, and there is no upper limit on the maximum number of owners allowed. General partners can set up without many formalities, though it is not recommended. Both limited partnerships (LPs) and limited liability partnerships (LLPs) require formalized legal setups, and that calls for plenty of paperwork.

Though they are the simplest structures to use when more than one owner will be involved, stay away from general partnerships. These are the only business structures where you can be held wholly financially responsible for someone else's actions; in some extreme cases, you could end up being personally responsible for a partner's unpaid personal debts. With a general partnership, you have no personal protection against the debts of the business, and no certain control over the way other partners run up those debts, making it the worst possible entity choice for your business. If for some reason it is your only option, you must put a formal partnership agreement in place and get plenty of insurance. Again, though, if you do have any other entities available for your business, use one; the enormous personal liability faced by all general partners should be avoided at all costs.

▶▶ **LPs offer personal liability protection to all limited partners, but the general partner is still personally liable for everything.** For this reason, in many cases an LLC or corporation is named as the general partner in an LP. Limited partners put up cash and walk away, being true silent partners. General partners run the business, hold all the power, and are subject to all of the liability claims. LPs need very structured setups, and involving a lawyer from the get-go is a must. These entities are very common for real estate holding companies.

LLPs are often the preferred business form for professional partnerships such as those formed by accountants or attorneys. In many states, these professionals are banned from forming limited liability companies (LLCs) or corporations, so LLPs at least offer them personal liability protection from the general debts of the business and from malpractice claims against the other partners. In virtually all other ways, including taxation issues, LLPs follow the form of general partnerships.

Corporations

Corporations are more than just business forms. They actually count as separate legal entities, meaning they exist all on their own . . . and they (technically) can live forever. Each is formed according to the guidelines of its home state. At birth, every corporation is a C (or regular) corporation. If no election is made to change that status, it keeps that structure. But corporations do come in other varieties. The most common alteration is the S corporation, but there are also personal service corporations (PSCs) and close corporations (a state designation).

The biggest advantage to incorporating is complete and total protection for the owners from personal liability for any and all business debts. No matter what happens, you cannot lose more than your investment, and no one can come after your personal assets (except in instances of malpractice—no liability shield can block that). This limited liability protection is common to all forms of corporations.

The big difference between the S and C varieties is tax treatment. C corporations pay their own income taxes. With S corporations, corporate income and tax liability flow through to the company's owners, hitting their personal tax returns. Other differences include some restrictions on ownership. For example, there can only be one class of stock. There are rules about who can be a shareholder, and there's a legal limit on the allowable number of shareholders.

The big downside of corporations is the paperwork and fee requirements. Corporations typically cost more to form and maintain than any other business entity. There are dozens of formalities to follow, from setting up a board of directors to keeping minutes from the annual shareholder's meeting. Failing to honor even one of them can invalidate your corporation and your personal liability protection. To help small corporations remain in compliance more easily, many states have developed a special entity called the close corporation, which allows for significantly reduced paperwork requirements.

Limited Liability Companies

What do you get when you cross a general partnership with a corporation? An LLC, which offers the best benefits of each without the worst drawbacks of either. This relatively new entity hybrid has quickly become the darling of small business advisors throughout the country.

Like corporations, LLCs are formed under state law, and those laws still vary quite a bit. Set-up is fairly simple. You file articles of organization in the home state, have an experienced attorney draw up your operating agreement, and you are in business. LLC owners are called members, and you can have any number of members that you want, even if it's just one (in almost every state). Set-up costs can run anywhere from a few hundred dollars (for do-it-yourselfers) to over $1,000, when you add in all filing costs and legal fees.

The big advantages of LLCs are the combination of personal limited liability and desirable flexible pass-through taxation. The biggest drawback comes with seeking equity investors—most investors (as opposed to involved owners) would rather put their money into corporations than LLCs.

Single-Member LLCs

A single-member LLC is basically a sole proprietorship with built-in personal liability protection. That added protection is huge, but to keep it securely in place, you must take every possible step to make sure that you don't inadvertently nullify your LLC status.

To ensure you remain protected, you absolutely must keep your business finances completely separate from your personal finances. That means no paying your home phone bill with a business check, no using your personal credit card to buy office supplies. Open a separate business checking account, and get separate business credit cards. And have an attorney prepare an operating agreement for your LLC even though you are the only member.

An Overview of Operations

In this section of your business plan, you will write a big-picture summary of your company's operational procedures, that is, how things run. In general, an operations section could include things like the following:

- How your company will control costs
- Definitions of your quality assurance procedures
- Plans for employee training
- Description of software integration with other business facets (like inventory ordering)
- Plans for selection and retention of key suppliers
- Strategies for customer service and support strategies

The most comprehensive operations sections are for manufacturing enterprises, as they may have to oversee massive activities to get production to promised levels. Since each stage of operations depends on full completion of the prior step, any slowdowns in the process can lead to serious backlogs. For that reason, having contingency plans in place is crucial for these types of companies, and those should be mentioned here as well. Also included will be descriptions of any major manufacturing equipment and production schedules (where applicable), the various locations and how they will interact, a synopsis of supplier delivery schedules, and any other external arrangements (like licensing agreements) that your company has entered into.

For service providers, this section will be particularly brief. Service companies sell time and experience, and their optimal production capability is much more flexible. Operational assumptions here will primarily be based upon available working hours that will be dedicated to paid-for client work, and what portion of time will be spent on non-revenue-generating activities. The main emphasis, though, will be on the proven efficiencies of those who will be generating most of the revenue.

Finally, this section would not be complete without a description of how your company's final product or service will make its way to the customer. You can describe that in a step-by-step manner, starting with initial customer contact and ending with postsale follow-up. One easy way to do this is to write a summary, in a narrative fashion, of the product's journey from concept to sale.

Briefly Define Your Products and Services

Though an in-depth discussion of your company's products and services will come later within the business plan, your readers will need a basic idea here to help them better understand the operations set up you have chosen. Think of this part as the Cliff's Notes version of your product/service description, and include only key factors. This picture will be a top-level, very general look at what you will be offering.

Even though this section will focus on the basics, it should convey the essence of the products or services you are trying to sell. Your business plan readers should have an instant grasp of the products and services, even if they are highly specialized or technical. If your product is still in development, mention that, including its current stage and approximately how long it will be until a full product should be available.

So what can the basics include? Make sure you cover the following:

- What it is
- What it does
- The purpose it serves to customers
- When it was (or will be) first introduced
- Any major modifications since inception
- What makes it unique

Multiple Offerings

When your company offers more than one product or service, this summary can quickly become unwieldy. Categorize wherever possible, focusing on product/ service lines rather than individual products/services, but making an exception for any standout offerings. To make this even more useful for your plan readers, you can list the offerings or categories in order of expected (or historical) sales volume, from greatest to least. For a company that offers both products and services, you can break this part down into subsections, still keeping each concise. You may also want to comment on how offering this broad range of products and services provides an added benefit for customers.

Consider Your Business Location

Readers of your business plan will want an idea of where your main headquarters will be set up—especially if you have or are starting a retail company. When it comes to retail stores, traffic is a main concern, so your location will be of primary interest to lenders and investors.

That doesn't mean that your space is irrelevant if you have a service or manufacturing business. These spaces are important as well, but they typically don't have as much impact on your daily sales. In this section, you will spell out your location parameters, whether you actually already have the space or not. You will include details like whether your company leases or owns the property, square footage, layout, and expected utility costs.

Points to Cover in Your Narrative

When you are writing up the section about your business location, jot down your impressions and any key words that will help you get writing. Then weed out any areas that either are not central or simply do not apply to your particular business. Take a minute to think about each of the following points:

1. Why did you choose this location?
2. What other locations did you consider?

3. Why did you decide against the alternative locations?

4. Does your proposed business (or business expansion) comply with local zoning laws?

5. Is the neighborhood suitable for your company?

6. Are there other businesses in the area?

7. Are you near any direct competitors?

8. Do you expect this to be your company's permanent location?

9. Are any renovations necessary?

Special Considerations for Home-Based Businesses

While it often seems like the simplest thing in the world, running your business—even part of it—out of your home is a bit more complicated than you might expect. Sure, it's a good way to save some precious start-up cash—that is, as long as it does not put any limits on your client base or productivity, making it a bad cost-benefit choice.

There are several important things to consider when you first look at your home as a possible base of operations for your business. You have to make sure there is enough space to do all the things you need to do, such as file business records, house equipment, and set up your desk and computer system. You also want to find a place that's free from distractions and temptations. Family members will interrupt you, the television will beckon to you . . . not to mention the fridge. If you can't block all this out or put a stop to it, reconsider working from home.

Once you've got the space and privacy issues squared away, you have some legal and financial issues to consider. Most important, you must make sure that your home is zoned for business use. Check with your city or county zoning department; they'll be able to give you the guidelines for operating a home business, if it's allowed at all. In most areas, you will be allowed to run a company out of your home if it doesn't impact your neighbors in any negative way, such as with pollution, parking, or noise.

On the financial side, you will probably need to add a specific rider to your homeowner's insurance policy, but that cost should be relatively minimal. A second phone line is a business must, both for convenience and tax deduction purposes. And speaking of tax deductions, make sure to clearly segregate your business area and activities from the personal.

Home office deductions are among the most often audited, so you may need to prove that your business space really is used only for that. That said, you can deduct a portion of all of your common household expenses as business expenses, including rent or mortgage, utilities, security, cleaning, and so on.

The People Behind the Business

To the readers of your plan, it may not be enough to understand how your business will operate. They will probably also want to know who will be running the company. They will want a picture of your organizational structure that shows who will be doing what and which responsibilities are linked to each key position. Your readers will want an in-depth look at the big guns behind your business, and that includes organizers, executives, managers, and any other key team members.

If you are not sure exactly who would count as a key team member, think about specific people without whom your company could not run properly. For example, if you own an interior design firm, the designers count as key personnel. Remember, the lenders and investors you will be approaching want to see the team you have in place. They want to know that you and the people you are surrounding yourself with have what it takes to make your business idea a successful one.

The key here is *people*. Do not represent your business as a one-man show to the readers of your business plan; they simply will not buy it. Yes, it is fine for you to take on the lion's share of tasks and the bulk of the responsibility. However, it is impossible for you to do everything, and it is even more difficult to do everything well. You don't have to take on partners or hire high-priced employees; paid consultants will do just fine to round out the edges. ▶ **Yours should not be the only name readers see in the management and key personnel section of your business plan.** If you have not yet filled in your experience gaps with suitable personnel, list all of the open positions with a description of how you intend to fill them. It is better to admit you have not yet found the right people than to act as if the gaps do not exist.

The Impact of Your Business Structure

The business entity you have chosen for your company can have a profound effect on the way it's organized. In fact, it virtually dictates the shape of your upper-level management team.

With a sole proprietorship (even those with the LLC label for liability purposes), you are the guiding management team. You are the sole owner, with 100 percent of the responsibility for how the business fares. In this section of the plan, you will include your experience résumé, highlighting what you can bring to the company and also mentioning the areas in which you will need help.

In a partnership—whether it is set up as a general partnership, an LLP, or an LLC—there are at least two people to share the organizational responsibilities. In the best circumstances, each partner brings unique skills that are complementary to the talents of the other partner(s). Ideally, one partner's strengths should offset the weak areas of another, even in the cases of a professional partnership where you are all licensed members of the same profession (like accountants or lawyers). For example, just because you are all lawyers does not mean you are all experienced with the same types of cases. One partner could be great at marketing while another excels in personnel management.

When the business is set up as a corporation, you have a whole list of official positions to run through, including the four main corporate officers (president, vice president, secretary, treasurer) and the board of directors. In very small, private corporations, it is very common for all of the corporate offices to be held by just one or two people. For the board of directors, though, it can strengthen your position when you populate those seats with people from outside your organization who can bring additional experience and insights into the business.

What Will Your Organization Look Like?

Every company (with the possible exception of those that truly have only one person involved) is set up in some structure. Someone is in charge, and someone else reports to that person. Work gets divided among different people. All of these factors come together to define your company's organizational structure. When your company has very few employees (less than seven, including you), you may not need to go into details about the organizational set-up and may instead focus on the key players themselves. If you have enough people working for you to merit an organizational chart, include that in your business plan.

There are several different ways you can choose to organize your company, with some being more formal than others. Larger companies may have different divisions or business units. Those may be further divided into distinct departments, with solid lines separating functions. Smaller companies may use less formal work groups or have a very relaxed organization based on particular responsibilities.

In the more structured setup, you would explain how the lines of responsibility work, who retains paramount accountability for each division, unit, or department, and which tasks each division will perform or oversee. For example, you could describe the customer service department like this: "Customer Service Department, headed by Thomas Vega, Vice President of Customer Relations, consists of eight customer service representatives. Each employee is responsible for answering customer phone calls, answering customer questions, solving customer problems, and encouraging additional purchases."

When you have an informal organization, state that up front. Explain that your company does not have distinct divisions or departments. If there are written job descriptions, you can include them here; if not, explain why you do not use them. This is very common in small companies with few employees, where everyone pitches in to do every job as needed. Let your readers know that, but also let them know who takes the lead for major business areas. For example, even if everyone helps out with the billing, there should still be one person in charge of the accounting function.

▶▶ **TEST DRIVE**

Consider the impact of each of these factors in choosing the optimal entity structure for your business. Even for an existing business, when it's time to expand, it may also be time to consider an entity change.

1. Is your product or service inherently dangerous?
2. Will your employees want a piece of the pie someday?
3. Do you feel like you already pay too much in income taxes?
4. How do you feel about paperwork?

Creating a Solid Marketing Plan

Part **one**

Part **two**

Part **three**

Part **four**

Part **five**

Part **six**

Chapter 14
Key Elements of Your Marketing Plan

Analyzing the Market

Market research will help you learn all about your customers, including who they are and why they might buy what you are selling. You need to understand how buyers behave, and the way to do that is by studying them. As part of your research, you will take an in-depth look at what goes into customers' purchase decisions, including their motivation and background. When you know what brings them to the marketplace, you can use that information to increase your sales traffic. How? By focusing your advertising and promotional efforts more specifically toward the things that motivate your core customers.

In addition to giving you a peek into the minds of your target customers, knowing their common characteristics can help you to identify new customers, which is a key component of growing your business. You can also learn about the types of new products and services your existing customers would be interested in trying, another way to expand your company.

Market analysis can help you to get an idea of what your customers think of you right now and how they rate your product or service in comparison to your competition. In fact, finding out what customers and potential customers think about your rivals can help your business compete more effectively. It can also help you test the waters of a new advertising direction.

In the business world, as in the rest of life, knowledge is power. The more you know about your customers, the better your chances of capturing their loyalty and making more sales. More sales means improving your company's profit potential, and (by extension) your personal financial well-being.

What Makes Your Business Unique?

The most important thing you need to know about your customers is that all they care about is making their own lives better. Your job here is to tell them how what you're selling is exactly what they need to achieve that goal. Pitch your company in these terms, and you're taking giant steps toward creating a winning marketing strategy.

No matter what you're selling, whether it is something that is truly one of a kind or something your customers can find almost anywhere, there is something unique about your product or service. Struggling to figure out what that is? Put yourself back in your customers' shoes and imagine what would motivate you to buy from, well, *you* instead of from anywhere else. Try to think of ways that your customers will benefit by buying your product or service from you. Even if a particular benefit seems insignificant, don't discount it yet.

What kinds of things can make your business unique? Start with yourself, especially if you own a service-oriented company. Your skills and experience (and possibly those of your co-owners or employees, if applicable) are unique. Next, look toward how you will get your product or service to the customer—maybe it's faster, easier, or more convenient. Consider the product or service itself. If what you're offering is one-of-a kind, your job here is done. Otherwise, think of other ways you can distinguish your offering—maybe it's more durable, lasts longer, or is easier to carry. Finally, you can always differentiate your product or service through price (though this can have other implications, as you'll learn in Chapter 16).

Market Analysis: Using Your Market Research

Here, the time, effort, and money you put in to developing your market research will come to good use. Now you will turn those piles of raw data into cohesive information upon which you can craft your marketing strategies. From your market research, you will put together an analysis that supplies the answers to these questions:

1. What is the current state of your industry?
2. Who, specifically, comprises your target market?
3. What will drive your customers to buy your product or service from you?
4. How will you define your pricing structure?
5. Who are your competitors and how are they doing?
6. Which types of promotions will best attract your target customers?
7. Which selling tactics will be the most effective?

Knowing the answers to these seven questions gives you a firm foundation on which to build your entire marketing strategy. All of the information you have collected will now be transformed into goals and plans, all designed to get your first customers in the door, to keep them coming back, and to let them do a large part of your marketing for you.

In addition, once the raw data has been converted into this more useful form, you will be able to determine the most cost-effective ways to reach your customers. You know that cash is your company's most precious resource. Precision marketing to the right people in the right way will get you the most revenue for each dollar you put out there.

Assess the Current Market Environment

While your marketing plan must grow from market research, all of that information comes from the past. While some of your analysis could point to upcoming trends and possible ways to target your customers, you need to add a pinch of "right now" to the mix. Regardless of past buying patterns in whatever industry you have entered, current economic conditions will influence what comes next. And what is happening both globally and locally will have a certain effect on your business right now.

Some Factors Affect Absolutely Everything

Think about summer 2005, when gasoline prices rose quickly and sharply, affecting virtually every business in the United States. Owners and employees had to get to work, delivery vehicles had to make deliveries—the list goes on. The take-away message here is this: Any business with a plan based on costs before the price hike had to do some serious recalculating to keep things afloat. That included the idea that customers would be making fewer trips to the store. Also, when product costs suddenly and sharply increased, product prices had to follow suit just to cover those higher costs. All of those factors directly impact any marketing plan.

Yes, the current market environment is an external, uncontrollable factor. That does not mean, however, that you cannot find a way to incorporate what is going on right now into your short-term marketing plans. Building in some flexibility will help your company handle these business-busting events in a way that does not hurt . . . or at least does not hurt quite so much.

Is Your Market Growing?

[handwritten: Yes   By How much   Industry vendor Ind Growth]

All the planning in the world can't change the tidal wave force of market trends. For a new or small business, though, riding the right trend in the right way can provide the lift it needs to soar. In a growing market, especially, there is plenty of room for newcomers to pick up precious market share. But where market share is already shrinking, and existing companies are digging in to keep what they have, the entry way will be paved with pitfalls. For the best shot at success—whether your company is a start-up or merely expanding into new markets—a market in the growth stage can bring your business along with it. You can enter a shrinking market if you have a surefire way of attracting customers . . . but be prepared for a fight.

There are only two quantifiable ways that a market can grow. The first is measured in unit sales, meaning people are buying more of what you are selling. The second is measured in dollars, which can be increased by either price hikes or sales volume growth. So how will you know whether your market is growing and, if it is, why? Check your research. It will indicate in which direction the market you plan to enter is moving and even how high it could move, based on the demographics of your target market and the current market saturation level.

Even if the market growth in your industry is stagnant or waning, though, opportunities may present themselves that can increase your market share. For example, your closest direct competitor could be closing up shop, leaving customers available and amenable to your marketing. Unexpected weather patterns could make particular goods and services more necessary than they would otherwise be. Knowing the current state of things is the best way—really the only way—to take advantage of opportunities.

The Window of Opportunity

No trend lasts forever, but some last longer than others, and some naturally prompt the growth of new trends. In the world of marketing, understanding the life cycle of trends can come in very handy. The hottest trends often cool down the most quickly, while those that build slowly can stick around for years. Either way, getting in during the uptrend is much better than starting out in the end stages.

The window of opportunity for marketing any product or service is closely connected to the industry. The speed of direction changes can also be predictable within an industry—clothing fashions tend to move faster than mattress styles, for example. Everyone needs clothes, and everyone needs a mattress. But from the marketing perspective, people buy new clothing much more frequently than they buy new mattresses, regardless of innovations in the bedding industry.

No matter what the specific product or service you will be selling, it will follow the same life cycle of every offering in the entire marketplace. Every product and service takes the same path. First comes development, then growth, which is followed by the maturity phase and finally decline. What may be different is the speed at which something evolves and the length of particular stages. To market successfully, you must know where your product or service stands right now, how long it's been there, how long it will likely remain in that phase, and what comes next.

Pinpoint Your Target Customers

In the current highly competitive business environment, you cannot put out a generic talking-to-everyone message and still expect to attract and keep customers. The giant general customer pool has thousands of segments and subsegments that pinpoint particular customer groups, which are sometimes called niche markets. To get these customers to buy your product or service instead of someone else's, you have to speak to them directly in language they want to hear.

Using a targeted market approach increases your chances of success in a very simple way: It directs your promotional dollars straight toward the people most like to buy from you. Instead of spending ten times as much money to reach ten times as many people, your cash is more effectively spent when your message reaches the right people. It's obviously better to spend $2,000 to get fifty customers than $10,000 to get the same fifty customers. Truthfully, there is no point in trying to sell your product or service to people who simply won't buy it. People without dogs are not going to buy dog food, for instance, so including them in your marketing efforts is just a waste of time and money. On top of that, when you are speaking to a smaller but more cohesive group, your message can be more specific and can address the audience more directly.

Start with the demographics. Even if the product or service you are offering could be sold to a wide variety of people, narrow your focus to what most of them have in common. Common demographic characteristics will help you set the tone for your marketing efforts. You would not speak to sixty-five-year-old grandmothers the same way you would speak to their fourteen-year-old grandsons, and your marketing should reflect that difference. ▶▶ **Knowing precisely who your target customers are helps you reach them on their terms, in a manner that is comfortable and attractive to them.**

Once you know whom you are talking to, you can switch your efforts toward the best ways to reach those prospects. Again, demographics can help define the kinds of communications your potential customers will listen to best. With so many options out there, choosing the best one gives you the best chance of making that initial contact. Does your target market tend to watch a lot of television, or do they listen to the radio? Are they Internet friendly? Do they read newspapers or magazines? The answer can be found in your market research, and it will make it easier to reach the people you want for your customers.

The bottom line is that the best way to reach the most likely prospects for the least cash outlay is to really know your target customers. Know who they are, what they want, and the best ways to tell them you have what they need . . . and you will soon see your sales begin to grow.

Identify the Competition

There's a lot you can learn from your competitors. They have already sat where you are sitting now, and they have already made the decisions you are trying to make. You can see what they have done well and what has not worked out. You can see where your product or service differs from theirs, and knowing this can help you to add some punch to your marketing campaigns. You can even figure out preemptive ways to defend your future turf from competitive poaching. First, though, you have to know who your competitors are, and whether or not they will have any real impact on your business.

Your business plan should address only those competitors who can have a real impact on your company's potential success. Through your market research, you uncovered every possible competitor: direct and indirect, current and possible. All of that information is necessary knowledge for you, and it can affect the ways you market and run your business. If there is a lot of competition out there, you may want to include a generalized list of all the rivals you may have to face. But significant competitors should be addressed fully and directly in your business plan.

Your business plan readers know that competition is out there. Even for a brand-new groundbreaking product or service, there will be competition; it just may not exist today. Potential lenders and investors want to know that you have carefully considered who else is out there and what you are going to do about it. They want to know how you will gain and preserve market share. A clear definition of your competitive advantages that takes into account intelligence about your most significant competitors will make your plan, and your planned profitability, more credible in the eyes of the readers.

Revisit Your SWOT

In your SWOT analysis, you analyzed your company's internal strengths (S) and weaknesses (W), as well as external potential opportunities (O) and threats (T). The S and W of the SWOT come from what you already have going, and these factors will help to direct your shorter-term planning, like your marketing plan. While the O and T also impact your business plan, they are more suited for long-term strategic thinking and what-if scenarios. So for the purposes of developing successful marketing ideas, go back to your SWOT analysis and revisit the strengths and weaknesses you have listed.

When it comes to marketing your company, you will want to emphasize your business strengths and downplay the weaknesses. These internal factors are under your control. You can determine the best ways to use your strong points and beef up areas in which your company is weak. In your marketing strategies, though, a look through the strengths can

How Not to Deal with the Competition

Eric Marsden turned his lifelong love of reading into a business. He opened a used bookstore, complete with out-of-print titles, cozy wing chairs, and a resident calico cat. His little shop struggled to turn a profit, but it was managing to break even—that is, until the new big-name bookstore a few blocks away turned part of its floor plan into a used book annex. That, added to their nationally recognized name, their overwhelming new book selection, and a popular in-house coffee bar, sent Eric into a panic.

Instead of turning to his business plan or his SWOT analysis, Eric simply reacted to his competitor's growing used-book business and his slowly dwindling sales. First, he began to lower his prices to meet or beat their price levels. But where they were able to get cut-rate prices by buying in much larger quantities, Eric was not. His price-cutting began to cut into his break-even success, making it even more difficult to compete. That sent him into an even greater panic, and he made further changes. He started providing free coffee and cookies, and he began to stock some current best sellers. These choices only cut further into his margins without bringing in the business he was trying to attract so desperately.

Eric's biggest mistake was in reacting to his competition without thinking about what was best for his company and his customers. Yes, he had lost some of his clientele to the chain store. But as he tried to copy them, he began to chase away those customers who had stuck with him. If he had followed the strategies he set out in his business plan and focused on keeping his happy customers happy, he would have been able to act from a place of strength instead of reacting, without a plan, out of fear.

prompt new insights that will help bring in customers, initiate sales, and start your business on the road to profitability.

Your goal here is to identify your target market and take it over, bringing your company more than its share of market share. You can do this by turning the strengths from your SWOT into clear and simple strategies, into actions you can take to begin the task of attracting and keeping customers. Not every strength will necessarily lend itself to marketing ideas, so focus your attention on three or four of those that will. The goals you set, and the actions you plan to take to meet those goals, will help you to formulate and solidify your marketing plan.

Meet the Four Ps

If you've ever taken a marketing course, you have already been introduced to the Four Ps. These four elements are essential to any discussion about marketing, and marketing is a crucial part of every successful business plan. The Four Ps make up your marketing mix, the parts of your marketing plan that are fully under your control. You cannot control the business environment, competitors, or potential customers; but you can manage your marketing mix, and doing so effectively can positively change your company's profitability (which, alas, is not one of the Four Ps under your control).

Just what are these all-important Four Ps?

- Product
- Price
- Promotions
- Place

In the following chapters, you will get an in-depth look at each of these key components of your overall marketing mix. You will also see how they work together to create your company's marketing plan. First, though, let's have a brief explanation of each.

Product

Intuitively, product seems to mean physical goods for sale. In the world of marketing, though, anything and everything you want to sell—be it goods, services, or ideas—counts as a product. For example, during a political campaign, the politician is the product. When you bought your gym membership, better health was the product.

Included in this P are all of the features of your product, as well as the customer benefits they convey. From its appearance to its packaging to follow-up customer service, everything attached to the thing you are selling is part of that product.

Price

Price refers to how much people are willing to give up (usually in the form of money) to get a product. Price sets a value for your product, but that value is more than just a number—it's an integral part of your whole strategy.

Many business people come at pricing from the backside by simply figuring out how much they need to charge to cover their expenses and make a profit. That overlooks two very important parts of the pricing consideration—the marketplace itself, and customer perceptions. The prices you set communicate to your customers, and they can ultimately affect the type of clientele you attract and keep. There is an unwritten price that the market will bear for a particular product, and unless you can clearly differentiate your offering from the pack, you'll need to work within that price reality.

The trick is to hit the pricing at just the right point. That's the number that customers will pay, that will keep them coming back to you, and that will keep your business in the black.

Promotion

You can have the greatest product in the world, but if no one knows about it, no one will buy it. So if you're going to go through the whole process of setting up a business, coming up with a product, and doing endless computations to come up with the perfect price, don't make all your work pointless by stopping there. ▶▶ **Promote your product as if it's the best thing on earth and no one can live without it.**

Promotion means a lot of different things to a lot of different people. When it comes to marketers, though, promotion encompasses every aspect of communicating with customers. You have to convince people of two things. First, your customers have to believe that they need something, and second, they must believe that you can provide it better than anyone else can.

Place

On the surface, place seems pretty clear cut. But in today's global wireless market, it can be anything but. And in marketing terms, place can mean something a bit different than just a spot on the map. What it really means here is both where and how you interact with your customers, including how you reach them.

Not that physical location is unimportant—it's not. Your place of business may be a crucial part of your marketing plan. But, again, the geographic spot is just one facet of Place with a capital P. You also have to be concerned with things like how easy it is for customers to get there, whether they can find parking, whether you are open at convenient times, and whether your shop/office is attractive to your clientele.

Believe it or not, even the smallest companies tend to do business in more than one spot. Maybe they have a shop and a Web site, or a Web site and a mail-order catalog. Consulting firms, for example, may do business mainly at customer sites. Wherever and however you deliver you product to your customer is part of your Place, even if it's not the same as your main business address.

▶▶ TEST DRIVE

Time to nail down your unique selling point . . . and that means it's time to grab your pen and paper again. Put away any feelings of modesty, as this is the place to brag ridiculously. Your unique selling point should sound like an ad; you can always tone it down if it goes too far. Here's a jumpstart for your brainstorm:

➲ Come up with five spectacular adjectives to describe your product or service—is it robust, inspiring, and enduring? Not big, green, and square?

➲ Write three sentences that give exaggerated reasons why your company is the best place for customers to come.

➲ Define yourself as if you were talking about someone you admire enormously.

A Detailed Description of What You're Selling

When it comes right down to it, the main business of every business is selling, be it products, services, or some combination of the two. At the very heart of your company is the something you are selling—and coming up with a concrete yet appealing description of it is one primary objective of your business plan.

This section provides the opportunity for the readers of your business plan to find out not only what you will be selling but also why anyone would want to buy what you're selling. Aside from the basics, you will tell your readers about the various features of your product or service and how those translate into benefits for your customers. More important, you will describe how your product or service solves a problem and/or fulfills a need for those in your target market. To really catch your readers' attention, though, include pictures (especially if they can facilitate an understanding of what you will be selling). They'll help your product—and your company—really stand out in your readers' minds.

You'll start the section with a general overview of your product or service and work down into the details. If you will be selling something that already exists and is widely understood (like sweaters or housekeeping services), your description can be concise. If the product or service you will be offering is either brand new or not commonly known, you will need to fill in all of the blanks here. Avoid using industry jargon or insider lingo; your business plan readers should not need a glossary to be able to understand the description here. (That does not mean you cannot include a glossary as an appendix to the plan, but your readers will probably not want to flip back and forth while they are trying to understand what your product is.) If your company owns any patents, trademarks, licenses, or copyrights, or has any of those arrangements pending, include them in the product description section along with any pertinent details.

At the end of this section, you can talk about products you envision adding to your repertoire in the future, particularly spin-off or add-on type products. Knowing that your vision extends beyond your initial idea can help convince your business plan readers (particularly prospective lenders and investors) that your business has long-term potential.

Describing Highly Specialized Products

Some products require the use of specialized language to describe them. Should your product fall into that category, it is all right to use the words you need—as long as you explain them as simply as you can within the text. Be aware of the knowledge level of your plan readers, and speak to that level.

You may have to walk a fine line here. You will need to explain in sufficient detail for your readers to have a clear picture of what your product is without disclosing extremely sensitive or confidential information. You may opt to leave out proprietary details here, focusing instead on what the product actually does and on convincing your readers that it will easily fulfill your customers' expectations.

Describing Services

If your company will be service-oriented, your description will center on addressing the following points:

1. What specific service will you provide?
2. Why is your company qualified to provide that service?
3. How will the service be presented to customers?
4. Who specifically will be performing the service?
5. Where will that service be performed?

From this list, choose the one item that, more than any of the others, truly sets your business apart. It can be more difficult for potential customers to distinguish service offerings from one another, especially when it comes to a new entrant into an existing market place. For that reason, it's important to differentiate your company in one primary way, even though there may be many secondary unique factors.

Even if the "who" will not be your primary unique selling focus, your readers will want to know what qualifies you (and any co-owners or employees) to perform this service. Include here descriptions of relevant educational background, additional training, professional experience, and anything else that adds to their comfort with your performance.

Also in your business plan, you must address the costs associated with providing your service. These include things like training, personnel, and professional license maintenance, for example. While these may not technically count as direct costs on a statement of profit and loss, they certainly count here for purposes of general discussion.

> ## Minimizing Misunderstanding
>
> If it is likely, or even possible, that your business plan readers will not understand the service your company will be providing, you will need to explain it in easy-to-digest terms. You will need to write up a comprehensive clarification, chock full of details, to enlighten them. If they cannot understand what you are offering, they won't believe that potential customers will understand either—even if the core of your target market is well-versed in the subject.
>
> As you describe this service, try not to use overly technical language. If certain terms must be used, define them right there in the text, making it as easy as possible for your plan readers.

Dealing with Multiple Products or Services

When your plan includes many products and services, it can be tempting to describe each in full detail. For two to ten offerings, this works just fine, but if you have more than that, this section of your plan will become unwieldy. Whenever possible, categorize your products and services into more general camps and describe those, then list a sampling of what belongs in that category.

In addition to the "what," your business plan readers will want to know *how* these offerings fit together, especially if they may seem unrelated at first glance. Include things like your floor plan and display ideas in this section, how long it takes to produce or receive each product, general costs associated with each, whether specialized staff members will be needed to assist customers, and how your product/service mix may change over time.

Why Yours Is Better Than Everyone Else's

You want customers to buy your product or service instead of looking somewhere else. To accomplish that goal, you must convince them that in some particular way, what your business is offering will satisfy their needs more than anything else out there. Even if you are selling something that can be found in a thousand other places, you have to find the one feature that sets your product apart from all the rest.

In marketing terms, this is often referred to as a unique selling point, or USP. The USP is something that clearly and easily tells the customer how he can benefit from what you are selling. Your USP should actually be phrased that way, in terms of the benefit to the customer, rather than in terms of product features. For example, instead of saying the product is lightweight, say the product is easy to carry. "Lightweight" is a feature of the product, but the way this feature benefits the customer is by making the product easier to carry.

It's very important to distinguish features from benefits. Features describe the product itself. Benefits speak to how the product will make the customer's life easier, better, or richer. For every distinct feature of your product, you need to come up with at least one benefit that feature will provide to your customers.

Come Up with Some Product Benefits

Get a piece of paper and a pen, and get ready to write. Write down every way in which your product or service can benefit your customers, even if it seems obvious or insignificant. Don't edit yourself as you put pen to paper here. Think of it as a brainstorming session, where every idea must be considered—you never know which can lead to your final USP. Here are some questions you can ask yourself to get your idea juices flowing:

- How does this product make life easier?
- Will the product save time?
- Is the product easier to use?
- Will the product last longer?
- Does the product look better?
- Is the product easily accessible to customers?
- Does the product offer convenience?
- Does it cost less?
- Is the product easy to pay for?

Remember to think as if you are the customer. Think about what things motivate you when you consider a purchase. Ask friends and family what can trigger their buying decisions. The more customer insight you have, the easier it will be to come up with key benefits around which you can build your marketing plans.

Developing Your USP

Take a look back at all the benefits you've come up with. If you managed to come up with a full-page list, it can be hard to turn the best of the benefits into one cohesive USP. Try to choose what will be most important, or at least what your target customers will likely perceive as most important. Consider which of the benefits will truly distinguish your offering, and your company, from the competition.

This single idea has a huge job, but it must be communicated in a very simple fashion. Your USP will convey what makes your business special and spell out why potential customers should come to you instead of going to your competitors. You also have to convince customers not only that they need what you have but that only you can provide the most important benefits. That's asking a lot of that single idea, and it may take you quite some time to melt this down into a unique and original USP.

That is key: unique and original. A general, generic USP won't distinguish your company at all. For example, saying that your company offers top-quality service really says nothing at all. Your USP must communicate specifics: "We back our service guarantee with thirty years of experience in the field." That USP gives your customers a reason to trust your company. It implies reliability and adds in a specific measure they can rely on.

Do You Need Inventory?

If you plan to open a retail, wholesale, or manufacturing company, you will need to have some inventory in place before you open your doors for business. So the short answer is yes, you do need inventory. The secret to success, though, is in knowing just how much you need.

▸▸ **Managing inventory effectively can make the difference between boom and bust for product-oriented enterprises,** particularly retail establishments. Inventory miscalculations are the number-one blunder, the biggest area of error for retailers, and here's why. You could end up with significant taxable income, a hefty tax bill, and no cash to pay it with because all your funds have gone into your inventory. Sound confusing? Keep reading.

Buying and holding inventory costs a lot of money. You have to pay for the goods themselves, storage and warehousing costs, delivery, and everything else you need to keep things in shape for sale. While inventory eats up cash flow, it does not hit your profit and loss statement as an expense *until you sell it*. That means you have a whopping cash outflow without a corresponding expense, a.k.a. a tax deduction. Lower expenses translate into higher income, which means more taxes to pay. That phenomenon, very common for novice retailers, can put your company out of business very quickly. The trick is to aim for balance. Have enough inventory to keep your customers happy, enough cash for you to meet your necessary expenditures, and enough deductions to keep your tax bill to a bare minimum.

Successful Inventory Management

To get a handle on the right inventory level for your business, you need to address a few key points. First, you have to maintain a selection varied enough to draw your target customers. Second, you have to pay attention and weed out any items that simply are not selling (no matter how much you love them). Finally, you must make sure that your inventory investment makes sense in relation to the rest of your goals, especially your profitability plans.

There is some method to inventory management madness. It may take you a while to get into the groove of it, but there are some basic pointers to follow to get yourself started in the right direction. The best, and most successful, retail companies focus on what customers want right now, and they make sure they keep the most-wanted items on the shelves. Bookstores stock the *New York Times* best sellers list; toy stores display the merchandise tied in to this season's hottest kids' movies. Know what your customers are looking for today, and have it on hand. At the same time, you must have enough of a selection to meet corollary customer interests.

Bookstores may also carry the classics, and toy stores will forever offer wooden blocks.

The flip side of stocking the right merchandise is cutting loose items that simply are not selling. If you see sales for a particular item lagging, mark it down, and get it out the door. Turn those cash flow drains into cash . . . cash that you can use to buy new and different items that may better appeal to your base clientele.

The size of your total inventory (both in items and dollars) depends on some factors unique to your business. Those factors include the type of retail merchandise you sell, the size of your company overall, how much customer traffic you see, and the average shelf life of the products you offer.

Striving for Inventory Turnover

Turning over your inventory at least three or four times a year is the goal here, at least for most typical retail establishments. "Inventory turnover" refers to completely replacing your stock, which you can also describe as how many times during the year your inventory is sold. It's more of an accounting phrase than a true picture of inventory movement. (It would be somewhat unusual to sell all of your inventory at one time and replace it all immediately afterward.) Some types of retailers have much higher inventory turnover than others—think produce market as compared to new car dealership; check out the standard for your industry, and company size, so you know approximately what number you should be aiming for.

The inventory turnover calculation involves two numbers: your cost of goods sold and your average inventory. If you are working with pro forma numbers, the easiest way to get your cost of goods sold is to multiply your projected sales by your average cost of sales when expressed as a percentage. For example, if you will buy an item for $1 and sell it for $2 your cost of sales percentage equals 50 percent. If your sales projection comes out to $100,000, your projected cost of goods sold would be $50,000. That number is then divided by the average inventory balance, which you can find on your pro forma balance sheet. Supposing your inventory is $12,000, your inventory turnover would be about 4.16 times per year ($50,000 divided by $12,000).

Evaluating the Competition

As you come closer to defining your strategies, you need to put a face on your competition. As part of your planning process, you must find out who is already offering something similar to what your company is going to sell. And among other things—such as their relative success, their general pricing strategies, and which customers they attract—you must consider how your competitors will react when you join the marketplace. When they prepare their SWOT analyses, you are one of the threats, and they will likely have some plan in place to keep you from stealing their market share.

The level of competition in your industry and in your area depends largely on what you will be selling. If you will be offering a product or service that's been around for a while, you may be up against some solid, established companies, and some or all of their existing customers could make up part of your target market. On the other hand, if you will be introducing a relatively new product or service, your competitors may also be new to the game, aggressively seeking market share to build their companies on. These factors are not mutually exclusive. There can be new, aggressive competitors in firmly established industries, and strong reputable companies can branch out in new directions. Your mission is to figure out just who and what you are up against and how they are most likely to react to your company.

The second important issue to look into is how your competitors treat their customers and how they position themselves uniquely. Regardless of how unusual your vision is, no matter how well you can differentiate your product or service from the masses of similar offerings, the way the customer views that difference is really what counts. If the customers don't see the difference, or if the difference you have chosen to focus on simply doesn't matter to them, they will not go out of their way to buy from your company, especially if their needs are already being met adequately somewhere else. Reread your market data. ▸▸ **Take a fresh look at what inspires your target market, and revisit your competitors' claims.** Then make sure your unique selling ideas address both what the customers want and why they cannot possibly get that from your competitors.

Don't Be Afraid to Face the Competition

In human nature, there are two basic responses to fear: fight and flight. ▶▶ **When it comes to the business world, fight is the only option.** Flight can only guarantee failure, and the same goes for simply ignoring the fact that your competition exists. In fact, pretending you don't have any competitors will do more than hurt your marketing plan—it will convince your business plan readers to not take your plan seriously. Competitors are a basic fact of the business world. They are out there, and they will try to keep you from gaining market share. Is that scary for a new small company? Yes, but ignoring it doesn't make it go away. So dig in, educate yourself, and get ready to fight.

The first place your battle plans will take shape is within your business plan. That will be based in the information you've gathered during the market research phase. Here, you will look particularly closely at your competitors and learn from what they are doing well and poorly. Your strategies should not be based only on those of your competitors, meaning you shouldn't copy what they're doing to the last detail. Still, you will find ideas and inspirations in your analyses of their tactics.

What to Include in This Plan Section

You may have heaps of information about your competitors, but not all of it belongs in the body of your business plan. Essentially, what you want to show your plan readers is that you know exactly whom you are up against and how you plan to best them. The rest of the details are best left in the research pile.

If you have relatively few direct competitors, list each by name. Should you have more than ten, you can categorize them instead. Regardless of how many competitors you have overall, your three main direct competitors should be listed individually. For each individual or category, include your take on their strengths and weaknesses, how well they appear to be succeeding in this marketplace, and what possible threats they may pose to your company. When you show your business plan readers that you truly understand the competition, they will trust your vision of how your company can succeed.

In addition to your direct competitors, include a section about your indirect competitors. As you learned earlier, indirect competitors come at your customers from a completely different angle. For example, if you open a miniature golf course, DVDs are indirect competition. You both provide entertainment to customers but in very different ways. Be aware of where your indirect competition is, how they attract the same slice of the market pie, and how to convince potential customers that your pie is better than their candy.

What Comes Next?

Once your business plan readers have a good handle on the products or services your company will be offering, and why they will be desirable to a substantial part of the target market, your marketing plan will shift toward other facets of the strategy. Before that, though, this is a good time to consider what comes next, meaning what will your next offerings likely be.

One of the best ways to help your company grow is to add complementary products and services to your menu. That strategy serves two major purposes. It gives your current customers more of what they want, encouraging them to come to you for a greater selection of products and services, and it attracts new customers who may think they need only this new product or service, but who may buy more once they see what else you have to offer.

When branching out, the best products and services to add are those most closely related to what you are selling now; they should logically flow from your current offerings. For example, a bookkeeping firm could easily add on tax preparation services but should not begin performing manicures. A candy shop could start serving ice cream but probably not French gourmet dinner cuisine.

To begin thinking about what comes next, make a free-flowing list of ideas based on logical outflows from your stable of products and services. Focus on related talents you bring to the table and how you can connect those with what you already have. You don't need to set any time frames or make any definitive plans. Should one or two ideas seem like great potential moneymakers that you might choose to implement within the time span covered by your current business plan, you can include a paragraph or two that gives a nod to this future idea.

▶▶ TEST DRIVE

Consider the following scenarios that can impact your company's inventory flow. How likely is each to occur? What can you do if it does?

1. You order 1,000 units and sell only 150 in the space of six months.
2. You have 300 units in the warehouse and customer orders for 500 today.
3. You order orange, and your supplier delivers yellow.
4. Your best-selling product becomes obsolete (or gets recalled).

How Much Can You Charge?

The price of your product directly reflects its value in the eyes of your customers. If they perceive your price to be out of line for what they feel like they're getting in exchange, they may be put off from buying. That goes both ways. If the price feels either too high or too low, it could make your customers think twice before making a purchase. The more they have to think about it, the more likely they will end up somewhere else. When you think about setting prices, put yourself in the place of your customers, and try to match that price to their perceived value of your product.

Of course, that's just one side of your internal pricing conversation. You also have to consider how much you need to charge for your products to make them profitable for you. At the very least, your prices must be designed to cover all of your company's expenses and provide a profit opportunity. That is the rock-bottom price you can afford to charge, the lowest you can possibly go. The basement price is based on numbers and facts and is backed up by your break-even analysis. (See pages 203–204 to learn how to calculate that break-even number.)

On the other side is your sky-high ceiling price, the absolute highest price anyone would possibly pay for what you're offering. That is the price you could charge for a product that virtually everyone wants but no one else is selling—the old supply-and-demand dance. In the end, your initial price will probably fall somewhere between rock bottom and sky high, but you need to know the boundaries and how to set them to find that happy medium.

A Quick Look at Supply and Demand

At the most basic level, supply refers to how much there is of something, while demand refers to how much of that thing people want. If you have ever tried to shop for a child's gift during the mad holiday rush, you already know a little something about the laws of supply and demand. In the perfect economic scenario, supply and demand match up. In reality, they rarely do, and if they happen to for a moment, market forces drive them apart again.

Demand, particularly in relation to supply, can drive prices. Sometimes, demand and price run in opposite directions. For instance, lower prices can increase demand for certain products. Other situations can affect price differently. For example, dwindling supplies coupled with constant or growing demand can lead to easily sustainable price increases, at least in the short term. For some products, high prices can even boost demand (particularly true for certain status symbol items).

Getting a handle on both the supply and demand for your product right now can help you set a proper price. Remember, though, that both of these factors change almost all the time. Building some flexibility into your pricing structure can help you react to these differences without doing any damage to your bottom line.

The Ripple Effect of Price Changes

When you change your prices, your revenues will change, at least initially. Price changes can bring in additional sales or additional profits. They can also change the way customers, and potential customers, look at your product. Price changes can also influence your standing in the race against the competition. With so much at stake, carefully consider price changes before you make them.

Though a price change may have many positive immediate effects, it may come with a longer-term downside. For example, if you have goods that did not move as quickly as you expected, you may be tempted to slash the price and stick them on the sale rack. That could get those goods out the door, but it could also change your merchandise from high-end to discount in the eyes of your customers. Another potential drawback of the sale price plan is that if you do it often enough, some (maybe many) of your customers may only shop when discount sales are in force. Yes, a good sale can draw in new customers (a benefit), but it can also slow down regular sales (a definite drawback).

Don't forget about price increases. They happen also, and customers may not take to them very well. ▶▶ **The fear of angering clients should not keep you from making necessary price increases**—to account for inflation, for example. Service-oriented businesses in particular are prone to regular price increases. When your prices are going up noticeably, you need to let your customers know. Most important, you need to tell them why. If your customers feel the increase is reasonable, they may still gripe about it, but they will be less likely to jump ship. Try to couch the news in terms of the extra benefits that will go along with the increase—even if you have to use some imagination to come up with them.

The bottom line is that price changes in either direction influence your customers and your customers' perceptions of your business. Consider all the implications carefully before you make any changes, and try to deal with potential pitfalls before they occur. Finally, try not to alter your prices often. Customers like to know what to expect, and they prefer stability to price-tag roller coasters.

The Danger of Pricing Too High

The main risk of setting your prices too high is that you might scare customers away. Even products and services that come with standard big price tags can be overpriced. Though a higher price can take some of the anxiety out of the cost-covering purpose of the numbers, the potential loss in volume may not be worth it.

That's not to say you shouldn't charge a fair, on-the-high-side amount for a product that can bear the weight. Expensive products and services should come with substantial price tags. Without them, people will question the quality of your product. The trick is in finding the right line and not crossing over from the merely expensive to the overpriced.

Not surprisingly, guessing is not the best way to figure out your price ceiling here. In fact, you already have the best tool to use in building your price structure: your market research. Knowing how much people are already paying for similar products and services helps set your standard. Customer surveys can help you determine how much your market would be willing to pay for the best version of the product or service. Look at the trade studies you have collected, and go back over questionnaires and polls. From this combination of sources, you will be able to glean the true price ceiling and charge what the market will truly bear. Whenever you can, set your sights on the ceiling.

Going for Volume

For new businesses, the lure of volume can be strong. But many novice entrepreneurs mistakenly think that the lowest possible prices will lead to the highest possible volume. Once the customers are drawn in, the

Don't Be Afraid to Charge What You're Worth   Inside Track

Setting prices for services can be tricky, especially when other businesses are your primary customers. And as Jane Halpern and Dave Sharp learned, these customers are only too happy to pay you much less than your work is worth.

Jane and Dave started a graphic design partnership when both became dissatisfied with the increasing overtime demands of their corporate bosses without a corresponding pay increase. Their old bosses quickly hired them on a contract basis; the two were so happy to get their first paying client that they accepted the job on the customer's terms. They got a lot of referral work and continued to charge the same low prices without a lot of thought to how much their services were really worth.

As they got a handle on their quickly growing workload, Dave approached Jane about setting new prices. Since their company had no inventory, minimal overhead, and few ongoing capital asset needs, the prices they were charging were bringing in profits. But some quick calculations showed that the profit margins were below industry averages, and Dave wanted to bring their prices up. That way, he explained, they could be more choosy about the jobs they accepted. He suggested a test increase of 5 percent.

At first, Jane was quite resistant to the change, especially when she thought he had randomly chosen an increase percentage that wouldn't change much of anything. After much discussion, the two agreed that their time was worth at least 25 percent more than they were currently charging. When the next contract came up, they introduced their new pricing schedule. Rather than the reaction they expected, which was an irate customer demanding the old price, their client grinned and said, "Well, I guess the free ride is over. But at least it lasted longer than I thought it would."

thinking goes, the business will be able to start bringing prices back up to more sustainable levels.

There is nothing at all wrong with competitive pricing, as long as it fits in with your overall marketing strategy and your complete business plan. Not to mention that no matter how competitive your prices are, they must still allow you to turn at least a modest profit. The volume strategy does often work for product-based retail businesses, especially those with a variety of relatively low-cost items for sale. Again, you should not necessarily set your prices to meet or best those of your competitors, but you should know what their price schedules are so you can effectively hold on to your market share (and maybe even grab some of your competitors') through your promotional campaigns.

What factors will go into a volume strategy? You should start by considering the following:

- ➲ Feasibility, based on what you are selling
- ➲ Competitor pricing
- ➲ Typical competitor responses to your pricing
- ➲ Standard demand levels for your product
- ➲ Your market share goals
- ➲ Your production or storage capacity

When you set your sights on volume, you must be able to back it up with availability. There is no point in trying to drum up volume business when you do not have the products ready for delivery—in fact, it can be counterproductive.

To attract volume buyers without building your entire pricing structure around that, you could try offering quantity discounts to your customers. For example, many grocery stores knock 10 percent off the shelf price when customers buy items by the case. This typically does not cut sharply into their margins because it saves them the cost of unpacking the case and pricing and shelving the individual contents.

The Danger of Pricing Too Low

Low prices not only affect your sales, they influence your profits and could also have long-range effects on your company's ultimate growth potential. Setting initially low prices, or implementing price cuts, can increase sales, but that will not necessarily help your profits grow. You have to sell more to capture the same revenue, for starters. Costs of a price cut (for example, hiring extra staff to cover the extra volume) can add up faster than sales—and that could lead to quickly shrinking profits or even losses on each item you ring up.

Your prices must, at the very least, cover your costs. If they don't, your business is guaranteed to lose money, no matter how large your sales volume or market share. That said, new companies (especially those that are product-based) are sometimes forced to set their prices lower than those of their well-established competitors to gain a foothold in the market. Unless you can convince your target customers that your product offering is in some way better than that of your rivals, or that your backup services are stellar in comparison, your company may have to endure a break-in period of low prices.

Even in that circumstance, though, you cannot set your prices so low that your company is not breaking even. Your prices must at least cover your costs. If they don't, your business cannot possibly succeed in the long run, no matter how many customers you attract at first.

Remember, too, that undercutting your competitors' prices can lead to two highly undesirable side effects. First, it could send the message that your products are not worth as much as your competitors' are, even if they are exactly the same. Customers in your target market could presume that you are selling inferior, more poorly made items, and that perception can turn them away for the long haul. Second, you could unintentionally spark a price war with your more established competitors, a war they will almost surely win.

If you plan to establish a low-price policy, carefully consider all the potential ramifications. Look to your nearest rivals, and try to determine ahead of time what their reactions will be. They could attack with even lower prices to run you out of town, or they could simply ignore you and carry on. A look at how they have reacted to other competitors in the past may indicate how they will react to your company's policies. Also, do not overlook the impact on the perceptions of your potential customers; a reputation of inferior offerings and service can keep them away.

Computing the Break-Even

Every business owner wants to know the answer to the question, "Will my business be profitable?" There's no definitive answer to that because you can't possibly know whether you'll make a go of it before the fact. That said, you'll still need to come up with some numbers to help all the other numbers—like pricing—fall into line. Preparing a break-even analysis is the first, and possibly most important, step toward determining whether your business actually can turn a profit.

A break-even analysis will show you just how much revenue you need to bring in to meet all of your expenses. Earning more than that target figure puts you on the road to profit. And since a break-even analysis is standard fare for business plans, creating one accomplishes two important tasks: getting your business plan closer to completion, and quantifying how much you will need to earn to turn a profit.

In theory, surpassing your break-even point indicates success. The reality may turn out somewhat differently, though, because your analysis is founded on assumptions about expected expenses and projected revenues. The more research you do, the more reasonable your assumptions will be, and the closer your numbers will be to the eventual reality.

Don't expect your break-even to be written in stone, though, as this is one very flexible number. Subtle changes in your assumptions will change your break-even. In reality, the underlying numbers you use to calculate this figure will absolutely change over time. In addition, you can change some of the numbers proactively by switching suppliers, finding ways to increase productivity, or increasing prices. Why would you try to change these numbers? Because lowering your break-even point means increasing your profitability.

Understanding the Numbers

To calculate your break-even point, you need to get a handle on some underlying numbers and then do a little math. These figures include your company's overhead, expected product price, and direct costs. The difference between the product price and the direct costs equals the gross profit margin (also called the contribution margin).

The most important number you need to come up with to compute your break-even is your overhead, or fixed expenses. These expenditures are the same all the time and do not vary based on sales or productivity—these are the bills you have to pay even if you sell nothing at all. Overhead costs include things like rent, insurance, advertising, interest, and administrative (or back office) salaries.

Direct costs, also known as variable costs, are directly related to and vary proportionately with your sales. Direct costs come in two flavors: product-related and sales-related. Product-related direct costs include everything you have to pay to get the product ready for sale to your end customers. The biggest factors here are typically the cost of the product itself, that is, the amount you pay your supplier per item. Add on to that sales taxes that you pay, freight charges of getting the products to you, unpacking and shelving costs, and all other expenses you have to incur to get that product ready for sale. Finally, postsale costs should be considered, like gift-wrap and shopping bags.

Costs That Aren't Wholly Fixed or Variable

Some businesses may be faced with costs that do not fall squarely into either the fixed or variable category. These are called mixed costs, and they combine elements of both. One example is postage, which can be attributed to product delivery costs and overhead expenses like billing and paying bills. Trying to figure out the true and exact proportions would be much too time-consuming for the benefit it would serve. So to make your life easier, and without causing too much distortion in your break-even analysis, simply allocate half of the total cost to each category.

The Break-Even Formula

To come up with your break-even point, you have to do a little math. First, though, you need to collect the numbers that you will use in the formula. Here is the basic break-even formula (measured in dollars):

$$BE = FC / (S - V)$$

In this formula, FC stands for your total fixed costs in dollars (a figure you can get from your pro forma statement of profit and loss). The S represents your total gross sales, expressed as 100 percent. The V represents your variable costs as a percentage of sales. If a product you sell for $10 comes with direct costs of $6, your V here would be 60 percent. The difference between sales and variable costs is commonly called contribution margin.

Here is how to use the formula. Suppose your first-year estimated fixed costs come to $15,000, and your variable costs are 60 percent. Your break-even formula would fill out like this:

$$BE = \$15,000 / (100\% - 60\%)$$

The result would be break-even sales of $37,500. To figure out your break-even volume in units, simply divide your total sales in dollars by the per item price. For example, if you sell vacuum cleaners for $250 each, your break-even sales volume would be 150 units.

Maximizing Profits

When it comes to boosting profit levels, there are three ways to make it happen. First, you can increase your sales volume above break-even levels. Once you pass that break-even mark, the entire contribution margin translates to pure profits. Second, you can increase your prices, thereby increasing your contribution margins. That has the effect of letting you hit the break-even level sooner, which in turn leads to quicker profit realization. Third, you can find ways to lower your costs, both direct product-related costs and overhead expenses. That way, more of your revenue earned will be preserved as profits.

Of course, you can also increase your profitability through a combination of these methods. However, to truly know which is doing the most to add profits to your bottom line, it's often best to tackle one approach at a time. Each tactic could provide significant financial benefits, but each comes with its own unique caution. So consider your choices carefully before implementing any of these plans.

Pump Up the Sales Volume

If bringing in more revenues by increasing your unit sales sparks your inspiration, think not only about how you can affect that change but also about how that change will affect your company. Again, there are three main ways to turn up your sales volume: lower prices (at least temporarily) to get more units out the door; sell the same products at the same price to a lot of new customers; or convince your existing customers that they need to buy more. While all of these methods can impact your sales in the short term, the one with the best chance of real long-term staying power is attracting new customers.

Each of these methods can help increase sales and maximize profitability, but each also comes with some potential drawbacks. The lower price plan also raises your break-even volume, so although you will be making more sales, it will take more sales to turn a profit. In addition, any new clientele who are drawn in by your temporary markdowns could hit the highway when prices rebound to normal levels. Tapping your current customers to buy more from you can also cause a momentary sales spike, but it could slow down sales afterward. When customers stock up, they may not need to come back as frequently, and that could impact other items they might buy from you as well. In addition, it is also possible that overselling to particular clients will turn them off from your business. The downside of starting a campaign to bring in new customers is that it will cost you money up front, and that will cut into your profitability at least initially.

When you are trying to increase your overall sales volume, be prepared to handle the response. You will need to make sure you have enough supply to meet the extra demand. Plus, you must ensure there is adequate staff to deal with the overflow. More sales could translate to additional requests for customer assistance (both pre- and postsale) and will necessarily require you have extra supplies on hand (shopping bags, for instance).

Increasing Prices

While you have already learned about the potential hazards of overpricing your products and services, your current pricing structure may still allow for some wiggle room. Once you have gained a strong foothold in the market and have begun establishing a loyal customer base, you will have more freedom to raise your prices without fear of losing everyone. The keys to a successful price increase are making it relatively painless and providing a good reason for the hike (in case anyone asks).

This strategy is much simpler to implement when your business offers services. There, you always have a built-in unique selling point: you, and the other professionals on your staff. Therefore, you can safely charge anywhere between 15 and 30 percent (depending on your industry) more than your competitors without losing core customers to them. That's not to say you should implement a 15-percent price hike in one fell swoop—that could easily turn clients away. Start smaller, and increase them gradually. If your prices are more than 30 percent higher than those of your direct rivals, you will no longer be targeting the same market.

When considering an across-the-board permanent price increase on products, focus your marketing on added-value services. Intangibles, like better customer follow-up, are harder for consumers to pin down when it comes to price. Think about the difference between buying new shoes at Nordstrom's and a discount shoe warehouse. The warehouse may stock the exact same shoes, but Nordstrom's charges a premium for their world-class service, and millions of customers are willing to pay the higher price for that.

Cutting Costs

The final way to maximize your company's profitability has less to do with your pricing structure and more to do with your costs. There are some costs you really cannot monkey around with, like the monthly rent on your five-year lease. Others, however, can be negotiated and renegotiated once you have developed a relationship with the companies that your company is buying from.

Typically, the primary cost-cutting target is inventory and those costs that are directly related to producing or obtaining your products. Since these costs are the ones that take up the biggest chunks of your revenue, they can have a huge impact on profitability. Don't assume that your suppliers won't budge on price—they are probably used to haggling.

▶▶ TEST DRIVE

This exercise involves putting down the book and interacting with other people. You are about to conduct a price survey and comparison. To do that properly, you will need to find at least five different places that sell what you're selling. If your company sells a product, find the most similar product you can and take note of its sticker price; if it's on sale, write down both the sale price and the regular price. To compare service prices, you'll have to make some phone calls and ask for estimates. Make sure you keep your facts the same for every call so that the prices you get are truly comparative.

Define Your Marketing Strategy

Your marketing strategy is really just the plan to get customers to buy what your business is selling. That overall strategy is made up of several components, such as your target market, your product, and your pricing schedules, just to name a few. All of these come together to help you develop a clear message, the one you will send out in your efforts to reach potential customers.

As you develop this marketing strategy, look back to your mission statement and consider your specific goals. Your marketing plans should support those goals and flow naturally from them. When you work from that central place, you will be better able to make sure that your marketing and sales efforts are consistent and interconnected, a crucial point to those business plan readers from whom you are seeking funding. A clearly defined marketing strategy compels all of the individual pieces to work together in a logical manner, and it helps to ensure that the program fits in with your comprehensive business strategies. For example, if in your top-level plans you decide to stress high-quality service over all else, you wouldn't want to develop a bargain-basement pricing schedule.

In addition, keep your budget in mind. Don't adjust your budget to your marketing plan. Instead, adapt your marketing plan to fit in with your existing budget. It's easy for marketing spending to spiral out of control. Image-building can be very expensive, and the exercise is better suited for national companies with huge bank accounts. Instead, smaller companies need to work within their budgets. They are better served by spurring customers to action—the action of coming in and buying now.

The bottom line is that your marketing strategy will be bounded by both your budget and your overall business strategies. It should be consistent all the way through, from the way you define your products and services to the prices you decide to charge for them. Taking a less structured, more haphazard approach can use up precious cash without achieving the results you were hoping for.

Positioning Your Products and Services

As in real estate, where location is everything, positioning is everything in the world of marketing. Here, though, position does not refer to physical position, or the place where people can buy your product. Instead, it refers to customers' perceptions about your company—its position in their minds.

With the hundreds, even thousands, of marketing messages that broadcast every day, people must filter out those that seem more important or interesting to them. They base that judgment on a quick glance at the product presentation and message. That message is the basis of your positioning. It is what will form customer perception about your company and what you're selling.

The point of your message is to create a positive image for your company in the minds of your target customers. On top of that general good feeling, you want to create the perception that your product or service is unique and that buying from you is the best way to satisfy a need your customers have. While the idea is simple, the implementation can be tough.

What Your Message Will Convey

Before you develop the actual content of your message, here are some basic guidelines to follow:

1. Keep it simple and easily understandable.
2. Make it memorable.
3. Create an unmistakable link to your product or service.

To come up with a good message, you have to get into the minds of your customers and know what will stand out in their minds. Standing out from the competition is crucial here. While knowing how your competitors position themselves is an important consideration in developing your own message, following what has worked for them will only strengthen *their* place in the market.

You can aim to position your business or product as higher quality, more convenient, superior personalized service, lower priced . . . the list

AGILE,

RAPID

INSERTION

is as long as you can imagine. Think long and hard before you settle on a position, though, as this core message will spread through every facet of your marketing and sales. From your advertising to your salesmen's customer interactions, everything will follow that positioning. Should that message be off, or unattractive to your target market, you will have a harder time bringing customers in.

Changing Your Position

Spend a lot of time on choosing your marketing position. Enlist the help of professionals if need be, and do not make a hasty decision based on what's currently the easiest position to take. This should be a long-term decision that will impact your entire marketing plan for years to come. Solid positions often take years to develop, and they should not be fiddled with lightly.

Although it is possible to reposition your business and your product, it is difficult and can make potential customers think your company is unstable. For that reason, it should not be a frequent occurrence. Rather than creating a clear picture for your target market, repositioning will cause confusion among them, at least at first. So before you decide to change your entire positioning stance, make sure the one you have already chosen is absolutely not working.

Should you come to that conclusion, revisit the entire process. When your originally chosen position does not reach customers in the way you envisioned, you must return to ground zero to figure out where that message fell short. Review your market research and your target market. Enlist as much help as you can: employees, mentors, or marketing professionals (if you can afford them, this is a good use of that allotted money). Especially since this is not the initial message you have put out there, it is crucial that this position be the one you stick with.

> ## Minor Adjustments Are Not the Same Thing as Repositioning
>
> Though repositioning your product or service is a huge undertaking, making small adjustments to clarify your main message is not. As long as these edits still impart the same basic ideas, they will not change your positioning. Rather, their point is to make the message easier for potential customers to relate to and remember.
>
> Staying consistent keeps customers coming. It may take them a while to get to you, and a repetitive message keeps your product and your company in mind. In fact, customers tend to react more positively to consistency than to change. So tweak your message if you must, but leave the meaning behind it intact.

Setting Sales Goals

How will you be able to tell if your promotional efforts are successful? By taking a look at the numbers. However, current sales statistics alone cannot measure your success; instead, they must be viewed in comparison to predetermined goals. Then you will be able to figure out not only if these efforts are working, but how well.

In some part, your sales goals will be related to your sales expectations, those that will make their way to your pro forma financial statements. But while those expectations are based on your realistic planning assumptions, and not on what you hope will happen, you can set your goals a little higher for the purposes of gauging the success of your overall marketing plan. Consider your pro forma revenue projections the lowest sales you hope to achieve, and set your sights on slightly loftier sales goals.

Your sales goals are, however, constrained by some basic facts. For example, with a mall retail shop, you will not be making sales around the clock seven days a week; your store will only be accessible when the mall is open. Other factors can put an upper boundary on your sales as well. For instance, most customers will only buy one car at a time; people typically don't buy snow shovels during the dog days of summer; and your store can only hold a preset amount of merchandise. Working within these constraints puts a natural cap on your sales goal, no matter how high your hopes soar.

Your sales goals will in part dictate the shape of your marketing plan. Relatively modest goals may be achievable with a low to moderate investment in advertising and promotion; aggressive sales goals may call for a more comprehensive marketing strategy.

All About Advertising

When it comes to getting customers in the door, advertising is typically the first tactic that comes to mind. Everyone is accustomed to seeing ads in the newspaper, in magazines, on television—virtually everywhere you turn you'll see an ad for something. Developing your advertising strategy, though, can be a lot tougher than that inundation would suggest.

▶▶ **The first basic rule of advertising is repetition.** Regardless of the media outlet you use to convey the message, it should be consistent and repetitive to allow it to sink into the minds of your target customers. The second rule is to test everything. Every ad is full of variables, and even slight changes can have a huge impact on sales. Third, ask for action. If you're going to shell out the cash for an advertising campaign, make sure it inspires your customers to do something, rather than just introducing them to your company. Finally, unless you are an expert marketer, hire this job out to an experienced professional at an established agency.

Advertising Medium

One of the first decisions you will make is where you want to place your advertisements. Where they will run can impact their style and message, size and length, and (of course) cost. And though television is probably the first thing that came to mind when you started thinking about advertising, it's often the last medium of choice for new or small businesses. If not television, where? Consider these options:

> **Newspapers** run the gamut from tiny local rag to regional, and the size and scope of your target market will determine which type is a better fit for your plans. Remember, larger newspapers typically come with inserts, another easily accessed form of advertising.

Signs and billboards will attract local traffic, but they may not reach customers outside of your immediate area. These call for easy-to-read, quick-to-absorb, eye-catching copy and design.

Radio ads can reach a large population, but getting the right population at the right time is critical. You have one chance in about thirty seconds to make a lasting impression, and it may take several placements before your ad registers among listeners.

Web advertising requires the existence of a dedicated Web site to catch customers. Forms of Web advertising include banner ads, click-through links, direct e-mail, and search engine placement.

Focusing Your Statement

Advertising is one of the most expensive ways to get customers, so it's important to reach as many as possible in a way that draws them in. The content of your advertising message is crucial—a single word can make the difference between sparking interest and being ignored. And you only have a few seconds to catch them before they move on to the next thing.

Let your advertising message flow from your overall marketing strategy, and make sure it reflects both the type of business you are striving to become and the personalities of the customers you are hoping to attract. Your unique selling position can be emphasized in your advertising, as that differentiates your company from any others. Regardless of who ends up actually writing the ad copy (and, again, if you are not experienced here, pay someone who is), the message should be comfortable to you and make sense inside your marketing plan.

Tips for Advertising on a Budget

With the mountain of costs associated with starting or expanding small businesses, stretching precious cash resources to pay for big-time advertising may be out of the question. Plus, while your business plan readers want to see that you do have substantial plans designed to bring in customers, they also want to see that you are keeping spending at a reasonable level. Translation: they want you to advertise, but not at the expense of profitability.

With a little ingenuity, though, you can run a full-scale marketing campaign on a bare-bones budget. There are literally dozens of ways you can promote your business without busting your bank account; you just have to know where to look. Later on, after the cash and profits are flowing in, you can look back and measure how well each of these strategies panned out for you and expand your efforts in these areas. For now, though, the trick is to bring customers in and get them to buy more, in the least costly ways possible.

For an existing business that's looking to branch out—either by adding new products and services or bringing in a different type of customers—there are even more ways you promote your business with minimal cash involvement. People already know about your company, and you already have a steady customer base; you have something to build on. A new business must take an entirely different approach. There, the primary goal is spreading the name around and telling customers why they should come to you. Some economical methods work well for either stage of business—it's just the message itself that will vary.

Let Your Customers Advertise for You

Word of mouth is a wonderful thing, but you cannot count on customers to sing your praises unless you provide them with a little incentive and a constant reminder. Of course, you must offer a unique and useful product and top-quality service in order for customers to want to recommend you to other people. Since that's already in place, ▶▶ **use your repeat customers to your advantage; after all, they are your best advertising outlet.**

There are some very simple ways to let your customers do your marketing for you, all designed to bring in new business with minimal expenditure on your part. For example, you can offer gift certificates, which provide a convenience for your existing customers and bring new blood into your establishment. Even better, since these are actually prepaid sales, your cash inflows get an immediate bump.

Other options include things like two-for-one deals, which work particularly well for personal service businesses (like "bring a friend for a facial"). You also can offer customers a bonus for every customer they bring in that results in a sale. For example, if they refer a friend who buys something, the original customer will get a 10-percent discount on his next purchase (and now you've gotten two sales out of this deal).

Use Your Computer to Create Marketing Materials

With all of the do-it-yourself design software available today, it's easier than ever to create and produce some of your own marketing materials. One case in point is flyers. You can very easily and cheaply make up flyers on your computer and print them as you need them. Eye-catching design is key here—use bright colors with a clear message, and print away. If you don't have a color printer, use colored paper. Include as much information about your company as possible (name, address, and phone number *must* be on there) without making the flyer seem difficult or time-consuming to read. If your cash isn't as tight as your time, you can bring a file over to a print shop and have them produce the flyers for you.

Once you have the basics under control, print up hundreds of copies, and put them everywhere you can think of. Use the bulletin board in the grocery store, telephone poles, community centers—virtually everywhere there is space. You can put stacks of them in lobbies, waiting rooms, and train stations. Even if people don't take them along, they probably will read them while they're waiting.

In addition, enclose a flyer into every single piece of mail you send out—not just promotional efforts, but everything you mail. You can put a flyer into your remittance envelope when you are paying bills. You can insert flyers into customer invoices. Add them into the envelope when you are sending a written purchase order to your suppliers. Don't stop there. Stuff a copy into every customer's shopping bag or hand them out with your receipts—anything you can think of. It's basic math, really. The more flyers you put out there, the more people will see them, and more visibility typically leads to more sales.

Other Cost-Effective Ways to Spread the Word

No advertising campaign would be complete without a mention in the Yellow Pages. Whether your company is brand-new or becoming established, there are hundreds of potential customers out there who will only find you while their fingers do the walking. Since these books are typically published only annually (though in some areas they may come out twice a year), you may not get your ad in until the next cycle. Though phone book ads are not free (as White Pages listings are), every business should have at least a line mention.

Another good resource is complementary businesses, which can offer cross-referrals. Talk to other local businesses about sending customers your way in exchange for the same service from you. You can place each other's flyers or business cards where customers are sure to see them, or you can mention each other to your clients should the topic flow naturally. This practice is particularly common among small service providers.

You don't need to limit your referrals to other businesses, though. Other types of organizations may also eagerly provide referrals, and you can pave the way with things like service bartering or offering modest discounts. Even without blatant referrals, some places may just let you leave flyers. The venues you'll use depend somewhat on the business you're in, but they could include things like the public library, the local college campus, community centers, social services offices, charitable foundations, and even government offices.

Using Special Incentives

Have you ever been to a bakery and gotten a little card with ten little pictures of a muffin on it? Every time you buy a muffin, the cashier punches a hole in your card, and when you earn ten punches, you get your next muffin free. That is a common special-incentive program that has been proven effective.

A special-incentive program rewards your customers for purchasing from you, and a good one can keep them coming back. The best programs encourage customers both to buy right now and to continue buying from you frequently. While the punch-card method works well for some types of companies, other types of incentives work better for others.

Additional types of special incentives programs include the following:

- Free gift with purchase
- Buy a certain number, get one free
- Purchase discount when total spending exceeds a certain dollar amount
- Discount coupon for the next purchase
- Add-on service packages for lower total price
- "Private" sales
- Free shipping with purchase
- Free samples

Finding Free Publicity

One of the best forms of promotion for small businesses is free publicity. It costs you nothing (or next to nothing), and brings your business to the attention of people you might never otherwise reach.

How can you drum up some publicity for your company? One good way is to write up a press release about something newsworthy and send it out to local newspapers. A successful press release will be concise and enticing. The title should be descriptive and compelling, and it should clearly impart the point of your release. For example, you could create a press release about the grand opening of your business. Newspapers, especially those with relatively small circulations, need content to fill their pages. When you supply them with a press release, you fill their needs at no cost to them, making this strategy a very attractive win-win part of your marketing plans.

Volunteering your services also helps spread your name. For example, you could offer tax preparation to seniors on a specific day during tax season. Yes, it means giving away business, but the word-of-mouth publicity that comes from that can more than make up for your time. Participating in community events and the like also gets your name out there at no monetary cost to your company.

You can also try to get yourself interviewed on the local television or radio station if they run a program about your field of expertise. Program directors are often on the lookout for fresh voices (and faces) as they try to fill up the time slots with something new. Offer your services as an expert for a discussion panel, submit to an interview, or let them do a profile on you and your company. Should you land a spot, make sure to issue a press release notifying audiences of your upcoming appearance. And make sure you are prepared. You should have memorized a targeted message that focuses on the unique selling position of your business, and mention it whenever it fits into the conversation.

▶▶ TEST DRIVE

You want your company listed in the Yellow pages, and now is the time to reserve space. Call the phone book publisher today, and connect with their ad sales department. Then get the answers to the following questions:

- Can you reserve the ad space right now?
- When does the ad have to be submitted to get into the next edition?
- How much does each size ad cost?
- Is there any prohibited text?
- How many box ads for each type of company may appear on a single page?

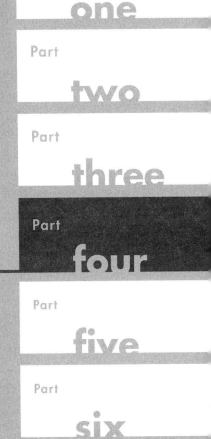

Part
one

Part
two

Part
three

Part
four

Part
five

Part
six

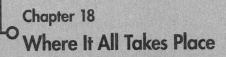

An Overview of Sales Tactics

No matter what type of business you have, it involves selling something to someone. The fourth pillar of marketing, called place, defines that selling process. This is distinct from promotion, which both introduces your company to customers and convinces them that they need what your business is offering. The actual selling itself, exactly how you and your sales team will close these deals, is what puts revenue on your income statement.

Selling requires planning and tactical strategies. There are many different ways to sell your products and services, and the techniques you choose will speak directly to your company's success. As you'd expect, the method (or methods) that will work best for your business depend on what your business is.

In your business plan, you will write out in detail any features of your chosen sales approach that can specifically spell success for your company. In addition, in this section you will also cover those aspects of your sales plan that are significantly different from the tactics your competitors use. For example, if the norm in your industry is to focus on catalog and Internet sales, but you have chosen to put phone sales in the starring role, you will need to explain your reasoning to your business plan readers.

The Terms of Sale

The language of sales can be confusing to the uninitiated, so here's a quick vocabulary lesson to help you get through this chapter. First, the most important word in the sales lingo: close (pronounced like the verb). Here, "close" means getting the customer to take a specific action, and the ultimate close results in a firm purchase commitment. Next, channels: this refers to how products get to the customer. For retailers and service providers, the channel is direct, but other business types could include one or more intermediaries, like wholesalers, distributors, agents, brokers . . . the middlemen. Finally, the reps (nothing to do with crunches). Reps are the frontline salesmen, either independent or in-house, and they are masters at closing deals.

What Are the Basic Sales Tactics?

Before you opt for one approach over another, even if you decide on a combination of tactics, it helps to have a basic understanding of the various sales methods.

Phone sales involve making calls to potential customers to let them know about and convince them to purchase your product or service.

Inbound phone selling relies on potential customers calling in to your company and your dedicated sales force ending the conversation with a firm sale.

Direct mail allows you to reach large numbers of prospective clients through the mail, in the hopes that a percentage of them will be interested in making a purchase.

Web site selling brings customers to an Internet store and uses screen copy to convince them to buy products or services.

An independent sales force uses face-to-face persuasion to entice prospective customers to make purchases and is typically used in business-to-business sales.

Retailers allow customers to come in to a storefront, look around, and directly choose what they will be buying.

Even if your business lends itself to a variety of methods, one will likely stand out as the primary approach. For many small businesses, tactics that place emphasis on direct selling to chosen customers can be the most cost efficient. So at a time when cash flow is the most crucial, consider your alternatives carefully before you make a choice.

Choosing the Best Approach

Without firsthand knowledge of which sales tactic works best for your business, a little learning is in order. First stop, check out what works for your closest competitors. They come backed with some requisite experience, and you may be able to gauge just how well their tactics are working. Next, find out what works best for the industry as a whole. Trade groups can be an excellent source of suggestions as they typically compile myriad statistics to help industry members prosper.

Some types of businesses lend themselves to particular sales tactics and will not work with others. In addition, your overall marketing philosophy can help guide this decision. As with everything else in your marketing plan, your sales tactics should blend in with the overall promotional strategy. For example, when you are offering a specialty product or service, your sales tactics will require a more personal touch. If you have a manufacturing firm, you will need sales reps to move your product toward wholesalers or retailers. When you have an informed, knowledgeable customer base, in-person interactions may not be as crucial, allowing you to use phone or print means to close sales. When educating the customer is part of the deal, though, a more personal approach is called for.

The bottom line is that choosing the optimal sales approach is more art than science, and the process may just involve some trial and error. Consider all the factors you believe will go into a sale and how you think your customers will best respond. Implement your first choice, but don't be afraid to make alterations if Plan A doesn't pan out.

Selling by Phone

The idea of selling by phone, a.k.a. telemarketing, may raise some eyebrows. At one time or another, you have almost certainly been the recipient of some form of telemarketing, and you may well have been annoyed by it. Don't let your personal perceptions and experiences turn you off of this proven, and often successful, sales method. There are some companies for which it truly works wonders.

This form of telemarketing, the outgoing call, takes a proactive approach to sales. Here, each phone sales rep starts with a customer list, honed to contain only those who belong to your target market and are most likely to be interested in what they have to say. These reps typically work off of a script, but the best can make it seem naturally conversational and can improvise to keep customer attention. Most important, though, is the ability to grab that attention in the first ten to fifteen seconds of the call—without that, the selling part of the mission will never take place.

Because all calls are made to target customers, some portion of them will be receptive to this approach. When you've reached those prospects, it's crucial to keep them engaged with the script and sales pitch. It's the job of this sales force to get people interested, develop a friendly rapport, keep them on the line, and convert any doubts into consideration. Should the customer decide to make a purchase, this process should be ridiculously easy—he should be able to buy right now, over the phone, without any follow-up necessary that could kill the deal. If customers have any questions, they must get thoughtful answers. ▸▸ **One key to successful sales talks is the ability to listen and understand customer concerns and then transform them into sales.**

At the end of the day, though, it all comes down to volume. The more calls that are made, the more potential there is for firm sales. And when the calls are made only to people likely to desire the product or service, the success percentage will be higher than with calls that are made more randomly (like directly from the phone book, for example).

Handling Incoming Calls

For some businesses, the inbound call approach can be the most successful tactic. In these cases, customers have basically decided to make a purchase (or at least be pretty close to making that decision) and have approached your sales force directly. However, inbound calls that occur for other reasons can result in sales as well.

Essentially, there are four reasons why someone would call in:

1. He is ready to make a purchase.
2. He is in the process of deciding to make a purchase and wants to compare the offerings of different companies.
3. He is just looking for more information about your product or service before he can decide whether or not he wants it at all from anyone.
4. He needs some other form of customer service, like lodging a complaint or reporting an address change.

With an experienced employee on the other side of the phone, any of these calls could be turned into a sale, and a done-deal sales call could be bumped up with add-ons ("Today only, customers who buy the scarf can get a matching hat for 20 percent off the standard retail price").

How do these sales prospects get the call-in number in the first place? Typically, your promotional campaign would stress the phone number and encourage potential customers to make a call. An advertising program directed toward making the phone ring could include things as simple as refrigerator magnets or as complicated as television ad jingles. That campaign, however, has to be matched with solid performance when the phone is answered.

Your best advantage here is a fully trained phone sales force. Many novice entrepreneurs mistakenly assume that if the customer is calling in, the deal is as good as sealed. But think back to times you have called in to ask a question or place an order. Think about being placed on hold, or how many menu options you had to wade through to talk to a person; think about a rude or ill-informed staffer on the other end of the line who either could not or would not help you in the way you needed. It's a lot easier to lose a customer here than most business owners think, and many decide to cut costs by using lower-level staff here. Don't make those mistakes. Instead, make sure that whoever is answering your phones knows what he's talking about and knows how to close a sale. Even better, aspire to develop a staff that can turn virtually any call, one that's come in for any reason, into a finalized sale.

Using Direct Mail

Direct mail walks the line between a promotional effort and a sales tactic, and the items it covers run the gamut from Val-Pak coupons to full-fledged Harry & David catalogs. Sending out direct mail pieces can serve multiple purposes, like adding to your company's recognition factor, spurring potential customers to call or come in to your main offices, or actually making a sale.

With direct mail, you send materials to a particular list of people, preferably those who share the primary characteristics of your target market. In focusing your attention on communicating with these people, you increase your chances of selling your product or service. Costs vary widely here, based on myriad factors like paper quality and color. Included somewhere in the mailer will be a sales letter, the most important component; it should be the first thing prospects see when they open that mail. You'll also want to make sure your piece includes some type of response card, postage paid, to make it as easy as possible for customers to respond. When credit card information or a check is required, make sure to include a postage paid return envelope for them to use.

When it comes to the *who* factor, the best bet is to use a mailing list comprised of people who most closely match your target customers. Better lists typically return better response rates, so use care in choosing which you use. You can also run small tests, using only a portion of the list, to determine what the response rate looks like before you spend a lot of money on a full-blown mailing.

Here are some quick tips for getting the best sales percentage out of your mailings:

- Offer your customers the option of a mail-back or phone response.
- Unless your mailing is 100-percent local, offer a toll free number for individual consumers.
- Accept all major credit cards.
- Use a respond-by date to spur people to quick action, preferably a number of days rather than a specific date.
- Make their purchase risk-free with a liberal return and refund policy.

On the Internet

It's impossible to track the exact number of Internet users in the United States, but it's certainly well over the 70 million mark and expanding rapidly each day. Selling your product or service over the Web can be very appealing to new and small business owners. You can reach a vast audience with a relatively minimal hit to your budget, make frequent low-cost changes as necessary, and handle customer orders from across the globe twenty-four hours a day, seven days a week.

Sound too good to be true? While Internet selling has truly been a boon for the business community, some aspects are not exactly as simple as they seem to be. What are some potential downsides? Web-site creation and maintenance costs can pile up; the more elaborate things get, the more expensive your site will be. When the site is down or running slowly, customers can easily surf over to another site and buy something else, possibly never to return. You still need to have another way for customers to reach you while they are at your Web site, in case they have trouble finishing their purchase—without immediate access to support, they will probably just walk away. Finally, don't fall into the excitement trap. Not everyone who surfs the Web will visit your site, and not all site visitors will become customers.

That said, ▶▶ **every company should have some level of Web presence, even if it's just a simple home page listing your offerings and some direct contact information.** Though absolute beginners will do well to retain a consultant experienced in Web site design, it is possible to create a simple home page on your own fairly inexpensively. If, however, your site has to be complex, use a consultant even if you plan to do some of the work yourself.

However, if you plan to sell only online, your Web site is everything. Though this method is the youngest, it is in no way the smallest. Customers spend billions of dollars each year making online purchases, from airline tickets to bestsellers. From the customer perspective, it's quick and easy, generally accepted to be safe, and enormously convenient. But making it work that way takes, well, a lot of work. Internet shoppers follow the same patterns as in-person retail shoppers: impulse buyers, window shoppers, preplanned purchases, bargain hunters. The tone of your site should meld seamlessly into your overall marketing strategy.

Here are five of the most important characteristics of a successful e-commerce site:

1. Very fast page loading
2. Easy navigation
3. Secure checkout

4. Customer technical support around the clock, seven days a week

5. An easy-to-remember domain name

A Face-to-Face Sales Force

Though most business consultants will tell you that in the world of business, everyone on your team has to be a salesman to some degree, a dedicated active sales force takes things up quite a few notches. There are several variations on the salesman theme: in-house, independent, on the floor, and on the road. What these all have in common is the ability to encourage and close deals face-to-face with customers, up close and personal.

The first factor that weighs in the decision of the type of salespeople your company will use is the main customer group: individual consumers or other businesses. The processes invoked to sell to these two groups are quite different, and it is important that the reps you choose know how to deal with your target clientele. For example, a rep who is selling raw materials to a furniture manufacturer plays a much different game than one who is selling perfume to people strolling through a department store.

But before any salesman will agree to work for your company (especially one paid on a purely commission basis), you have to sell him on the potential of the product or service you are offering—his livelihood depends on its success. To make your point, you may want to share the marketing section of your business plan. It will demonstrate exactly the type of marketing support his efforts will have and could help convince him that the prospects of huge profits truly exist.

Independent Sales Representatives

For new and small businesses, independent sales reps can be lifesavers. First, they typically don't require any up-front money; rather, they tend to work on commissions, getting paid only after a sale has been consummated. Second, though they may need some specific product education, sales training is unnecessary. These guys are professionals, and they already know how to sell. And the benefits don't end there: no associated administrative costs (like travel or phone expenses), minimal (if any) management needed, and you can count on them to stick around (they are already familiar and comfortable with the sales life).

As with anything, there are some drawbacks as well. For example, independent sales reps typically care more about closing a sale than any follow-up customer service needs. That's not to say they don't care about customers (they do want repeat business), but their job ends with the sale. Also, they will likely have other clients, probably in the same general industry, and possibly your direct competitors . . . unless you have them sign an agreement forbidding that. Finally, they are beyond your control. If you sell three products and one is the most stellar seller, that's where they will focus their efforts (more sales means more commissions) regardless of your desire to get rid of slower-moving merchandise.

An In-House Sales Force

Maintaining a dedicated sales force can be very expensive, and it is not a decision to be made lightly. Consider all the added-on costs, when compared to independent reps:

- Telephone expenses
- Travel and meals
- Office space
- Payroll taxes and preparation
- Management costs

On top of those, this choice will cost more of your time, and it may even cost you some lost sales for territories left uncovered as you try to build a strong staff.

With all of those disadvantages, why would anyone want an in-house sales staff? For starters, you have control over things like which products they sell, their travel schedules, and what sweeteners they can add to deals, to name a few. In addition, you can rest assured that they are not selling a stitch for your competitors, either direct or indirect. Finally, they will develop loyalty to both the company and its products, and that can push them to push products that don't take off right out of the gate.

Paying Commissions

There are two ways you can pay commissions to your independent sales reps. One is strictly personal: they make a sale, they get a commission. The second is territorial. Also called ledger commissions, this way reps reap the benefits of any sale that occurs within their territory, no matter how that sale was closed.

The next common commission question centers around percentages. Typically, independent sales reps receive somewhere between 5 and 15 percent of net sales (which equals total gross sales less any discounts, allowances, and returns). Business owners can negotiate the specific terms with their sales reps, and factors influencing those terms include the experience and contacts (of the rep), product price, and average customer purchase.

Going the Retail Route

Retail sales have two distinct sides: selling to the retailers, and retailers selling to customers. Each side of the retail coin calls for completely different sales tactics and involves very different players. What they have in common is that products are always involved.

Selling to Retailers

To get down the pipeline to a retail outlet, a product often travels through a few interim destinations. Here are some of the main players involved in this trek:

Manufacturers create the product from raw materials.

Wholesalers (a.k.a. jobbers) play middleman between manufacturers and retailers.

Distributors act like independent sales reps to move products from manufacturers to wholesalers, and from wholesalers to retailers.

Importers facilitate the movement of products from overseas.

Inside Track   The Invisible Cashier

Donna Maxwell had finally opened the bakeshop of her dreams. Every morning, she and her assistant baker, Ted, would come in to work hours before the sun came up, preparing award-winning pastries, home-style muffins and rolls, and hearty loaves of bread. When they finished in the back, Ted would load up the van and make deliveries to the local restaurants and grocers that stocked their baked goods.

Donna would venture out front, greet the first customers, and begin ringing up breakfast sales. That worked well . . . in the beginning. But as word spread, the store got too packed for one person to handle. So Donna hired a cashier to ring up the customers. Donna got customer orders packed and ready to go, and Sara (the cashier) would collect the money to help busy businessmen get on their way.

Once Sara appeared well trained on the cash register and had learned to fill customer orders, Donna began to leave the store as soon as the morning rush subsided. After a few weeks, Donna realized that her 10:00 to 2:00 sales had seriously slacked off. She asked Sara about the drop in traffic, and Sara told her that very few customers came in during that time. Donna's experience with that time block was very different, and that got her thinking.

Donna sent in some "spy" customers at 11:00 one day to see what was going on. When they entered the store, it seemed that no one was there. They waited a few moments, shouted "Hello," then walked out. After twenty minutes, they headed back in, with the exact same results. Then Donna herself went in and found Sara in the back, reading a book with her iPod headphones on . . . and promptly fired her.

The moral of the story is that if customers can't buy what they want, when they want it, your business will lose sales.

There are other considerations when selling to retailers, where competition can be fierce. For example, a manufacturer who has successfully sold his products to a wholesaler has no assurance that those products will end up in retail outlets. In fact, many retailers are hesitant to stock products from small, new, and unproven companies. Their floor space is precious, and they want to fill it with items practically guaranteed to fly off the shelves. That can take some extra convincing on your part;

selling a retailer on your product's potential can take it further than even the deepest discount.

Selling by Retailers

Retail shops mean storefronts, where customers walk in and buy products directly from the company. Good salespeople can play a part in increasing overall sales, encouraging customers to make purchases and pointing out corollary items that they might want to add to their shopping carts. In some retail situations, those with higher-end products, helpful salespeople are considered a must-have. But even bargain stores should train all of their employees on the art of leading customers to the buy decision—at the very least, store personnel should not pose a hindrance to purchases.

▶▶ TEST DRIVE

Getting your company up on the Web is a great way to reach a lot of people with a single investment. To slash costs to a bare minimum, you can come up with great copy and design ideas all by yourself. It doesn't matter if you can't draw—start to sketch out your home page by following these steps:

1. Draw your company's style: posh or discount, technical or artistic.
2. Pick three to five graphic images you want on the page.
3. Write some bullet-point text to convey your unique selling point.

Put it all together, and you have a home page!

Preparing Financial Statements

Three Statements You Must Include

Every business plan contains the big three financial statements: a balance sheet, a statement of profit and loss, and a statement of cash flow. No business plan will be considered by a lender or investor without them. Typically, you will include both historical and future projected versions on each statement when you have an existing business. For a start-up company, all of the company's numbers will be projections.

Even if you will not be preparing financial statements on an ongoing basis, you will need to have at least a working knowledge of them to effectively run your own company. Financial statements provide you with critical data about your business: where it stands (the balance sheet), how it's doing (the statement of profit and loss), and how you'll pay the bills (statement of cash flow). If you don't have a basic understanding of these numbers, you will not be able to realistically evaluate the state of your business.

Don't Let Financial Statements Intimidate You

For those of you who have a numbers phobia, don't worry. These statements are easy to compile, and the actual math is straightforward. Once you have all the information gathered and sorted, it's really just a matter of putting the right number in the right spot; you can use the worksheets in Appendix 3 to help you get started. Every business decision you've made up to this point has a number attached to it—now you just have to organize those numbers and plug them into the financial statement format.

To make your job even easier, grab some basic spreadsheet or bookkeeping software, such as Microsoft Excel or QuickBooks. Using computer programs should quell some of your math anxiety, as calculations are their specialty.

How These Statements Fit Together

All three basic financial statements are intertwined, and the numbers from one often flow into another. For example, the bottom line from your statement of profit and loss (called your net profit) is incorporated into the equity section of your balance sheet. The total cash asset on your balance sheet must equal the final cash number on your statement of cash flow.

And various numbers from the statement of profit and loss will appear on your statement of cash flow.

At the very heart of all the financial statements are the accounts themselves. Accounts are used to help keep track of and summarize financial activity. The statements build on that, by combining like accounts to present a financial picture. The balance sheet reveals the overall financial position of your company at a specific point in time. The statement of profit and loss speaks directly to the success of your plans over a given time period, ending with the literal bottom line. The statement of cash flow demonstrates how money moves into and out of your business. The three statements taken together make a definite comment about both the health and potential of your company.

Because the statements are interlinked, and because some pull numbers from others, the order in which you prepare them makes a difference. The order sometimes varies, though, depending on whether you are working with actual historical numbers or with pro forma projections. For example, your actual balance sheet cannot balance until you know the results of your operations. By the same token, your actual statement of cash flow gets information from both the statement of profit and loss and the balance sheet. When preparing projections, it can be easier to start with your expected cash budgets and let those numbers flow backward on to the statement of profit and loss and the balance sheet.

Follow Generally Accepted Accounting Principles

To help make sure that financial statements are universally understandable to their users, a uniform set of guidelines, called generally accepted accounting principles (or GAAP), was developed. GAAP covers all the rules, definitions, and guidelines for standard accounting practices in the United States.

The GAAP rules are not written in stone. Instead, they incorporate some flexibility where it makes more sense for different businesses to account for things slightly differently. For example, there are two major ways to account for transactions, cash basis and accrual basis, and each is best suited to different types of companies. In addition, GAAP rules are modified as necessary to keep up with real-life business situations rather than remaining applicable only to problems in old textbooks.

The bottom line is that the underlying point of GAAP is to make financial statements comparable across time periods and among companies. So when you create your financial statements, try to make sure that they comply with GAAP guidelines. If you are unsure, check with your accountant for guidance.

Cash Basis Accounting

When you set up your books using the cash basis, you only record transactions when actual cash exchanges hands. Many small businesses find this system simpler to deal with, as income and expenses are simple to track by just looking through your checkbook.

Here's how it works. Suppose Customer A orders a hand-carved cabinet from your company in January for $2,500. You complete and deliver the work and invoice in February, and you finally get a check from the customer in March. You would record the transaction in March, when the cash payment was received.

The Time for Financial Statements

Balance sheets are really snapshots of account balances on a particular date. In the heading of the statement, that single date is included. The other two major financial statements each cover a time period (and in almost all cases, they should cover the exact same time period). In those cases, the financial statement heading contains an entire phrase, typically worded like this: "For the three months ended March 31, 2005" (for instance). That phrase means your statements of profit and loss and cash flow cover the three-month period from January 1 through March 31, 2005. Typically, when the three statements are presented as a set, the ending date for the two period-related statements matches the date of the balance sheet.

Accrual Basis Accounting

Under the accrual method of accounting, revenues and expenses are recorded as you incur them, regardless of whether cash has yet changed hands. Many types of businesses fare better using this form of accounting, regardless of their size. Some examples would be product-based businesses, companies that extend credit to customers, and companies that run tabs with their suppliers.

Using accrual basis accounting, the transaction described in the previous section would actually be recorded in two distinct parts. The first transaction gets booked when you deliver the product and invoice to the customer, and the second transaction is recorded when the cash comes in. Handling your books in this manner gives you a truer sense of your company's profitability.

Setting the Time Frame

For each financial statement, you'll include both historical and current numbers (wherever possible) as well as pro forma future figures. Each statement is typically organized into different date columns so the reader can easily see patterns of growth.

In addition to that, though, is a type of time frame appropriate to each statement. A balance sheet is a financial snapshot taken on a specific date (for example, as of October 1, 2006). On the other hand, both income statements and statements of cash flow represent the activity that has occurred over a specified period of time (for the year ended on October 1, 2006).

Due to the uncertain nature of financial projections, most lenders and investors will not want to look at pro formas further out in time than the upcoming three years. For companies that come with a track record, plan readers will expect to see current and historical statements (going back three years, or as many as you have if your business has been in existence for less time). Before you put your final version together, check with your individual readers to make sure that what you have chosen to include meets their requirements. Do not offer more than they are asking to see. If they want more, they will let you know.

As to the statements themselves, show monthly projections for the first year, followed by quarterly projections for the second year and finally by annual projections for year three for both your pro forma statements of profit and loss and cash flow. As to historical statements, include both a year-to-date current statement and full annual statements for the past two years. Where the steadier balance sheet is concerned, prepare quarterly numbers for the first year going forward, then annual figures for the next two years. You will include a current balance sheet as well as those from the past two years for already existing companies.

Where the Numbers Come From

If you have never done this before, you may be wondering how you will ever be able to create financial statements and projections for a company that does not even exist yet. Never fear—your company may not be up and running, but the sources of your numbers are all around you. Some of them will depend on the planning assumptions you make (as described in Chapter 9), while others come from published information (like supplier price lists). All of them, though, are available to you with just a little looking.

Start with easy-to-define expenses and work your way out from there. The simplest number to pin down is rent. If you already have a lease in place, pick up the rent expense from there. When you haven't yet settled on a location, call around to any places you are considering that are currently available, and make an estimate based on those rent figures.

Personnel Expenses Include More Than You Think

When novice entrepreneurs start considering the costs of hiring employees, they start with salaries (or wages), maybe continue on to payroll taxes, and usually stop right there. Employees, though, can come with myriad other expenses on top of just base salary costs. Here are some very common additional expenditures that you will need to include in your estimates if you plan to hire employees:

- Workers' compensation insurance
- Unemployment insurance
- Health insurance benefits
- Life insurance benefits
- Retirement plan setup and maintenance costs
- Retirement plan contributions
- Increased liability insurance premiums
- Vacation and sick pay

Current Statements from Your Existing Business

When you are working with an existing business, you have a head start on record gathering. Your company has prepared financial statements—at least statements of profit and loss—every single time you have put a tax return together. Chances are that if you had a tax professional prepare your returns throughout the years, he has also been providing you with a full set of financial statements every year. Those are your starting point, and you can easily use them to help you with your forecasts.

But before you begin to use your current statements as a basis for future projections, look at them from an outsider's perspective. Collect three years' worth of balance sheets, statements of profit and loss, and cash flow statements, and see how they have changed over time. General patterns can be helpful, but putting numbers to the changes can be light years more beneficial, even providing insights that you will want to share with your business plan readers. Whenever possible, import those statements into a spreadsheet program to make calculations easier, quicker, and more accurate.

Your first line of comparison should be the straightforward annual change for each number or category on each statement type, where (hopefully) revenue numbers will increase while costs and expenses remain stable or decrease. To perform this calculation, use the earlier period for your base numbers. Subtract the figure for year one from the corresponding figure for year two, then divide the difference by the year-one figure to get the percentage change. Once you can see specifically in which direction your business is headed, it will make the entire financial section of your business plan easier to put together.

Every Business Needs Financial Forecasts

Whether your company is brand new or has been around for years, you will have to prepare financial forecasts to make your business plan complete. Of course, if you have existing financial statements to work from, you already have a big part of the job done. Still, you need to project out into the future based on the changes you will be making to your company.

Financial forecasts serve a big purpose. They force you to quantify your ideas and how much they will cost to implement. They make you examine all of the expenses that are necessary to the creation of revenue, the revenue that will lead to eventual profits. To create these statements, you will have to assign realistic dollar amounts to every one of your expectations. And this is where you will really learn whether your company has true profit potential.

In addition, forecasts set benchmarks against which you can track your company's progress. You can use them to see where your estimates have been far off and where they've been dead on, both of which will help with planning further out into the future. This comparison process allows you to gauge areas with room for improvement and make better budgetary judgments going forward.

Every Number Comes from Somewhere Traceable

In the initial stages of contemplating your business idea, you may have grabbed some numbers out of thin air and tossed them around. This preliminary exercise showed enough potential to get you here, but now you need some backup for the numbers you have chosen. For example, if you said to yourself, "If I can bring in $10,000 the first year, that will cover my initial $7,500 cash outlay and give me back a little extra," now is the time see if any of those dream figures have legs.

On the face of your pro formas (or in an attachment, if the pages get too busy), you will include notes about where each individual number has come from. These figures will have grown out of your planning assumptions, so you should be able to easily document your sources. Most important, ▶▶ **your sources must be traceable, as it's entirely possible that the person reviewing your plan will randomly verify figures.** If a number is little more than a guess, say so, and be sure to include on what information you based that guess.

More Than One Set

When you are just starting out as an entrepreneur, it can be helpful to develop more than one set of financial forecasts. One can serve as the worst-case scenario, where sales lag while expenses pile up—this version will help you decide if you and your personal financial state can handle the fallout if your company fails. Another picture can reflect your most hopeful scenario, with sales levels backed into by how much profit and cash flow you hope to generate. Yes, this version is wishful thinking, but it also gives you something to shoot for. Finally, you will develop a wholly realistic scenario, and this is the version that will become part of your business plan.

Why bother putting together more than one forecast? One good reason is to force yourself to get in the practice of dealing with what-if scenarios. As you develop these variant pro formas, you will see what flows out of them. For example, if sales don't add up as you've expected, you will have to find other sources to beef up your working capital while you employ alternative strategies to attract more customers and more sales. Or if your company brings in more customers, and generates a ton of sales, you will have to think about how to deal with potential inventory shortfalls, hiring additional personnel, and the like. No matter how realistic your plan version is, it's still just a guess. Thinking about different possibilities can help you deal with them if they occur.

Revisiting Your Planning Assumptions

As you begin to put your pro formas together, you will go back to the planning assumptions you have developed (as described in Chapter 9). These building-block figures will come together and help determine the expected financial shape of your company for the first few years of its existence. As you begin to put the statements together, you will see that some numbers naturally flow out of others and that some follow through from one statement to the next. Here's where all the research that went into your budgetary planning comes together, and you will be able to determine whether your company has a hope of becoming profitable.

Most business planners want to jump right in with the statement of profit and loss, but it's common accounting practice to start with a beginning balance sheet. This reflects what you have at the outset, including money you (and any co-owners) will contribute, and what fixed assets you have or will get and how they will be financed. This statement will mark the bare-bones starting point for your company, and the activity on the other two pro forma statements will hit this one and transform it into the period-ending balance sheet.

Now, on to the statement of profit and loss. On this statement, the overhead expense figures are the most predictable, so start with those. As your direct costs will be a direct result of your sales projections, sales figures will have to come next, and (as you'll recall) they can be the hardest to nail down. Accept that it's impossible to absolutely accurately predict sales, so come up with the most realistic scenario that you can, preferably based on knowledge of industry averages and local sales trends for similar-sized companies that you've included in your planning assumptions.

Cash flow can result directly from income and expense activity (though those are not the only factors affecting it). The most important planning assumptions here are those involving your credit terms (to customers), which impact your company's cash inflow, and your payables assumptions (to vendors), which direct its outflow. On this pro forma, you will also have to revisit your financing assumptions, both cash that you expect to receive from both lenders and investors and that you will need to pay back. As you fit all of these assumptions into your cash flow statement format, they will bring you back to your expected cash balance at the end of the period . . . and tie directly in to your ending balance sheet, neat and tidy.

▶▶ TEST DRIVE

To get comfortable with financial statements, you have to immerse yourself in them. Go online, go to the library, and start by just looking at them to get a feel for how they flow. Then take a closer look and see how they work. You'll know you've got it down when you can pick one set of statements and answer these questions:

1. Which is the least current asset?
2. Does phone expense constitute an operating expense or part of cost of goods sold?
3. Do credit sales count as sources or uses on a statement of cash flow?
4. Which number appears on both the statement of cash flow and the balance sheet?

Part

one

Part

two

Part

three

Part

four

Part

five

Part

six

All About Assets

Everything your business owns that's worth money is an asset. From your three-drawer file cabinet to your delivery truck, if it belongs to the company and comes with a price tag—no matter how small—it belongs on your balance sheet.

Assets are typically separated into two main categories: current and long-term. A current asset is one that will likely be converted into cash within one year, like inventory. Long-term assets are around for the long haul and include things like buildings and vehicles.

This works the same way whether you're talking about your business or your personal finances. When it comes to the personal side, which usually must be disclosed when you're trying to get money for a start-up business, the actual assets will be somewhat different but the underlying principle will be the same: what you own.

What Is Not an Asset?

As you glance around your office or shop, you will see a lot of things owned by your company that don't quite make it into the asset category because they are consumable. Simply put, if you can use it up, it is not really an asset. To qualify for the balance sheet, an item has to have some lasting value, and the ability (on some level) to help you generate income.

Paper clips, trash bags, postage stamps . . . items like these, though they have value, probably won't be around for any substantial period of time. Those things that don't fit into the asset category can be found on the income statement, in the expense section (as you will see in Chapter 21).

Current Assets

Current assets are very liquid, meaning they can be exchanged for cash very quickly. They are listed first on the balance sheet, and typically in the order of liquidity. If it will turn into cash sooner, it comes higher up on the list.

Cash, therefore, comes first—or cash and cash equivalents, to be more precise. This asset group includes all the cash you have lying around (in the register, or a petty cash envelope), all the money you have in the bank (both savings and checking), and money market funds.

Next in line are accounts receivable. This is the money your customers owe you as part of your normal course of business, and you have a legal right to receive payment promptly. These are not credit card transactions, where a customer has paid by credit card and you are waiting for your check from American Express. Instead, accounts receivable crop up when your business has extended credit directly to a customer—putting the sale on their account, like running a tab for them.

Inventory is typically the next item you'll see in the current assets section of a balance sheet. This category includes everything your company is currently holding for resale. Most business types will need only a single line entry here, but manufacturing firms may have three distinct groupings: raw materials, work-in-progress, and finished goods.

Finally, many companies have one more catchall category called "other current assets" to hold those items that don't really fit into any of the first three groupings. Usually what you'll find in here are what's known as prepaid expenses. As the name suggests, these assets are really expenses that have been paid for in advance—that extends their usefulness long enough to place them in the asset category. The classic example is insurance, where you pay a premium annually that covers your business for the whole year.

Long-Term Assets

Long-term assets are tangible assets that will be useful to your company for at least one year, sometimes more, and that cannot be immediately or easily converted into cash. Even when you are planning to sell or otherwise get rid of an asset in this category within the next year, it still belongs in the long-term section of your balance sheet.

First, you'll have a depreciable assets category, which may also be referred to as "fixed assets" or as "property, plant, and equipment." These are assets that depreciate (or lose value, at least according to accounting guidelines) over time. Included would be items such as vehicles, buildings, land (the only fixed asset that does not depreciate according to GAAP), and equipment. This section typically has three lines: fixed assets, accumulated depreciation, and net fixed assets.

The proper way to list these fixed assets is at their purchase prices rather than at their current market values. Next, you'll have a line item for accumulated depreciation, which equals the total of all of the depreciation that has occurred so far. (You will learn how to calculate current depreciation in Chapter 21.) Finally, the net fixed assets number is equal to your total fixed assets minus your accumulated depreciation.

Some companies have a different type of long-term assets that cannot be included within the fixed assets category. Here you will find intangible assets such as patents and copyrights, for example. These assets have long-term use, and they can generate revenue for your business for many years, but because they have no physical form, they simply don't count as fixed assets. Like fixed assets, though, intangibles also lose value over time (again, according to GAAP). Here, that value loss is called amortization, and the asset version is called accumulated amortization.

Why the Assets Are So Important

When it comes to securing a loan, the assets section of your balance can make all the difference to your banker. He'll look to see what you have that's easy to sell, on the off chance that you are unable to make payments from your company's cash flow. ▸▸ **Sometimes, a lender may even ask you to put up some assets as collateral, specifically naming them as property of the lender if you don't make payments per your loan agreement.**

A Look at Liabilities

Liabilities represent all that you owe: all debts and obligations your company must satisfy either with cash or other assets, or by performing some type of service in the future. These are all legal obligations, meaning that the people or companies to whom your company is indebted can sue you for payment or performance.

Just like assets, liabilities come in two basic flavors: current and long-term. Current liabilities are those that must be satisfied within the next year. Long-term liabilities take longer than one year to be paid off. To make things a bit more complicated, the current portion of long-term liabilities (the part that does have to be paid this year) gets transferred over to the current liabilities section.

Current Liabilities

Current liabilities signify cash on the way out within the next twelve months (except in those cases where your company is obligated to supply something other than money). The biggest source of this type of debt comes from your suppliers and will be much more prevalent in inventory-oriented businesses than straight service providers.

Accounts payable is made up of the amounts you owe your vendors for items you plan to resell. That includes your inventory itself and any other items you need to complete a sale, such as shopping bags, customer invoices, and gift-wrap. When you buy these items and the vendor extends credit, you have an obligation to pay him according to his terms.

Then comes the list of other types of payables, none of which is directly part of inventory or other cost of sales items. Other payables can include things like the following:

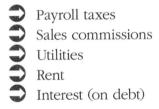

- Payroll taxes
- Sales commissions
- Utilities
- Rent
- Interest (on debt)

Most standard monthly bills fit neatly into the other payables category. You get the bill, along with the obligation, today but don't have to pay until the due date. Sometimes income taxes are included in this section, while other times they are highlighted on their own line. The positioning depends on the amount due compared to other payable items. If the balance due is very big, give income tax payable its own line.

Finally, you'll list any short-term debt. This includes both the current portion of long-term debt and any other loan or note obligations due within the year. What separates these debts from the others in your current liabilities section? They represent borrowed funds, as opposed to expenditures made on account in the normal course of business.

Obligations That Do Not Involve Cash

Sometimes a business will incur a liability that has nothing to do with sending a check. There are two other things your company can be indebted for: goods and services. One simple example is a magazine subscription. Typically, subscribers pay up front for a year or two of magazines. Once their payment is accepted, your company will be obligated to fulfill the terms of the subscription, basically sending out each monthly issue.

Any time a customer prepays your business for something (yes, this is the flipside of a prepaid expense), your company has to provide that something . . . or else send them their money back. Because there is a contractual obligation, this counts as a liability for your balance sheet.

Long-Term Liabilities

Long-term liabilities are obligations further out on the time scale than the next twelve months. These debts are almost always the result of borrowing, and they often correspond to long-term asset counterparts. The most common examples of long-term business debt include mortgages, financed equipment purchases (or installment notes), business start-up or expansion loans, and long-term leases. Some companies, usually medium-sized to large, also have long-term pension obligations.

Another common form of long-term business debt is bonds. Many companies issue bonds to raise capital without diluting ownership or tapping into a single financing source (like a bank). This type of debt is typically incurred by large, long-standing companies.

Why Your Liabilities Matter

Any potential funding for your business, whether it comes from a lender or an investor, involves someone who wants to get paid back. They will want to know who's in line ahead of them, meaning who has a previous claim against your company's assets and earnings.

From a lender's point of view, if their loan isn't secured by specifically named assets, they can only collect after others with previous claims or more highly secured claims get their money back. From an equity investor's point of view, a lot of interest-bearing debt (loans and notes, for example) means less profit to go around.

Don't panic if you or your company has debt—it's expected. And some forms of debt are better than others, to the readers of your business plan. Mortgages and other fixed asset-related debt is considered standard and won't really raise any eyebrows. Payables incurred in the normal course of business, and paid off regularly, won't even cause a blink. A lot of unsecured debt, on the other hand, can scare the money guys away. That includes previous business loans and high credit card balances, which indicate an inability on your part to meet obligations with existing cash flow.

Understanding Equity

Equity represents the true ownership or net worth of a company. At the simplest level, equity equals the difference between what you have (your assets) and what you owe (your liabilities). In most cases, that result will be positive, but it is possible to have negative equity.

The equity section of your balance sheet shows the details of the company's net worth. What it looks like, though, depends on how your business is structured (the entity type). For sole proprietorships, the equity section contains a single line called owner's capital (your name goes where the word "owner" is). Partnership balance sheets look similar, except that each partner has a line reflecting his or her capital account balance. Corporations, though, are completely different. These sections contain two separate items: investment and retained earnings.

Calculating Equity for a Proprietorship or Partnership

The main difference between a sole proprietorship and a partnership, at least on the balance sheet, is the number of owners. A sole proprietorship has only one owner, and a partnership has at least two. Calculating capital balances is the same for both, except for one additional step needed for partnerships.

First, let's look at the basics. In these businesses entities, the capital balance equals the initial investment into the company by the owners plus any subsequent additional investments plus any profits earned by the business (or minus any losses sustained by the business). For sole proprietorships, the math ends there.

For partnerships, any profit or loss has to be allocated according to agreement. It could be exactly evenly among the partners, or there could be special percentages to apply. Each partner's capital account is computed separately, based on the money or property he has put into the business and his or her share of profits (or losses). For this reason, partnership capital accounts may not be equal; in fact, they frequently are not. When the partnership has more than ten partners (common in professional partnerships and limited partnerships), there may be a single line item on the balance sheet representing total capital supported by a separate detailed schedule of individual capital balances.

Equity for Corporate Entities

Ownership in corporations is represented by shares of stock. Whether there is one owner, fifty, or 500,000, only the total value of outstanding stock is listed on the balance sheet—not by each owner as with the other business structures. Sometimes there are different classes of stock, and those would be listed separately but still as overall totals.

The total stock value is calculated by multiplying the number of shares outstanding (those owned by anyone, including you, other than the company itself) by the par value (or stated face value) of a single share. Sometimes an investor will buy shares in your company for more than the dollar amount stated on the face of the stock certificate, a practice known in accounting terms as additional paid-in capital. That excess over par gets its own line in the equity section.

Figuring Out the Numbers

Three guys got together and formed a corporation. At the outset, they authorized the corporation to have 5,000 shares of stock, each with a par value of $10. They each invested $10,000, and got 1,000 shares each in return. After a while, their company had grown and they were ready to take on a new investor. He put up $12,000 for 1,000 shares.

In this example, the total stock outstanding has a value of $40,000 for the 4,000 shares. In addition, the company has additional paid-in capital of $2,000 thanks to investor number four. Assuming these are the only relevant numbers, the total shareholder's equity would equal $42,000.

Retained earnings equals the accumulated total of each year's profit (or loss) minus any portion of that which has been distributed to shareholders as dividends. In simpler terms, retained earnings are any profits that have been kept inside the company to help it grow.

How It All Adds Up

There are two reasons a balance sheet is so named. One is that it contains a listing of all the permanent account balances on a particular day. The other is that the two sides of the report must balance according to the basic accounting equation: assets equal liabilities plus equity. If your balance sheet does not balance, you are not done with it yet.

Of course, it's a little more complicated than the three summary figures that make up the accounting equation. Each main section is comprised of subtotals, and those calculations are also spelled out under GAAP. (See the section called "Standard Balance Sheet Format" on page 254–55 for a detailed example.)

In the assets section, you will have subtotals for both current assets and long-term assets. Also, in the long-term section, you'll have minicalculations for depreciable fixed assets and amortizable intangible assets. Each of these sub-subsections will look pretty much the same: you'll start with the assets themselves, deduct any accumulated depreciation or amortization, and finish with a total net asset value. At the very end of the main section comes the overall total for your assets.

The other side of the report contains the total liabilities and equity. The liabilities section is somewhat simpler than the assets section, but it still has two main subdivisions: current and long-term. You'll show subtotals for each and then add them together to get the final total liabilities amount. The equity section has one or more line items, but no real subsections, that get you to the final number. Finally, you'll have a number that captures the total liabilities and equity—and that number *must* equal your total assets.

Getting to Projected Numbers

When it comes to projections or pro formas, the balance sheet is the least important statement. Why? Because it has less impact on your every-day business operations than either the statement of cash flow or the income statement. That doesn't mean it will be ignored—bankers will look at your prospective balance sheet(s) to see how you plan to handle expanded operations as your company grows and where you expect additional funding to come from. In fact, in some cases, obtaining that first cash infusion from the bank will depend on your company's ability to meet particular balance sheet conditions—like keeping your net worth above specified minimum levels.

For you, though, the projected balance sheet is an excellent planning tool. Essentially, it's a peek at how you plan to use your assets over the next few years. Maybe you're starting out with used or outdated equipment and want to know when it makes sense to replace it; maybe now your company has a sixty-day collection cycle for accounts receivable and you want to see how things would shape up with a shorter collection cycle; or maybe you want to see what your balance sheet could look like when your first business loan is paid off. Any potential change in assets or liabilities directly impacts your company's net worth and your ability to stay in business . . . and grow that business.

Getting down to specifics, here are a few key points to remember:

1. Your balance sheet must always stay in balance.
2. Expected changes to your balance sheet will impact your other financial statements, and the opposite holds true as well.
3. You need to make well-informed, reasonable assumptions for each projected number.

▸▸ **There are specific standard projection methods for each type of balance sheet account.** Some are quite simple, some take a few steps, and some require the creation of other statements first.

Projecting Assets

When it comes to forecasting asset values, it's easiest to just run right down the balance sheet. First comes cash, and your future estimated cash position can be plucked right from your cash flow projection for the same year. Second is your accounts receivable, and this figure also requires information from another statement. Since your receivables balance depends on your credit sales and your typical collection lag (thirty days for most businesses), you'll need to look at your sales projections for the appropriate prior period to estimate your receivables balance.

Your inventory projection comes directly from your projected income statement—use the estimated ending inventory figure for the proper period (demonstrated in Chapter 21). To come up with projected prepaid expenses, base your estimates on the current numbers and add on a small percentage for those you believe will increase. For example, if you have a ten-year lease on your office and pay one year in advance, you'll know the exact prepaid rent for the next ten years. Insurance premiums, on the other hand, tend to rise slightly every year, so add a small percentage onto the existing annual prepaid balance.

Existing long-term assets keep their value; it's only the accumulated depreciation and net fixed assets figures that will change. Again, periodic depreciation figures come right from the pro forma income statements, and you just need to add them up. If you plan to purchase any new assets as your company grows (remember, these are future assumptions), add them in here. Just don't forget that the payment method has to be accounted for as well, usually by an increase in your liabilities.

Projecting Liabilities and Equity

Estimating future liabilities follows some of the same principles as forecasting assets. First you'll look at accounts payable. This number combines the credit purchases that went into your ending inventory balance and the typical amount of supplies you purchase on account each month. Figure in how quickly you normally pay your suppliers, and you'll know how many months' worth of bills to include.

Other payables can often be estimated based on your typical monthly balance, such as average phone bill and electric bill, for example. Payroll, however, depends on your pay cycle. Look at your calendar to see which day of the week the end of the period falls on. Then take your periodic (weekly, biweekly) payroll expense, divide it by the total number of workdays in the period, and multiply that by the number of days that fall before the period end. For example, if you pay employees $5,000 each Friday and the period in question ends on a Wednesday, you would estimate $3,000 of salaries payable.

For any type of installment loan, just add up the number of payments you will have made by the end of the pro forma balance sheet date, and subtract the principal portion from the last period's account balance. Then place your calculated balances in either the current or long-term liabilities section as appropriate. Interest payable works in the opposite manner. Add up the interest portion of payments for the upcoming year, and list that total in the current liabilities section. Remember to add on any new liabilities you expect to incur as a result of projected future asset purchases.

Like fixed assets, some parts of your equity section will remain constant from year to year. Unless you issue new shares of stock, your stock value will stay the same, as will the additional paid in capital. What changes here is the dollar amount of retained earnings, and this is where the balancing act comes in. First, your balance sheet has to balance, meaning that the total equity must be equal to the total assets minus the total liabilities. Also, though, the retained earnings should be reflective of activity on the income statement. When everything flows properly, the ending retained earnings should equal the beginning balance plus the current period's profits (or minus the current period's losses).

Standard Balance Sheet Format

At the top of every balance sheet is a three-line heading. That heading will always include the name of the company, the name of the statement, and the appropriate date. For example:

ABC Company
Balance Sheet
December 31, 2006

Following that comes another heading, "Assets," under which all of the company's assets will be listed in order of liquidity. At the bottom of the list will be a total, labeled "Total Assets." After a little space, another heading will appear, "Liabilities and Equity." As you'd expect, this section will house first the liabilities (in order from current to longest term) with a subtotal, then the equity section. Finally, those two categories will be summed and labeled "Total Liabilities and Equity." And, to make the balance sheet live up to its name, the total liabilities and equity must equal the total assets for the statement to be in perfect balance.

ASSETS	
Current Assets	$2,000
Fixed Assets	$4,000
TOTAL ASSETS	$6,000
LIABILITIES	
Current Liabilities	$1,000
Long-term Liabilities	$2,500
TOTAL LIABILITIES	$3,500
Owner's Equity	$2,500
TOTAL LIABILITIES & EQUITY	$6,000

▶▶ TEST DRIVE

Time to make a practice balance sheet, based on everything you will contribute to your business. Make three columns: one for assets, one for liabilities, and one for equity. Start with the assets, listing them in order from the most current (cash) to the long-term (land). If you own each of those assets straight out, the other side of the equation is 100-percent owner's equity. If any of those assets come with attached debt, slide that figure over to your liabilities section. Total each column, then cross-total them to make sure that the summed up liabilities plus equity equals the total assets.

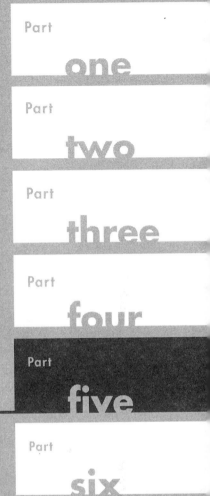

Statement Components, and a Little Math

Profit and loss statements range from ultrasimple to utterly complicated. Service businesses have the most straightforward statements, while manufacturing companies have the most complex, and retailers and wholesalers fall somewhere in the middle. But they all have some basic components in common: revenues and expenses.

When products are part of your business design, your expenses need some sorting out. Some expenses, called cost of sales, are directly connected to the products you are making or selling (such as component parts). Others, referred to as operating expenses, are just standard costs of doing business: rent, phone and utility bills, and insurance, for example.

The Name Game

Like most things in accounting, profit and loss statement components are called by many different names. People tend to use the terms "revenues" and "sales" interchangeably, sometimes even coining the phrase "sales revenue." Other monikers include gross sales, gross revenues, and sales income.

Expenses also come with plenty of nicknames. The cost of sales type can be called cost of goods sold, variable costs, direct costs, or direct product costs. Operating expenses may be referred to as general and administrative expenses, fixed expenses, overhead, or discretionary costs.

So which of these terms are preferred by accountants? For service businesses, revenues and operating expenses are usually used. In product-based businesses, the standard terms are sales, cost of sales, and general and administrative expenses.

The Other Line Items on Your Statement

In addition to the basic sales and expense categories, your profit and loss statement will show other information. Some of these line items are to add clarity to a section, and some are placeholders for calculated numbers needed to get to the bottom line. Not every business will have every one of these line items, but the general flow is standard.

At the top of your statement is the revenue section. If you have more than one line of revenue (for example, you offer both résumé writing and term paper editing services), you may want to list them separately. Companies that sell products will sometimes include a line for sales returns—that way they can see both how much they sold overall and how much of their merchandise came back. In those cases, the revenue section would have three lines: gross sales, sales returns, and net sales.

Next, for product-based businesses, comes the cost of sales section. For a start-up business, you can just use an estimate on your pro forma statement, based on your planned mark-up percentage. An ongoing business will draw from its prior period statements and include existing inventory numbers (both beginning and ending) and purchases made during the period. The final line at the end of this section is called the gross profit or gross margin. .

Expenses come next. Depending on how you segregate your expenses, you could have one or more subsections here, such as selling expenses and general and administrative expenses, for example. Once you've listed all the expenses, the next line will be your profit (or loss) from operations, sometimes also called the profit before income taxes. Then you'll include a line for estimated taxes, followed by the net profit—the real bottom line.

Statement Math

The mathematics of the profit and loss statement is uncomplicated, really just some addition and subtraction. The key to getting the correct result is keeping the numbers in line, literally, especially for the more complex-looking statements. If you create your reports using spreadsheet software, pay attention to the columns you enter numbers into. And if you plan to stick with paper and pencil while you're getting everything together, use accounting paper with prelined columns. Take a look at the format for profit and loss statements at the end of this chapter to see how the numbers should line up.

The sales math is pretty simple: gross sales minus sales returns equals net sales. If you don't have returns (for an existing company) or think they will be so minimal as to not impact the numbers, don't include a line for them or for net sales. Simply go with the single sales line (but then take out the word "gross").

Next comes the math for the cost of sales. Essentially, cost of sales equals beginning inventory (what you started with) plus purchases (goods you bought during the period) minus ending inventory (what you have left). If you're basing your cost of sales on a markup percentage, you'll have only a single line item here. When you've computed your final cost of sales number, that figure is subtracted from your net sales to give you the gross profit (as expressed in dollars). Gross profit percentage may also be shown and is always calculated as a percent of revenue (gross profit divided by net sales).

Expenses are really just columns of numbers to add up. Each category of expenses will be subtotaled separately, and then you will add those subtotals together to come up with your grand total expenses. That sum will be subtracted from the gross profit to show your profit (or loss) from operations. The next line will be an estimate of the tax due on that income, based on current tax rates. (If you project a loss, no income tax will be due.) Finally, you'll subtract that income tax figure from your profit from operations to get down to the net profit.

A Realistic Sales Forecast

Anyone can come up with a sales number that will make their projections look good. Your job is to come up with a number you can prove that will make your projections look achievable. Whether you are turning to lenders or investors to infuse your company with cash, you are going to have to tell them exactly how you came up with your sales forecast figures. That goes for both existing companies and start-ups; your business plan readers will demand backup.

Your business stage will impact how you develop that forecast. An existing company that is looking to expand will base projections on its historical sales and expected growth rate. That expected growth rate can be based on expanded advertising efforts, the addition of new products or product lines, or growth in your target customer base. To get projected sales here, simply take the last period's total sales and multiply that number by one plus your expected growth rate percentage. For example, if your sales were $50,000 and you expect sales to grow by 5 percent, multiply $50,000 by 1.05 to get $52,500.

A brand-new company, on the other hand, has no sales records to pull from, so its information has to come from different sources. This could include data collected while you were doing market research, such as market size and buying propensity. It could be based on the revenues of similar businesses (like your direct competitors). Your projection could even be based on "presales" to particular customers, as sometimes happens when a professional leaves a firm and takes his clients with him.

Whichever method you use to estimate your future sales, make sure you have some facts to back up your numbers. Write down the steps you took to come up with your assumptions—even if you don't include them directly in the business plan. Remember, this document is not just for the money guys—it's for you to learn whether your business idea is feasible. Creating overblown sales estimates, especially if you come to rely on them, can lead to business failure.

Units First

It can be daunting to come up with a full-blown dollar-based sales forecast. To make things easier, start with quantity. Consider how many products you can sell in a day or a week; think about how many billable service hours make sense. Once you can determine a reasonable sales quantity—based on a combination of your research and some common sense—you can extrapolate to come up with monthly units, and then the total revenue dollars those sales represent.

For example, if you paint custom T-shirts, and each takes five hours, you can't produce more than eight in a forty-hour workweek; eight is your maximum number of units. If each shirt sells for $75, your maximum weekly revenue will be $600.

Cost of Sales

Virtually every time you sell a product, you've had to buy it first. Maybe you've bought raw materials, or maybe you've bought finished goods. In either case, the product you sell has cost you something. In fact, there may be multiple costs associated with a single product in addition to the product itself, such as finishing materials, sales tax paid, and delivery charges (to your place of operations).

To be counted in this category, an expenditure has to be directly related to obtaining the goods for resale and getting them customer-ready. Any costs incurred after that, even if they seem to be directly related to the sale of that product (like a customer invoice), do not belong here. Also, if your company is strictly a service enterprise, you will not have any cost of sales since you are not selling physical products. (Your labor, or that of employees, does not count as a cost of sales on a formal profit and loss statement.)

Do not confuse cost of sales with inventory; they are not the same thing. When you purchase products, they go into your inventory—and sit there until they are sold. Only after they've been sold do they convert to cost of sales.

Figuring Your Selling Expenses

When selling expenses will make up a substantial part of your total expenses, it's common to list them in their own subsection of your profit and loss statement. The heading for this segment is typically "Marketing and Sales Expenses." If you only have one such expense, though, it should be included in the general and administrative grouping.

Unlike most other expenses, which fit squarely into the overhead or direct cost categories, selling expenses tend to have one foot in each camp. For example, sales commissions will vary by the level of sales generated by your employees, but these commissions are not considered to be part of the cost of sales. Or perhaps you give away a free pen with each purchase—the cost is associated *with* the sale but does not count as a cost *of* the sale.

In addition to sales commissions, this section may also include such items as these:

 Sales salaries
 Promotional materials

➲ Advertising and publicity costs
➲ Credit card costs

You may also want to have a catchall "other marketing expenses" line for anything that is sales-related but that does not quite fit into the other categories (like delivery service) and is not big enough to merit its own.

Computing Sales Salaries and Commissions

In an ongoing business, you'll already know your salesmen's salaries and all of the other business expenses tied to that, such as payroll taxes, retirement contributions, and company-paid insurance, for example. You'll also already have an established commission structure in place. For your projections, all you need to consider is whether those salaries will increase over the next few years and by approximately how much. You'll also apply your existing commission rate to your projected sales. If you have more than one salesperson, each entitled to a different percentage, you can use either a simple average or a weighted average to calculate the projected commission expense.

For a new company, you'll first have to figure out how much you plan to pay your salespeople, including seasonal workers. Add to that standard payroll taxes, plus any benefits for which the company will foot the bill. Next, you need to decide whether your business will pay sales commissions. If so, choose a reasonable percentage of sales that will be paid. If you think that not all sales will qualify for commission (for example, sales that you handle yourself), carve out an estimated portion before applying the commission rate. ▶▶ **Remember that commissions count as payroll and are subject to the same payroll taxes.**

Promotional Materials, Advertising, and Publicity Costs

This expense category is reserved for items designed to promote your business. Such items would include things like T-shirts, free samples, coupons, brochures, catalogues, and even business cards. Virtually everything you give away to attract customers—and to encourage them to buy—is a promotional material.

Sponsorships also fit into this category. For example, if your business sponsors a Little League team by providing their uniforms (with your company's name stenciled on them, of course), that counts as a promotion. Instead of including these with charitable donations, put them in with your selling expenses.

Next comes advertising. Whether you choose direct mail, newspaper ads, television commercials, or radio announcements, any campaign designed to drum up business fits into this expense category. Other examples of advertising expenses include flyers, phone book ads, window displays, banners, and signs. Here you would also include any fee paid to the company that designed your ad campaigns and arranged for any publicity (free or otherwise).

Credit Card Costs

Sometimes, if your company doesn't accept credit cards, you can lose a sale. So most businesses do set up merchant accounts so they can process credit cards, as a convenience to customers. That comes at a cost—several costs actually. From the original set-up to the everyday processing, the credit card companies will charge you a veritable menu of fees. All of these fees will end up in this expense category on your profit and loss statement.

For new companies, there's an extra fee to be considered: the one-time set up costs charged by your bank to get your account up and running. (Any deposits required by the bank don't go here—they count as assets, not expenses.) Once you've gotten started, typical ongoing expenses include the discount rate (the percentage charged by the credit card company to process your sale, usually one to five percent), transaction fees (a minimal fee for each credit card processed), and a minimum monthly fee (if you don't hit a target transaction fee figure).

Account for General and Administrative Expenses

Getting a handle on your general and administrative expenses helps fill in the bulk of your pro forma profit and loss statement. In this section, you'll include the regular everyday expenses of running your business, and most of these expenses will be the same (or nearly the same) every month. The working assumption in this section is that you will be renting office, retail, and/or storage space. if you plan to run your business out of your home, check out the section entitled "Working From Home Expenses" on page 265–66.

First you will gather your company's written-in-stone expenses, those that are contractually the same every month. These fixed costs include rent, salaries, and related payroll expenses, insurance, equipment leases, service contracts, and loan interest. There are two things to keep in mind for salary expense. First, don't double-count any amounts already allocated to selling expenses; second, remember to estimate the costs of wage-based (or hourly), temporary, and seasonal employees. Depreciation (and amortization, when applicable) expense fits into this predictable category as well; learn how to calculate it on page 266.

After the predetermined expenses have been listed, you'll begin to estimate those that will vary somewhat from month to month. These expenses include things like phone bills, utilities, postage, professional fees (like accounting and legal), general business supplies, repairs and maintenance, vehicle costs (like gas, parking, and tolls), travel and entertainment, and fees, licenses, and taxes (not including income or payroll taxes).

Working from Home Expenses

When all or part of your business is run out of your home, a portion of your household expenses should be allocated to the business. As much as you can, try to keep expenses that can be clearly separated separate. For example, get your business its own phone and fax number. Also, setting up a distinct, dedicated area for the company (as opposed to working on your laptop on the kitchen table) makes it easier to designate specific portions of household expenses to the company—not to mention making it easier for you to separate your life from your work.

▸▸ **When it comes to mixed costs, you'll have to determine the portion applicable to business expense.** The IRS method (meaning the one you are supposed to use when you fill out your tax return) is based on square footage. Divide the square feet of your designated business area by the total square footage of your home; the resulting percentage will be applied to mixed expenses. Mixed expenses include things like gas and electricity, heating oil, alarm systems, house cleaning, rent (if you don't own your home), and mortgage interest and property taxes (if you do).

Calculating Your Depreciation Expense

Depreciation is the one expense that will lower your tax bill without costing you a dime out of pocket. It represents the wear and tear on your fixed assets and is supposed to approximate their loss in value over time. (Yes, this applies even to those assets that increase in value, or appreciate). Each period, you'll charge some portion of your fixed assets to expense, with a corresponding increase in accumulated depreciation.

The IRS has specific guidelines for depreciating assets. Their rules cover two distinct angles: the useful life of the asset (how long it is supposed to be productive) and the applicable depreciation rate (specific percentages to apply to the original cost). Like most rules posted by the IRS, these are subject to change, and they often do. For the latest rules, you can talk to your accountant, or visit the IRS Web site at *www.irs.gov*.

Once you've gotten the rules on how to proceed, you will know the numbers you have to work with. For example, computer equipment has a useful life of five years. According to current IRS tables, your depreciation expense for year one is 20 percent of the asset value. So if your business computer system cost $3,000, the depreciation expense in your first year of operations would be $600.

Section 179 Deductions

Once you have been in business for any length of time, you will hear the buzz about another "gift" from the IRS: the Section 179 deduction. This special rule allows you to deduct the entire cost of fixed assets in the year you purchased them. The deduction has two limitations. First, it can't cause your company to sustain a loss (though it can be used to zero out your income), and second, it's subject to statutory maximums—$105,000 for 2005.

This deduction can be very helpful for fledgling companies, allowing them to spend precious cash on profit-building equipment rather than using it to pay taxes.

Your Profits, Before and After Taxes

Once you have subtracted all of your costs and expenses from your total revenues, the remainder represents your profits. (When your costs and expenses exceed your revenues, your company has incurred a loss, and your statement will end there.) Just like when you make money in your personal life, when your company earns profits, there will be a tax bill.

Who pays that tax bill depends on the underlying structure of your company. If it's the company itself, a provision for income taxes will appear on your financial statements. If, on the other hand, you (and your co-owners, if applicable) will be footing the tax bill, you can skip that line here.

When your company foots its own income tax bill, you will need to lay that out for your financial statement readers, starting with the income itself. The profits on which your company's income taxes are based are referred to as "Profits Before Income Taxes" on your statement of profit and loss.

The next step is to figure out your tentative tax bill, tentative because the IRS can make changes to your calculations after the fact. Corporate income taxes follow a sort of ladder system. As your income hits different preset levels, the tax rate changes. Basically, you apply the matching tax rate to the income you have in that step and add those subtotals to figure out your ultimate federal income tax tab. List that number on your statement of profit and loss across from the "Income Tax" heading.

Finally, you'll calculate your true bottom line by subtracting the income tax bill (if applicable) from the profits before income taxes.

Who actually pays taxes? In the land of business and federal income taxes, there are two basic forms your company can take. One is called pass-through, and in those companies, any tax consequences pass through to the business owners' personal income tax returns. The other is considered tax-paying, and those companies are responsible for their own income tax bills.

If your company is a regular (or C) corporation, it counts as a tax-paying business entity. S corporations, partnerships, and sole proprietorships are all pass-through entities and therefore will not shoulder any federal income tax burden. The tax treatment of LLCs depends on a tax election made by the owners. It can be treated as either a C corporation or as a partnership for federal income tax purposes.

Calculating Margins

Margins, in the financial statement context, mean the same thing they do when you're setting up a page before printing—the extra amount left over. In the business sense, margins contribute to your company's profitability. Since that is crucial to the future health, and the future existence, of your business, it is a good idea to pay attention to your margins, all three of them.

There are three basic margins you will need to keep track of: the gross profit margin, the operating profit margin, and the net profit margin. Any snafus along the way can turn your company's potential profits into losses.

The Flip Side of Margin Is Markup

The only way to have any margin at all is to charge your customers more money than it costs you to serve them. The only way to do that is to add on to your cost before you sell something, and that add-on is called markup. Though this term typically applies to merchandise, service businesses can use it (albeit internally) as well. How do you get your markup? Start with how much the product is costing you directly (using service hours as a basis for service companies), then add on enough to contribute to your other expenses and to profits.

Standard Profit and Loss Format

The accounting industry likes uniformity and comparability; hence the design of standard financial statements, including the statement of profit and loss. Like the balance sheet, this statement starts with a three-line heading. What's different is the time frame. While a balance sheet reflects information on a specific day, the profit and loss demonstrates activity over a time period. Here's an example:

ABC Company
Statement of Profit and Loss
For the Year Ended December 31, 2006

Though there are variations among these statements for different business types, they all still follow the same basic path. They all start with revenue, subtract costs and expenses, and end up with the bottom line profit or loss. Here's an example of a shell statement for a retail company.

Sales	$XX
Less: Returns and Allowances	$(XX)
Net Sales	$XX
Cost of Goods Sold	$XX
Gross Margin	$XX
Operating Expenses	$XX
Net Profit (Loss)	$XX

In most cases, the statement will be filled in with much more detail, including a listing of individual operating expenses (or expense categories) and an amplification of the cost of goods sold section. For service companies, the cost of goods sold section will not appear. The statement will contain merely revenues and expenses, which net to the bottom line.

▶▶ TEST DRIVE

Sales forecasts are tricky, so here's an exercise to help you transform them from could happen to probably will happen. Write down each of the following:

1. How many days per year do you want to work?
2. How many hours per day do you want to work?
3. Will your company generate sales when you're not there?
4. How many hours each week can your office or shop be open?
5. How many customers can reasonably be served in this time frame?
6. How many units can each customer buy at once?

The Importance of Cash Flow

Most people who decide to strike out on their own in the business world dream of earning megaprofits. Once they're up and running, though, that dream quickly changes into one of positive cash flows.

▶▶ **The first rule of the business jungle is this: If you have no cash, you cannot survive.** Therefore, managing your cash flow—meaning the way money moves in and out of your business's bank account—is one of the most important skills you must learn. The most important step in positively controlling your cash flow is understanding it, and that is where detailed cash flow projections come in. At the outset, monthly (maybe even weekly) statements are called for, so you can keep a close eye on the situation. Later on, once your cash is flowing the way you want it to, you can switch to less frequent statements.

No matter how successful your business appears to be on its statement of profit and loss, a lack of ability to pay the bills can cause your company to fail. At the very least, your company needs to have enough cash on hand to cover its monthly expenses.

Cash Consumers

No matter how carefully you plan, know that your startup expenses are going to cost more than you think. There is always some expense that gets overlooked when the forecasts are created. For example, maybe you didn't count on your warehouse being overrun by ants and the added cost of an exterminator. Perhaps your help-wanted ads didn't bring in appropriate candidates as quickly as expected, and you had to run them for a few extra weeks, costing the company an extra few hundred dollars. The reason behind the overrun is not as important as planning for it. To avoid falling short, increase your estimated start-up costs by somewhere in the 5 percent range.

When you're already up and running, the cash challenges are a little different. One of the biggest holdups for new companies is inventory. New businesses, especially when coupled with novice entrepreneurs, often overstock because they simply don't yet know how quickly sales will occur. Suppliers may not care that product is not moving out the door; they still expect to get paid on time. In fact, until a new business has established itself, it may have to pay cash on delivery for its inventory. Either way, if you have to pay for your products before your customers pay you, you are looking at a cash crunch.

That's the other common factor in cash flow mishaps—inaccurately predicting when you will receive payment from customers. When you extend credit to your customers, you let them walk away with your product (or completed service) without paying on the spot. Most of the time, you'll get your money according to the agreed-upon credit terms (the most common is within thirty days).

Then there is always the possibility of sustained losses in the early days of a new business. In fact, many companies that turn it around and eventually rake in the profits often suffered opening-phase losses. Depending on the industry you enter, you may want to add a few months' worth of possible losses into your start-up budget. It's impossible to predict when the tide will turn—your company could be the one that hits the ground running and earns profits from the start, or there could be six months of losses before profits make an appearance. Once you start operating, you'll have a clearer picture and will be able to adjust your projections accordingly. For now, to remain conservative, expect early losses to suck up some cash flow.

Cash Savers

It can be tough to control the cash flows that keep your company liquid, but there are ways to manage it. What seems like the simplest solution, cutting expenses, takes a lot of thought. You don't want to cut back in areas that will bring in sales (and money), like advertising or delivery services. But you also need to maintain a pleasant business environment and pay your rent and phone bills to keep things going. Consider all the things you are spending money on, how much you really need them, and whether you can figure out a way to buy now but pay later. (Beware of running up too much credit card debt, though). Trim off any expenditures that may not be necessary for now; you can always add them back in later when cash is more plentiful.

Try to work out better payment terms with your suppliers. In this context, better for you means longer payback time. If they currently offer you thirty-day terms, ask for sixty days. Even better, some suppliers may let you pay as you sell, sort of the way consignment shops work. If your current suppliers won't work with you, shop around.

The flip side of that is cutting back on your inventory holdings. Keeping $50,000 of inventory on hand when your current sales cycle only supports $25,000 is not necessary. Buying in bulk for lower per-unit cost is great when you have the cash flow to handle it, but for now, it may be a better idea to pass up the discounts and only stock what you can afford. When sales pick up, you can always increase your inventory levels to meet customer demand.

Finally, stay on top of your credit customers without scaring them away. One simple way to get the cash in quickly without alienating your clientele is to offer early payment discounts. For example, you can let them take 1 or 2 percent off their invoice total if they pay within ten days instead of thirty. Pay attention to late-paying customers, and do not let the amount they owe you get out of hand just to boost your sales. A sale that never gets paid for doesn't count.

Profits Don't Always Mean Cash

In the business world, there is a big difference between earning profits and having cash. Your statement of profit and loss can show clear, even large, profits while your bank balance remains paltry. Without ample cash, though, those profits won't be showing up for long, so you need to figure out where the cash is being held up and make adjustments accordingly.

How does this happen? The bottleneck usually starts with credit sales because the revenue hits your income statement before the cash hits your balance sheet. That's not to say that your company shouldn't extend credit to customers—it should, especially if that is the industry norm. But you also need to deal with the time lag and pay attention to the cash aspect instead of merely focusing on sales and profits.

In addition, major asset purchases can have a big cash impact without making virtually any dent on your income statement (except for current depreciation expense). Even when you finance your asset purchases, you may be required to hand over a cash down payment. The new asset, the related debt, and the cash outlay show up only on the balance sheet and don't affect your bottom line profits.

A Case of Big Profits and Little Cash　　Inside Track

Jenna Andrews and Linda Frye started a small catering company together—Jenna handled the party plans, Linda took care of the food. They struggled to book dates for the first few months, but then word of mouth began to spread and new customers were quickly added to their client list. The women accepted almost every job that came in, including two weddings larger than they'd ever handled before.

They carefully considered the costs of each job and added in a healthy profit for themselves. Looking at the schedule, the women realized they needed more freezer space. They shopped around and found a great deal on the right model if they paid cash for it. They bought the freezer, continuing to prepare for the parties and book new ones.

For the two large weddings, Jenna and Linda had to hire extra serving staff. They also needed to rent additional glassware, place settings, and table linens as their in-house supplies were too small to cover the number of guests. Both parties went off as smoothly as possible, and the women sent out their final invoices. By the time they received full payment three months later, they were scrambling for cash.

On paper, Jenna and Linda had scored big profits. But their bank account had not yet caught up. While they had incorporated the extra big party expenses into their planning budgets, they had not really considered the cash implications. The temporary waitstaff had to be paid immediately, and the rental company had required a substantial deposit. On top of that, the freezer, purchased with cash, hit the books as an asset and did not figure into their profitability, just into the cash flow. While their income statement looked great, they had almost no cash left to buy the next round of supplies.

Breaking Down the Sales Forecast

To get your cash flow projections going, you'll need to revisit your sales forecast. Look at your expected revenues for each period to start. Then you will determine which of those comes from a pure cash sale, which from checks or credit cards, and which were made on account (generating an account receivable). This breakdown will help you figure out the impact of your sales on your cash balance, immediately and in the near future.

For the purpose of generating pro forma statements of cash flow for your business plan, consider customer checks and credit cards as instant cash. Only credit sales, where your company extends credit to a customer, will show up as delayed receipts in your projections. The big trick is predicting the extent of that delay.

How long it takes your customers to pay you depends mainly on the credit terms you offer, usually based on the industry standard, but it is also determined by the current economic climate and on their individual financial situations. Typically, service businesses and companies that cater directly to consumers offer standard thirty-day terms, while product-oriented business-to-business sales often come with sixty-day terms. Companies that want to hasten cash inflows can offer early payment discounts ("Take off 2 percent if you pay within ten days").

But specified terms don't always mean predictable payments. It's very common for customers to pay late, so factor at least some level of lateness into your projections. For example, you could presume that 50 percent of customers will pay on time, 25 percent will pay up to thirty days late, and so on. Document your assumptions so your business plan readers will fully understand where your cash-in numbers come from.

Minor Delays

Cash sales technically include customer checks and credit cards handed over at the time of purchase. However, in the sometimes day-to-day cash struggle of new and small businesses, a delay of even a single day can have some repercussions. While you won't want to call attention to this in your business plan, recognize this: what counts as cash in the accounting world may not translate into immediate cash in your bank account, against which checks you write will be honored.

Be aware that customer checks can take as long as five *business* days to count as available cash in your account. And while some credit cards are treated as direct deposits, they can still take up to twenty-four hours to clear.

Other Ways to Bring in Cash

The optimal way to infuse your company is by making sales and collecting money for them. But sometimes, especially in the infancy of a business's existence, there's a dry spell to get through. You still need cash to pay others, such as your employees, suppliers, or the phone company. If the cash is not yet coming through the door, you will have to come up with another way to bring it in.

The most common way that novice entrepreneurs bring cash into their company's coffers is through personal resources. They tap into their home equity, they max out their personal credit cards, they raid their Christmas Club accounts. Beware of getting yourself (and your family) too deeply in debt in the hopes that your business will turn around quickly. Before you add more of your money into the mix, try to figure out why your business is experiencing this cash crunch, and see if you can find a way to turn it around. If you firmly believe that a temporary tiding-over is all that is needed, putting up your own money keeps your equity from getting diluted, and it keeps your business from sinking further into debt.

Other ways to beef up your cash balances include the following:

- Getting a bridge loan
- Selling off some of your equipment, then leasing it back from the purchaser
- Factoring your accounts receivable

Sale and Leaseback

For companies with large, expensive fixed assets on the books, entering into a sale-and-leaseback arrangement can provide a large infusion of cash. In these arrangements, the owner of the asset sells it to a third party and leases it back immediately. The asset itself doesn't move at all, and its use doesn't change, either. All that really occurs is a paperwork shuffle.

The new owner has paid a tidy sum to get title to the asset but not the use of it. The original owner loses ownership but keeps using the asset as before and makes regular lease payments to the new owner per their financial agreement. Though there are many details involved in these complex arrangements, they can be worked out for the benefit of both parties. And for the business owner facing a cash shortfall, it's a boon. He gets a bounty of cash for the sale, without losing use of the asset through the leaseback.

Factoring Receivables

For businesses suffering a temporary cash crunch, factoring outstanding accounts receivable can offer a quick solution. What exactly does factoring mean? It's a common business finance term that refers to selling your accounts receivable to another company, kind of like when another loan company buys your mortgage from the lender who originated the loan.

The factoring company pays you an advance on the cash they expect to collect. This process gives you money right now, though it's less than you'd get if you just waited for your customers to pay. The factor holds the receivable, and the customer check is sent to them. This can help you immediately, but the lost cash flow (the money you would have gotten next month) must be taken into account so as not to throw your cash planning off any further.

The drawback is that you don't get the full value of your accounts receivable. Factors pay you only a percentage, even for those highly collectible accounts, and the percentage goes down, sometimes pretty far, for accounts that have a history of paying late. In addition, there are often processing fees and buyback conditions (meaning you have to repurchase any account they deem uncollectible) that can cut deeply into your profits.

Forecasting Your Cash Outflows

When it comes to projecting your cash outflows, consider this: You are probably underestimating them, maybe by a significant percentage. It is as common as dirt for a fledgling company to send more cash out the door than it brings in, at least initially, so do not be surprised if this occurs in your pro forma statements (as long as you can foresee a shift in the balance before your company goes bust). While the numbers you use are important, as well as where they go on the statement, the absolutely most important thing here is to have a realistic idea of just how much cash will be heading out the door every month.

You already have the groundwork done for this. A large number of your cash disbursements will flow directly from the pro forma statement of profit and loss. Expenses, however, may not be the only items that suck cash out of your checking account. For example, asset purchases are strictly balance sheet transactions, but they still eat up cash reserves. Principal payments on loans also won't show up on your statement of profit and loss, nor will any draws or dividends taken by you and your co-owners. So though these cash outflows are not considered expenses, they will still appear on your pro forma cash flow statement.

On the standard statement of cash flows, the section that details the outbound money (often called the "Uses" section) will follow that of the inflows. The operating expenditures come first, followed by asset purchases and owner withdrawals, and then any debt repayments. For product-related businesses the cost of inventory items often pose the biggest drain on cash; however, it is customary for these types of purchases to be made on credit. Therefore, the month of purchase—as expressed on the statement of profit and loss—comes a good thirty days before payment time. For instance, inventory purchased in January will show up as a cash outflow in February. (If you cannot find a supplier who will extend credit sales to a start-up business, you won't have that time delay.)

Operating expenses typically form pretty predictable patterns, and you probably won't see too much fluctuation. Asset purchases are most often planned for and are easy to see coming—they won't happen monthly. Debt repayment, too, is scheduled and predictable. (In any case, accounts payable, buying inventory and supplies on credit, does not count as debt—only loans do.) The biggest question mark is owner withdrawals. In corporations, owners who work at the company must draw salaries, which flow out with the other payroll expenses. However, other withdrawals (called *dividends* for corporations) can come whenever shareholders choose; the same goes for owner draws in other business structures. As best you can, include your true expectations of cash-outs on this pro forma statement. Base them on your personal budgetary cash needs, and if they put your cash situation into the red, consider asking for additional financing until operations alone can provide sufficient working capital.

Creating a Buffer

One of the most common mistakes made by novice entrepreneurs is underestimating expenditures. Things will almost always cost more than you have planned to spend, and cash will often be demanded sooner than you expect. A lot of research has gone into the numbers you used in creating your pro forma financial statements, and stress has been placed on using realistic numbers that can be traced easily. That's all well and good, but now you will have to add a fudge factor. This made up add-on provides a financial safety net. Add a cushion of 10 percent extra to your projected cash outflows, and include it in this statement. If it ends up being unnecessary, congratulations!

Getting to the Projected Cash Balance

Now you have all the pieces you need to come up with your projected cash flow balance. You'll start with your opening cash balance, which comes of the beginning balance sheet, and work down from there. For start-ups, this initial cash balance may be zero; early deposits from owner contributions and loan proceeds would then show up as cash inflows. For companies already in business, you can pick the number off of your prior statement of cash flows, where it will have been the ending cash position.

Okay, you have your starting figure. Next, you'll form a section for sources of incoming cash. First come operational sources, which usually means any revenue your company earns in the normal course of business—mainly sales. This will be split between cash sales and credit sales. That will be followed up by any short-term (meaning less than one year) loan proceeds. Next come any proceeds from long-term loans, and finally any equity contributions. After these are all listed, you'll sum them and list the total amount of expected cash inflows.

After that section is complete, you'll begin the "Uses" (or outflows) section. Again, you'll start with the day-to-day costs and expenses, such as inventory purchases, payroll expenses, other operating expenses, and interest. Next, you'll address planned asset purchases, then owner withdrawals or dividends. Last on this list comes payback, with short-term debt installments first followed by long-term debt payments. Now you will sum this listing, and call it "Total Uses Before Taxes."

If your corresponding statement of profit and loss is showing a profit, you'll have to plan to pay income taxes. The only plus to posting a loss is that you'll have no income taxes to deal with (though other types of taxes may apply). List your estimated income tax accrual. The easiest way is to figure out an estimate for the whole year, then divide it by the appropriate period and record it in the payment periods (typically quarterly). Subtract that tax figure from the previous subtotal to come up with your total outflows (labeled "Total Uses After Taxes").

At the very bottom of this pro forma comes your "Net Change in Cash," calculated by subtracting your total uses after taxes (outflows) from your total sources (inflows). Whether negative or positive, that figure represents what has happened with cash during the period. That result will be added to your starting cash, for the bottom line: your ending cash position, which should match exactly the cash balance on your ending balance sheet.

Standard Cash Flow Projection Format

The top of a statement of cash flow looks very much like that of a statement of profit and loss:

ABC Company
Statement of Cash Flow
For the Year Ended December 31, 2006

The cash flow statement also leads with what's coming in, followed by what's going out. But it also comes with an anchor, the cash balance at beginning and end. This is how it looks:

Beginning Cash Balance at (Date) $XX

Sources of Inflowing Cash:
Cash Sales $XX
Credit Sales $XX
Loan Proceeds, Short-Term $XX
Loan Proceeds, Long-Term $XX

Capital Contributions	$XX
Total Cash Inflow Sources	*$XX*
Uses of Outflowing Cash:	
Inventory Purchases	$XX
Payroll Expenses	$XX
Other Operating Expenses	$XX
Interest Expense	$XX
Asset Purchases	$XX
Owner Withdrawals and Dividends	$XX
Debt Payments, Short-Term	$XX
Debt Payments, Long-Term	$XX
Total Uses Before Taxes	*$XX*
Estimated Income Taxes	$XX
Total Uses After Taxes	*$XX*
Net Change in Cash	$XX
Ending Cash Balance at (Date)	**$XX**

▶▶ TEST DRIVE

To keep your business going, you may have to do things you'd rather not. Consider whether you could bring yourself to do the following things:

- ⟳ Ask your parents for money.
- ⟳ Take on additional personal credit card debt.
- ⟳ Refinance your mortgage with extra cash out.
- ⟳ Take out a home equity loan.
- ⟳ Ask friends for money.
- ⟳ Break into your retirement account.
- ⟳ Go back to work for someone else on the side.

Rations Summarize the Financials

For quick answers about a company's financial potential, bankers and investors often perform ratio analyses of the financial statements. The way the numbers work together can provide important insights into the current financial health and future profitability of a company. In addition to helping the money guys make a decision about whether they're willing to part with any money and if so, how much, they may set add some strings to that funding in the form of ratio maintenance.

Bankers Look to Ratios

Bankers, in particular, can be very strict when it comes to meeting ratio requirements. It may be in your loan documents that failing to meet particular ratios can put your loan into default. However, what matters to one banker (or to one bank, for that matter) may not be as critical to another. Even if your ratios seem to be coming in a bit under par, a strong case for the ability to pay back your loan as scheduled can be very persuasive.

Pay particular attention to the ratios your loan officer appears most interested in. Should they fall under the bank's "acceptable levels," explain why, and try to refocus attention on your company's strong points, particularly if positive projected cash flows are among them.

For smaller ventures, ratio analysis may not be required. But it does make your business plan look more professional and polished. On top of making you look like you understand the financial numbers game, it also saves the readers of your plan the work of calculating the ratios for themselves.

Ratio analyses tie your financial statements together, giving the most complete picture. They are, however, not required to be included—even without them, your business plan will be considered thorough by its readers. If you understand ratio analyses fully, and they add emphasis that will help you get the money you are looking for, include them. However, if they do not make sense to you, if you are not sure how to properly calculate them, if you will not be able to answer direct questions about them, or if they just don't look good, do not include them in your business plan.

What the Ratios Will Show

There are several basic categories that these financial ratios fall into, each covering a different area of importance. For example, some ratios help measure liquidity, meaning how well your company will be able to meet its upcoming financial obligations.

Each number adds to your company's overall financial picture, both on its own and when looked at in concert with the whole package of ratios. But you should not try to evaluate these ratios only as they appear for your company. You need something to compare them to see if they make sense for both the size of your company and the industry you are in. For example, one would expect a service firm to be more liquid than a company with a substantial inventory investment. When you compare your results to those of similar companies, it helps you to see where your company is doing well and where it can use improvement.

Other Ways to Analyze Your Financial Statements

In addition to performing a ratio analysis, there are other ways to evaluate your company's potential. One way is to look at your financial statements over time, called a horizontal analysis. Essentially, this methodology gives you a percentage analysis of the ups and downs on your comparative financial statements. For example, you could see the percentage growth in sales from period five to period six. For display purposes, the numbers for comparable periods would be shown in columns next to each other, typically with the earlier period on the left; the final column would be dedicated to percentage increases and decreases. What is the purpose of this type of analysis in your business plan? It can help illustrate your prospective growth in a clear, numerical fashion. For your own purposes, horizontal analysis of actual numbers can alert you to potential problems while they remain easily handled. For example, if sales increase by 14 percent and cost of sales increase by 36 percent, you may need to take a closer look at your pricing schedule and gross profit margin.

Another common evaluative measure is called the vertical financial statement analysis. In this method, you compare the relationships of connected items on a single financial statement. For example, you could measure each asset in relation to total assets to see how all assets stack up proportionally and in expected ways—you would not expect to see a disproportional investment in fixed assets in a service company, for example. Or if your company is holding on to an excessive amount of cash, you may want to look into ways to turn that cash into future profits. On the statement of profit and loss, each line item is turned into a percentage of total net sales. These numbers can help you look for ways to increase profitability in the coming years. In addition, comparing these percentages to industry standards can provide insights into more efficient ways to conduct your business.

Finally, some key financial figures like the sales break-even number and your company's available working capital should be included with your analysis. These calculations provide your business plan readers with critical information about the potential of your company, especially when looked at together. For example, they can answer the question, "Will I have enough working capital to carry me through the break-even period?" That's a question both you and other business plan readers will surely want answered.

Which Ratios Should You Compute?

Should you decide to include a ratio analysis, there are some absolutely must-haves. Make sure to include at least all of the following (each of which will be explained in detail below):

1. Current ratio
2. Quick ratio
3. Debt-to-equity ratio
4. Debt-to-assets ratio
5. Return-on-equity ratio
6. Return-on-assets (or return on investments) ratio
7. Sales break-even level
8. Cash-flow-to-assets ratio
9. Cash-flow-to-sales ratio
10. Working capital

There are additional ratios you may choose to include, especially if they will help to present your company in the most attractive light. For example, if you will have a very strong cash inflow from your credit customers, you could include a ratio called receivables turnover. Other potential inclusions are inventory turnover and net profit margin. Here are the ways to calculate each of the supplementary ratios:

Receivables turnover demonstrates the effectiveness of your company's credit policies. It is calculated by dividing accounts receivable by net sales.

Inventory turnover refers to how many times each year the inventory is completely replaced, a measure of the relative size of your inventory. To compute this ratio, divide your cost of goods sold by your average inventory (figured by adding beginning inventory to ending inventory, then dividing the sum by two).

Net profit margin shows the truest measure of your business success by demonstrating your bottom line profitability with respect to sales. Divide your net profit into your net sales; a higher result indicates more profitability.

Calculating Key Balance Sheet Ratios

As you would expect, the key balance sheet ratios focus on numbers culled from the balance sheet. Here, you will find figures crucial to calculating one of the most important measures of your company: liquidity. For a small start-up company, liquidity will mean the difference between life and death, making it even more important (at least initially) than profitability. Your company cannot survive without liquidity because that is the measure of how well it can pay the bills. Businesses that are not liquid often end up filing for bankruptcy—regardless of their apparent profitability on paper.

The flip side of the liquidity coin is debt. The debt position of your company denotes the amount of outside money that is being used to create profits. New companies commonly take on too much debt too quickly in an effort to show early growth, but this can have the opposite effect, with high debt payments choking their cash flow. Basically, the more debt the company carries, the higher its risk of failure. The important point to remember here is relativity: The ratios are better indicators of what is really going on than the straight numbers alone. Debt totaling $100,000 may have a lot of impact on a company with $1 million in assets, but for a business with only $120,000 in assets it can be like a noose.

The Current Ratio

One of the most important ratios any new small business should keep track of is their current ratio; in fact, your bank loan may require it be maintained at a particular level. The current ratio measures your company's liquidity, meaning how capable the business is of meeting its current financial obligations. The ratio is calculated as follows: current assets divided by current liabilities.

Though there is no one right number for every type of business, look for a current ratio of at least 1.0, meaning your company has $1 of liquid assets for every $1 of current liability. There is great variability, however, among industries. For some, a current ratio of at least 2.0 is the norm, and for others the average may hover around 0.75. The higher your current ratio, the more liquid your company is and the better able to pay its bills on time. Banks often look for a current ratio of 2.0 when they are considering making loans. This means that even if half of the company's current assets were lost, it could still cover all of its current liabilities—a healthy safety margin.

The Quick Ratio

While the current ratio is used by virtually every form of business as the prime measure of liquidity, product-based businesses are better served by calculating the quick ratio. The quick ratio is similar to the current ratio, but it removes one current asset from the equation: inventory. Even though inventory is considered a current asset, it is the most difficult to quickly convert into cash. Therefore, the quick ratio can present a truer picture of actual liquidity for companies carrying inventory.

To calculate the quick ratio, subtract the value of inventory from the total current assets, then divide that result by the total current liabilities. Like the current ratio, there is no one right number for every type of company. In most cases, aim for a quick ratio of at least 1.0; again, for this ratio, bigger is better.

The Debt-to-Equity Ratio

If you remember the accounting equation, you know that total debt plus total equity equals total assets. Assets are what you have, and the debt/equity breakdown shows who actually owns those assets: the owners of the company, or outsiders. When people or institutions are considering extending credit to your company, they will look at this ratio to see where they will be standing in line should things go awry. ▶▶ **Businesses that owe more than they own make bigger credit risks**, so if you plan to look for debt funding both now and in the future, keep an eye on this ratio—your bankers certainly will.

To compute the debt-to-equity ratio, you simply divide your total liabilities by your total equity. In this case, a lower number is a better number. A higher result indicates a higher failure risk for your business. When profits are earned and cash collected, and more of it goes to paying down debt than back into the business, it will be harder for the company to stay afloat—and it may even instigate the need for additional debt. Bankers typically look for a debt-to-equity ratio of less than 1.0 before they will even consider extending additional credit.

The Debt-to-Assets Ratio

Similar in nature to the debt-to-equity ratio, the debt-to-assets ratio shows the relationship of what you owe to what you have. This ratio should not exceed 0.5, but standards do vary greatly across industries. For example, companies that have large investments in fixed assets typically hold more debt than those without. Again, for this ratio, the lower the better. When the ratio is high, it indicates increasing risk of failure.

This ratio is computed as follows: divide total liabilities by total assets. The results speak to your company's long-term solvency, just as the current ratio addresses short-term solvency. Does that mean you should avoid all debt? Not at all; debt is a normal part of doing business. The trick is not to let the debt overwhelm everything else you are doing. Keeping an eye on your debt-to-assets ratio can help you see in the early stages when the debt level is getting dicey, so you can take steps to ensure ongoing solvency.

Analyzing Profitability

The key profit-related ratios focus less on profits themselves than on how those profits were generated. Sometimes referred to as the investment ratios, they clearly show how well you are using what you have to sustain profitability for your business. You have poured money into this business, and you deserve to see a reward for your efforts. These ratios help measure your returns in a precise way.

When you invest your money in anything, you expect returns (even if they do not eventually materialize). Regardless of your reason for wanting to go into business for yourself, the business itself represents an investment. For that reason, any good financial planner would tell you that the expected returns should be high enough to cover the very high potential risk of loss.

Return on Assets

When your company is managing its assets effectively, your financial returns will be higher. Ideally, your return-on-assets ratio—sometimes also referred to as return on investment—should be higher (hopefully quite a bit higher) than the interest rate you are paying on your debt. At its most basic level, though, the return-on-assets ratio measures how much income each dollar's worth of assets generates, an indicator of the overall earning power of the business.

To calculate the return-on-assets ratio, divide your net income by your total assets. For a more accurate inside view of how well your assets are performing, recalculate the ratio using only active assets in the denominator. For example, a warehouse that is under construction counts as a company asset, but it is not yet contributing to profitability. For external business plan readers, though, stick with the same number that appears on your balance sheet.

Return on Equity

Return on equity shows how much bang you are getting for your investment buck. Should you choose equity financing to fund your business, your plan readers will be especially interested in how this ratio pans out. As you would expect, higher returns are more attractive to investors, particularly when they are taking on the already high risk of putting their money into a small business. The returns here should show the promise of being substantially higher than one could earn by investing in a large, stable, established company.

Return on equity is computed by dividing total equity into net income. The result here is almost the opposite of the return-on-assets ratio. Return on assets shows how well the company is generating profits, while return on equity shows how much profit flows toward each dollar an investor puts up.

Sales Break-Even Level

Though this technically is not a ratio, this number is often included in the financial statement analysis section of a business plan. Even if you have addressed your business's break-even number in the body of your business plan, putting the summary number in with the rest of your analyses saves the readers the trouble of having to flip around to find it. The break-even number is important to all readers of the plan, both internal and external, because it indicates how much sales volume is needed *before* the company can finally begin turning a profit.

Break even, as you learned earlier, is the point where your sales bring in enough money to cover all of your company's variable and fixed costs. Every dollar earned after that sends a portion to profits. Earlier, though, your concern was simply figuring out your break-even scenario. Here, you will have to analyze it—and it should be substantially lower than your most feasible sales projection. Why is that? If the sales level you can most reasonably expect to meet falls short of breaking even, your company will lose money.

Cash Management Ratios

Both potential lenders and investors will want to know the adequacy of your cash flows. Without sufficient cash, everything else can become irrelevant. You need cash to pay your debts, both short and long term. For that reason, cash flow is the best predictor of current liquidity and long-term solvency.

Here's the kicker. Your business plan readers want to know that cash flow will be generated by the company and not merely brought in from outside (from either them or you). Without a sustainable influx of cash, no business can succeed in the long run. These ratios speak to how well your company is handling its cash.

Cash Flow to Assets

This ratio compares one number from the statement of cash flow to one from the balance sheet: your operating cash flow divided by your total assets. The purpose of this ratio is to demonstrate the ability of your existing assets (that is, your company's investment) to generate operating cash inflow.

Cash Flows to Sales

This ratio measures how well your revenues are generating cash inflows. Remember, sales do not always mean cash. If your company makes a lot of its sales on credit, this number will be significantly lower than that of a company that only makes sales for cash.

To compute this ratio, divide your cash flow from operations by your net sales for the period. This will help you measure just how much actual cash each dollar of sales is bringing in and speaks directly to how efficient your operations are.

Working Capital

Technically, the working capital is a key indicator of your company's liquidity. Working capital equals the excess of current assets over current liabilities. The more working capital you have, the lower your company's chance of facing insolvency, which means your business has enough current assets to cover all of its current liabilities as they come due. To risk stating the obvious, it's essential for your working capital to be a positive number. Negative working capital (and it does happen) is a serious sign of trouble.

Ideally, your working capital should have a built-in cushion, just like a personal emergency savings account, to draw from in case sales don't quite reach the levels you have expected, at least initially. Your working capital should be sufficient to be able to get your company through short-term slowdowns, a normal part of running any business.

Put yourself in the shoes of a loan officer. A small business owner has come to you for a loan, and his business plan included the following financial information about the current state of his company. Would you approve the loan?

- The current ratio was 0.75.
- The debt to equity ratio was 2.25.
- The return on assets was 20 percent higher than the industry average.
- His company had positive working capital, in line with the industry average.

6

Using Your Business Plan to Get Money

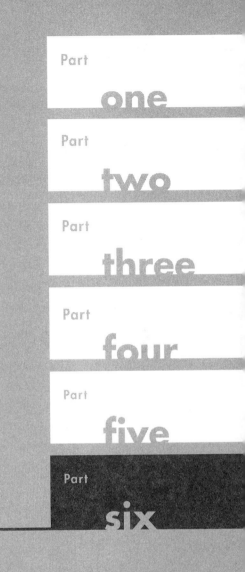

Part
one

Part
two

Part
three

Part
four

Part
five

Part
six

Figure Out Your Set-Up Costs

In this chapter, you will learn how to figure out how much money it will cost you to get your business ready for opening day. There are literally dozens of expenditures to consider, from the legal costs of incorporating your company to little odds and ends that virtually every business needs but no one really remembers to think about. As you begin to put together your start-up cost estimates, you can stick to ballpark figures—there is no need to come in right on the button. What you are really trying to do here is come up with a general idea of how much money you will need to get things going, whether it is $12,000, $120,000, or $1,200,000.

In addition to calculating how much it will take to be able to open your door for business, you will also need to take a look at how much money you will need to keep things running for the first few months—before any reliable, steady cash starts flowing in. Finally, you need to account for your personal living expenses during this startup time. If you don't have enough money to live on, it will be very hard to focus on your business.

To come close to your actual eventual cash needs, you'll need to consider the costs of items in at least the following categories:

1. Professional advisors
2. Adequate insurance
3. Pre-opening marketing
4. Staffing needs
5. Your place(s) of business
6. Basic business needs
7. Your personal cash requirements
8. Your first few months in business

If you are expanding an existing business, you may have a better idea of some of the costs you will need to consider. Many of the expenditures will be known quantities, while others may take a little research. The basic premise, though, is the same. It takes money to expand your business, and you need to know around how much money your plans will consume.

You can start thinking about where to get the money once you have a handle on the approximate total capital you will need to fund your business. First, though, you have to come up with a reasonable figure to work with.

Using Professional Advisors

Whether you are starting up a brand-new business or expanding an existing company, you are heading into unknown territory. ▸▸ **Even if you have years of entrepreneurial experience under your belt, you may not know all the ins and outs of the unfamiliar parts of your upcoming undertaking. This is where professional assistance can come in very handy.**

Regardless of the type of business you will be involved with, there are some core professionals you will want to have on your side. This is not a good place to cut corners—professional advice from the start can help you avoid pitfalls and success-killers later on. The key members of your professional advisory team could include an accountant, a lawyer, a marketing consultant, and an insurance agent. (Insurance agents and marketing consultants will be discussed in depth later in this chapter.) A good working relationship with your professional advisors will play a direct role in your company's eventual success.

If you have significant experience in one of these fields, you may be able to forego hiring an outside professional. You need to figure out if you have enough knowledge and expertise to take the place of a focused professional, whether you will have enough time to devote to this one area of your company's needs while you are also trying to get operations up and running, and whether you can actually save money by hiring out. (Remember, your time costs money, so factor that in when considering this point.)

Your Lawyer

A lot of new small business owners try to avoid using lawyers as much as they can because they fear the high costs of legal representation—but don't let that scare you away from hiring competent legal help. Most lawyers require retainers (sometimes sizable) to start working with you, but that can be a good thing. They know about how much the complete job should cost, they know their hourly rates, and they set their initial retainers accordingly.

This can help you accurately budget for your legal costs, even though it does call for a chunk of cash (often in the range of $2,500) up front.

What can a lawyer do for you that you may not be able to do for yourself? In the first place, he can help you determine the best entity for your business (for example, whether you should form an LLC or an S corporation). Once that decision has been made, a lawyer can help you make sure all the proper paperwork is filed, and filed correctly, which will help protect you from legal problems down the line.

In addition, a lawyer can look over all of your business contracts—including any loan paperwork or leases—to make sure you are not signing something you shouldn't be. He can help you draft the contracts you will require your clients to sign. Your lawyer can advise you when you are faced with making major business decisions, defend you if you find yourself on the wrong side of a lawsuit, and let you know whether you should be taking legal action against another party.

Make sure that you choose an attorney with plenty of small business experience, preferably working with start-ups. Even better, look for a lawyer who has worked with companies in your industry and who will be able to provide you with helpful advice and insights based on the successes and failures of other clients (though no legal professional will provide you with specific information, as that would violate confidentiality).

Your Accountant

Sure, everyone calls on the accountant after they've been in business for a while, when they need help figuring out payroll taxes or income taxes. But having an accountant on board before you start your business can offer up a lot of benefits. Adding a professional accountant to your team to help with the start-up can save you a lot of hassle and a lot of money in the long run.

Here are some things your accountant can help you with:

➲ Choosing the best bookkeeping software, and showing you how to use it

➲ Setting up your books, and teaching you how to make regular bookkeeping entries

➲ Helping you set up your payroll system (even if you are the only employee)

➲ Obtaining all the applicable tax identification numbers

➲ Advising you on the best business choices to help keep your eventual tax bill at a minimum

➲ Assisting you with the financial projection portions of your business plan

➲ Helping you develop a reasonable operating budget for your first few months in business

➲ Determining optimal starting inventory levels

➲ Introducing you to amenable bankers and helping you prepare bank loan applications

On top of all of the business benefits, your accountant can also help you on the personal front. Competent financial and tax planning can help keep you and your family afloat during the initial lean days of your start-up.

Working with your accountant before the fact will help your business greatly in the long run. He will already be familiar with your systems and will know that they have been set up properly. He will also be able to tell how well your business is doing in comparison with similar, local companies—and be able to help focus on areas that can improve your profitability. And as for his costs, ask him for an overall estimate of small business start-up advisory costs. An experienced professional will be able to give you a good idea of the total amount to budget for.

The Right Insurance

Whether your business will involve a manufacturing plant with dozens of employees, or you in your kitchen with just a laptop for company, your business will need insurance. To help make sure you have adequate coverage in every area where you will need it, working with an independent insurance agent (as opposed to a different company for each type of policy) can help you find the best mix of insurance products.

The type of business you have will largely dictate the kinds of insurance you need. Product-based businesses require different policies than service-based companies, and companies with employees have different needs than those without. High-risk operations (like working with toxic chemicals) may call for specialized policies. Not only will the types of insurance you need be unique to your company, so will the costs. This, again, is where a good agent can come in handy. He'll do the shopping for you to help you get the best quotes on the policies you need.

If you don't already have an insurance agent that you work with regularly, find one that you can trust. Ask around among local small businesses. Check with your accountant, and talk to your banker. Another option is to contact your industry trade association, as they often offer bundled insurance packages for members at discounted prices. The only downside is that you may have to purchase one-size-fits-all policies instead of something more personalized.

Once you have some names, call around for bids from both agencies and insurance companies. Look through each proposal, and make sure that they include comparable information before you make any decisions. Check out the coverage amounts, applicable deductibles, and coverage types. Make sure to find out whether running all of your policies through a single company can help reduce costs; many insurers offer discounts for companies that maintain multiple policies.

Property Insurance

Property insurance covers all of your physical assets. With these policies, your company will be protected from losses due to things like damage, theft, and other things that prohibit you from using your property.

Many small business owners cover their buildings, but they neglect to make sure that building contents are included in their policies. That can be a very dangerous oversight, as it's very common for machinery, equipment, and inventory to cost more than the building they are housed in. Plus, business records themselves are invaluable, and the costs to recover them can be quite substantial.

Beef Up Your Homeowner's Policy

Many small business owners run at least part of their businesses out of their homes. They mistakenly believe that their basic homeowner's policy, the one covering their personal assets, covers business assets as well. They're probably wrong—and that can be a very costly mistake, in more ways than one.

In addition to your business assets *not* being covered, you may actually be violating your existing policy by having an uncovered business in your home, and that could mean the insurance company won't pay if you suffer personal damages. To avoid potential problems, contact your insurance company before you start running your business from home. A simple added binder, with a small bump in premium, can help you make sure that everything is covered properly.

Liability Insurance

Liability insurance offers coverage for instances when your business gets sued. Typical costs included in coverage are damages (payable to the complaining party) and legal fees (incurred to defend your company and yourself) up to the total amount allowed in the policy. Liability potential exists in virtually every type of business, but some are more susceptible to problems than others. Those companies, in particular, should make sure they are adequately covered in the event of an incident.

Liability insurance is important for all businesses, but it is especially crucial for business entities that do not provide limited personal liability to their owners—namely, sole proprietorships and general partners in partnerships. For these types of business structures, the company's owners can be sued—and their personal assets put at risk—if they have neither adequate liability insurance coverage nor sufficient business assets to cover the damages due. Because some businesses are inherently more risky than others (a delivery service with ten drivers can get into more trouble than a lone graphic designer, for instance), many entrepreneurs choose to build personal liability protection into their business structures by forming their companies as corporations, LLCs, or LLPs. Even these companies, though, should have comprehensive liability coverage. In most cases, it costs less to pay insurance premiums than damages.

What kinds of things might your company be liable for? The list is fairly long, but some of the most common problem areas include the following:

- Products that cause an injury even when used properly
- Vehicular accidents and resultant property damage or injuries to people
- People getting injured in your place of business
- Malpractice (typically requires a separate, specific liability insurance policy)

To cut down on costs, consider purchasing an umbrella policy in addition to your standard liability insurance. Umbrella policies kick in after your other insurance policies have paid out, on the occasion that your company gets hit with a claim greater than its coverage. Since they really back up policies, you can usually get a lot of coverage for a very reasonable premium.

Employee-Related Insurance

When employees enter the mix, some types of insurance are mandatory and some are optional. Theoretically optional, anyway—these days, to attract desirable employees, you may have to offer competitive benefits packages, and that typically includes some insurance coverage. In addition to insurance for your employees, there is also insurance to help protect your business should you lose a key employee.

First on the list is health coverage. Health insurance helps to pay the bills associated with illness and injury. This type of insurance tends to be very expensive, and it can be hard for small business owners to swing the steep premiums. However, group plans typically cost less (per person) than individual policies, and offering this insurance can help attract the best employees. If you want to provide this benefit for your employees, you can offset some of your costs by having them contribute pretax salary dollars toward premiums.

One must-have policy is workers' compensation insurance. This coverage is typically required by the states of any business that has any nonowner employees (yes, even a single employee prompts the need for this coverage). How much coverage your company will need depends on

Limited Liability Business Structures
Don't Cover Everything

Todd and Lisa Gormley started a landscaping business together. On their lawyer's advice, they originally formed their company as an LLC. After all, they would have heavy equipment at other people's houses and they intended to hire employees, so they wanted to protect themselves from liability claims.

The business did well. Lisa handled the landscape design issues and performed much of the delicate detail work. Todd took care of all the heavy lifting and most of the manual labor. They both loved their company, and they took great pride in the effects they produced.

After a while, Lisa decided she wanted to take a more natural, organic approach to garden maintenance. She researched several fertilizers, finally settling on the formula she felt most comfortable with. To save money, she bought ingredients and mixed the fertilizer herself instead of purchasing the more expensive commercial preparation. She tested her creation at the next job they had scheduled.

Two days later, Lisa got a call from that (very angry) customer. It turned out that the fertilizer reacted badly in this environment, and it killed thousands of dollars worth of plants, including a prize-winning rose bush. The customer sued Todd and Lisa's company, as well as the two of them personally, for damages in excess of $10,000; the customer won her lawsuit.

The company coffers only had $1,000, and their low-budget insurance only provided another $5,000. The remaining cash was due from Todd and Lisa's personal assets, which effectively wiped out their savings and filled their credit cards to the maximum. How could they be held personally responsible? No business entity can shield you from your own malpractice or negligence. Lisa herself caused the problem, and Todd and Lisa would have to pay up.

which state(s) you operate in, the type of duties your employees will perform (for example, office work versus working with explosives), and how many employees you have in each performance category. As you might expect, more dangerous duties come with a higher insurance price tag. However, this is not a place to cut corners. The government is very serious about workers' compensation, so you need to make sure your policy at least meets the minimum statutory requirements.

While the previous two policy types cover your employees, key-person insurance covers your business in the event that someone crucial to the daily operation of your business dies or becomes disabled. Typically, these policies cover the heavy hitters in your organization: chief financial officers, chief operating officers, managers, even owners who participate in operations. In the simplest terms, a key person is someone without whom the company simply cannot run properly. The purpose of key-person insurance is to help your business function following such a major loss. For example, you can use the proceeds to hire interim replacements or conduct a high-level search for a permanent replacement. In addition, the insurance may be structured to buy out the interests of an owner who has died.

Business Interruption Coverage

A commonly overlooked policy type, business interruption insurance can save your business from a seemingly unrecoverable disaster. ▶▶ **This insurance policy basically covers all of your company's regular bills during periods when the business cannot operate normally due to a covered event such as a fire or flood.**

The main purpose of this policy is to get your business over the hump; just because your company cannot operate does not mean you can stop paying the regular bills. You still have to pay for phone service, trash pickup, and gas and electric, for example. You may also have to pay your employees, even if they can't come to work, to have them available when you can reopen. Plus, you will have to keep making lease and debt payments to keep both your loans and your leases active and avoid default. Finally, for an extra (usually pretty substantial) premium, you can get a profit protection clause written in, which covers you for the profits you will lose while your business cannot operate.

These policies do not cover repairs, replacement property, or liability claims. They exist solely to keep your business in business during the recovery period.

Determine a Marketing Budget

All new businesses have marketing needs, but the size of their marketing budgets varies widely. Various factors come together to determine how much money you will need to spend on start-up advertising, including these:

- The size of your company
- How much competition your company faces
- The industry you are in
- Your personal attitudes about marketing

Some fledgling companies have virtually no money set aside for marketing, while others throw the bulk of their cash into promotional efforts. At the very least, your company needs an ad in the Yellow Pages and an initial supply of high-quality business cards. Even the most meager marketing budgets should contain enough resources to cover these two crucial items.

If you have more marketing dollars to play with, you can look into additional forms of attracting customers, like print advertisements, radio spots, and even television commercials. Direct mail marketing is another very effective way to reach customers. You can also get more elaborate with your signs and displays—though these are considered marketing tools, many people include them in the "housing" section of start-up costs. Another great option is to develop a Web site for your company, especially if you provide a service for which performance location is irrelevant (like résumé writing as opposed to interior decorating) or have products than can be shipped anywhere.

Some of these methods are easy to price out, but others may take a lot of legwork. For example, you can call your local Yellow Pages and request a price sheet. You can contact a few printers and find out how much they charge for a set number of business cards. If you simply don't have time to deal with tracking down costs, or even determining which means of marketing will work best for your company, hire a marketing consultant, who will easily be able to help you determine an appropriate start-up marketing budget.

Paying a Staff

When you begin planning for a new business, one major decision you will face is whether or not you will hire employees. Once that choice is made, you may have to think about some related issues, not the least of which is how much help you will really need. Many novice entrepreneurs put off the decision about employees, trying to see if they can do everything themselves. However, the best time to make this decision is in the planning phases, especially because having employees is usually the biggest operating expense a company will incur.

To accurately estimate this portion of your pre-opening costs, you will first need to realistically assess how much you can do on your own and how much you will need to hire out. Part of this question depends on whether you have a scheduled opening day or there is flexibility built in to the timing. Consider all the tasks involved in getting your business ready for opening day, how many man hours each is expected to take (being sure to add on some time to account for the unexpected), how much time you really will have to devote to these activities, and which things you actually know how to do.

If you find you may need to hire some help, take some time to figure out exactly how much you need. Hiring several full-time, permanent employees can be very costly, and it requires immediate outflowing cash—not to mention that firing people can be very tough, both emotionally and legally. For those reasons, it's often advisable to hire temporary employees, outside contractors, or part-time help to get you through the opening until you know definitively how many employees you will need on an ongoing basis.

Things to Consider If You Do Hire Employees

Should employees turn out to be a must-have for your business, there are a lot of factors you will need to consider. As you are determining your staffing needs, consider the following questions:

1. If you only need forty hours per week of help, is it better to hire one full-time employee or two part-time employees?

2. Will you offer vacation pay and sick leave?

3. Who will take over when your employees are absent?

4. Will you offer benefits like health insurance or a retirement savings plan?

5. Will your employees need training, and if so, will you pay them for their training time?

Housing Your Business

In most cases, the physical space needed for your business will call for the biggest cash outlay. Whether you are opening a store, a professional office, or a restaurant, both the space itself and everything you need to turn that space into your work environment costs money. Even if you will start by working from your home to cut down on initial cash expenditures, you will still need to outfit your work area with some basic business necessities.

Though the space itself will eat up the biggest chunk of your business's housing budget, it is not the only expenditure you need to consider. Other big-ticket items in this category include equipment, fixtures, remodeling, and decorating. Don't forget the small-ticket items crucial to getting your space together—things such as signs and everyday supplies.

For some of these expenditures, one major decision you will need to make (typically regarding space and equipment) is whether to rent or purchase. You also need to be aware of your physical space requirements, especially when equipment is involved. For that reason, figure out the specifications of every piece of machinery and equipment you will need to operate your business before you calculate your square footage needs.

Rent or Purchase?

For start-up businesses, renting usually makes more sense for a couple of reasons. First, purchasing fixed assets calls for a lot of initial cash outlay (think down payments) and can send your start-up budget into an entirely different arena. Leasing, on the other hand, typically requires a much smaller initial deposit. Second, it's typically easier (though not necessarily cheaper) to modify a lease than to sell an asset, should things not work the way you expect. This logic holds for both space and equipment.

When you are expanding your business, purchasing fixed assets may be the more sensible decision. In this case, you have proven cash flow, you know what it takes to run your business profitably, and you know what equipment is the most useful to your company. For these reasons—plus the fact that assets you own tend to pay you back over the long run in revenue generation—purchasing could be a better choice for a business expansion.

A Look at Equipment Needs

Every business—manufacturing, retail, even service—has equipment needs, each unique to the company in question. ▶▶ **Each individual company needs a distinct mix of assets to help assure its profitability.** There is no single right answer that covers every business, even among companies ostensibly doing the same thing. You will need to decide what your company needs to prosper, which could be anything from huge machines to waiting-room sofas. That doesn't mean you can't scope out the furniture and fixtures of your competitors to get some ideas; they can be a great source of inspiration. You may also want to talk with members of your trade association or search the Web for additional ideas. Once you have a general idea of some of the standards, you'll be better able to assess what will work best for your business.

Your specific line of business dictates what types of assets your business will use. As a basic example, manufacturing concerns call for production equipment, while retail establishments call for merchandise displays, and food service businesses require refrigeration and cooking equipment. At the outset, stick with those fixed assets that your business really needs, and stay away from those that are not true must-haves.

Some assets, though, are common to virtually every type of business. These include computer equipment and communications hardware (like phone systems and fax machines). Depending on your other fixed asset needs, your own cash supply, and the overall size of your business, you may want to lease even these assets instead of buying them. Especially consider leasing computers and related equipment (like scanners and printers), which become obsolete relatively quickly.

Specific Costs to Account For

Now that you know what you need to house your business, and whether you will lease or purchase, you can start tallying up the necessary cash payouts. Remember, you will have to have your space, equipment, and machinery in place and ready for action *before* (maybe even a couple of months before) you open your doors for business.

Whether you have decided to lease or buy, include three to six months worth of monthly payments in your pre-opening budget. In addition, add in any necessary down payments or deposits. Don't forget to include delivery fees, closing costs, and any other expenditures (like required training or set-up) for your equipment and machinery. Include the costs of all fixtures, including assembly and installation, needed to get your space ready (display cases, shelving, or lighting, for example).

If your space needs to be remodeled, get competitive bids from a few contractors and maybe even some interior designers. Once you have plans in place, bids should be offered to you free of charge. Include the estimate from the contractor you plan to use. As for decorating, even if you plan to do most of the work yourself, use estimates from interior designers to give you an idea of what your ideas may really cost.

Signs and supplies make up the final portion of the costs associated with this section of your starting budget. Sign costs can run the gamut from $50 to a few thousand dollars, depending on your needs. If your business calls for signs that will cost more than $500 in total, get some competitive bids. As for supplies, consider what you will need to have on hand all the time to keep things shipshape: cleaning supplies, trash cans, and office supplies, for example. Include everything from soap in the restrooms to paper clips in the desk drawer, and remember to account for the fact that some of these supplies will need to be replenished regularly.

The Odds and Ends That Add Up

While they may not take as much cash as renting a warehouse, the little things that you will need to get your business running smoothly can add up to a fairly substantial sum. Some of these little things are bigger than others, and all of them are easy to overlook when you are trying to get a grasp of the big picture. These diverse expenditures don't really fit neatly into any of the other categories, so they get lumped together here under one catchall label.

Probably the most important items to cover in this category are the requisite licenses and permits. ▸▸ **Whether your business is subject to licensing at the federal, state, or local level (or maybe even all three), you must have these permissions in place before you open for business.** In some cases you may have to fill out a lengthy application; in all cases you will have to pay a fee. When your business is part of a highly regulated industry (like gas stations or liquor stores), expect to provide more paperwork and pay higher fees.

Another big kind of expenditure that comes in here is various deposits. Typically, utility companies (including phone, electric, and cable) will require a deposit, often sizeable, before they will hook you up. Some of these deposits are based on expected usage, some are based on the number of outlets you will need. The utility companies you will be working with should be able to help you estimate your deposit needs and let you know the conditions under which you will get your money back.

Next come the miscellaneous items your business simply cannot run without. These tend to be unique to the type of business, but some items are needed everywhere. Included here may be things like customer invoices or receipts, postage stamps, and coffee service.

Finally, just to account for all the things you forgot to include (and there will be some), the costs you underestimated (there will certainly be some of these, too), and the inevitable surprises that you could not have anticipated, add a little extra to your total cash needs. The basic rule of thumb is to tack 10 percent on to your total expected set-up needs.

Retailers Need a Few More Things

Retail businesses have two unique requirements that must be present on opening day: inventory and cash. You will not be able to operate unless you have ample supplies of both.

Beginning inventory covers the merchandise you have to have in place on day one before you open your doors. If you have done some pre-opening advertising, your store must at least contain the items that are supposed to draw the customers in. The amount of stock you'll carry could be quite substantial, so make sure you have a reasonably accurate estimate of the total costs (including any taxes and delivery charges you will have to pay). The suppliers you have been talking with may be able to help you with your initial orders, even give you an idea of the amount of inventory you'll need to start with.

As for cash, you will need to fill your cash register with enough money to make change for customers. You should also have adequate cash on hand to pay for small, last-minute purchases like lunch for you and your employees. Depending on the general price range of your merchandise and your expected turnout, you should have between $100 and $500 in cash available for change and petty cash needs. If your merchandise has change in the price tag ($8.75, for example), make sure you have rolls of coins close by.

Now that you have those two items covered, remember that you will also need things like price tags on your merchandise, the right kinds of hangers and enough of them (if you will be selling any items of clothing), gift boxes and wrapping paper, packing supplies, and shopping bags. If you are worried that you're leaving out something important, go shopping in a similar type of store and make note of all of the little details you wouldn't normally notice as a customer unless they weren't there.

Don't Forget Your Living Expenses

In trying to figure out how much cash they will need to get their companies up and running, new business owners often forget to take themselves into account. Especially if you will be giving up your primary source of income to focus on getting this business started, you must cover your family's needs as part of your start-up planning budget. If you have sufficient cash flow from your already-existing business, and that level of cash is expected to be sustainable during your expansion, you don't need to add this into your proposed funding needs.

In business plans for corporations, this expenditure falls squarely under the heading of salary. Since corporations are distinct legal entities, anyone who works for them (including owner-shareholders) gets paid a salary just like any employee of any corporation. Other business entities (sole proprietorships, partnerships, and LLCs) do not consider owners to be employees, and any money owners take out of the business for themselves is called a draw on equity (sometimes called a distribution) rather than salary expense. Since an owner's draw does not show up on the profit and loss statement, many novice entrepreneurs forget to include money for themselves when they start crunching the numbers.

The readers of your business plan, particularly lenders and investors, expect that you will need to receive cash from the business to live your life outside of work. They expect to see your personal budget requirements—even if just as a lump sum—somewhere in your cash requirements. The amount you decide on should show up on your pro forma statement of cash flows and balance sheet.

Ask for Enough Money to Work With

Contrary to what you see on television, almost no business earns enough revenue or brings in enough cash in the first few months of operations to take care of the requisite outgoing expenses. In creating your pro forma financial statements, you will have found spots where cash was tight and profits appeared only on the horizon. To fill in these gaps, you have to anticipate them—and you have to add enough funds to cover the shortfalls to the total amount of financing you are seeking for your company. Even if you have an existing company, one that's been successful enough to merit an expansion plan, you may end up with temporary cash shortfalls as you implement your new plans.

People asking for money are often afraid that they're asking for too much and that those they are approaching will balk at sums that seem extravagant. With small business financing, though, the opposite is equally critical. If you don't ask for enough money, you will throw a sizable scare into potential lenders and investors. They will notice if your request comes in lower than the figure that makes sense, based on your projections.

If you did add buffers into your projections, you can comfortably base your loan request on those results. If not, add an ample cushion to whatever number you did come up with. Chances are that you have overestimated revenues and underestimated costs and expenses; it almost never works out the other way. Realistically speaking, it is virtually impossible to foresee every impending expenditure, no matter how thoroughly you have planned. Protect yourself, and your business, by asking for more than you think you need.

Remember, it's much easier to add a buffer to your loan request now than to have to come in three months and ask for an additional loan. That underscores the flaws in your planning, and it may make the money guys nervous—not to mention that it will undermine their confidence in your company's ability to make good on its currently outstanding loan.

▶▶ TEST DRIVE

Think about the potential impact on your business as you ponder these insurance issues:

Deductibles: Will it be easier to pay a little more every month to get a lower deductible or to shell out a lump sum if an insurance event occurs?

Umbrellas: Is your industry the type where litigants will sue to the extent of your available insurance?

Timing: Do you want or need coverage to commence before your doors even open?

Which Bank Should You Go To?

When it comes to asking for huge sums of money, many novice entrepreneurs feel intimidated. Since your banker will be working with you for the long haul, it's important to choose both an institution and a loan officer with whom you feel comfortable. If you have an existing, mutually beneficial relationship with a banker (whether from an existing business, a prior professional relationship, or personal affiliation), start with him.

In other cases, you will have to do some bank shopping. Seek out an institution that has a reputation for working with new or small businesses. Ask your accountant or lawyer for a bank that he has worked with successfully in the past (especially if he does not mind facilitating an introduction). You can also ask other small business owners which banks they have had the most success with. This works particularly well at social/business functions (like local chamber of commerce events) where bankers often show up to see their clients in less formal settings.

Check out your local hometown banks. Many new entrepreneurs mistakenly assume that bigger banks offer more small business loans. In fact, smaller community banks often look to finance new local businesses that will be opening in their area, especially businesses that will create new jobs and expand their potential customer base. Plus, the loan officers in hometown banks can probably give you a lot more personal attention than a big commercial banker who has dozens of high-end clients.

Applying for a Bank Loan

The best-written business plan in the world can only help you get a bank loan if you can convince the loan officer to read it. You need to get into his head, understand what goes into his decisions, and focus your attention on getting him to focus on your plan. When securing a business loan is the primary purpose of your business plan, understanding what motivates your loan officer can be just as important as your plan itself.

Keep in mind that the loan officer's job is to make loans that he feels sure will be repaid. His career literally depends on making sound decisions when weighing loan applications just like yours. While he can't be successful if he consistently makes bad loans, he also won't succeed if he continually passes on good loans. Placing your proposal squarely in his "good loan" pile is the way to get the money you want; you do that by removing any doubts he may have about your company's ability to repay its debts.

Some Small Business Statistics

Bankers are understandably wary when it comes to making small business loans. Couple their traditional conservatism with typical small business survival rates, and you can begin to understand their cautiousness. For example, according to the SBA, approximately 572,900 small businesses were opened in 2003; an estimated 554,800 small businesses closed in that same year; and over 35,000 small business bankruptcies were filed (again, for 2003).

Those numbers may sound dire, but here's some positive data (also according to the SBA). A full two-thirds of new employer companies (meaning those with hired employees) were still in business two years after they started, and nearly half were still alive and kicking four years after opening their doors.

Knowing just what your loan officer's concerns are—and addressing them directly—can make all the difference toward securing your financing. So once you have completed your business plan, before you submit it to any loan officer for review, conduct a thorough critique using the cautious eye of a banker.

Believe it or not, the way you present yourself can add comfort for the loan officer as well. When you sit down for your interview, the way you look and how you are dressed form a strong impression. Wearing conservative attire, like a suit, will help put any banker at ease. It doesn't matter what kind of business you own. Whether your company is casual or avant-garde, whether you'll be working outdoors or with your hands, dressing like your banker does conveys a professional and trustworthy feel.

Improve Your Chances of Getting the Loan

You are already working on the number-one thing that can increase your chances of walking away with a pile of cash: creating a solid business plan. The business plan can get you through the door and convince the loan officer that your company is the one worth backing. Remember, focus your attention on preparing a brief, convincing executive summary to land your plan in the "must read" pile. In addition to writing your business plan, though, there are other things you can do to get the bankers on your side.

Putting up some of your own money is one of the best things you can do to convince a lender that you are serious about success. When you have your own investment on the line, lenders know that you, too, have a lot to lose, and that fact gives them comfort that you are really in this for the long haul. Especially for a start-up business, and even more so with a novice business owner, a heavy investment on your part (think 20 to 25 percent of necessary capital) can help you get the rest of the funding you need without having to sell off ownership interests in your company.

Another thing that can impress your banker is knowing which assets to rent, and which to buy. Assets that can actually create income, like production equipment and inventory, are looked upon more favorably when it comes to big purchases. On the other hand, buildings, furniture, and the like don't really generate sales. ▸▸ **Think twice before you make a decision to purchase real property or make a substantial investment in décor or renovations, and go with a lease whenever possible.**

Finally, asking for the right amount of money earns points in your favor. Yes, the facts and figures are all included in your business plan, but when you are face to face with the banker, you need to show that you understand how much it really takes to start a business and get it off the ground. You need to be the expert on your company. You need to know how the amount you are asking for, whether it's $20,000 or $200,000, will last until your company is bringing in sufficient money on its own. Know how much you really need, why you need it, and why it will be enough.

Types of Small Business Loans

There are three main forms of bank loans for new or expanding small businesses. Know which one you want, and why that type makes sense for your business.

First is the short-term, or bridge, loan. These loans have terms of up to one year and are typically used to supply capital for a company that needs cash to begin operations. Second are intermediate loans, which come due anywhere between one and three years. Intermediate loans are often used to help small businesses cover very large initial cash outlays and equipment purchases. These first two loan types may come with a single lump repayment (which includes principal and all the applicable interest) at the end of the term, or regular interest payments followed by a single principal payment at the end.

The third loan type, the long-term loan, usually requires installment payments over the life of the loan. Typical payback time is three to seven years. This type of loan is common for businesses with substantial start-up costs, like commercial mortgages and heavy machinery and equipment purchases.

Bankers Look for the "Three Cs"

Banks are conservative and traditional. They tend to rely on time-honored practices when it comes to such things as loaning money, especially when the person or business asking for that money does not come with a long-standing, sterling reputation.

The three Cs are part of bankers' tradition. These three pillars help them determine who will get a loan . . . and who will not:

1. Character: Bankers want to know that you are responsible and reliable, with solid ties to the community. They want reassurance that you can be counted on to pay back the loan and to stick around and work through any problems if your business suffers some setbacks.

2. Credit: To get a loan, you need to have a record of paying your debts, and that means a clean credit history. Occasional late payments are not deal-killers, but a record of skipped and tardy payments calls for a very compelling explanation.

3. Collateral: Character is subjective, and credit ratings can be quickly turned around, but collateral is here to stay—and bankers will overlook a lot of other issues if you have solid collateral to offer up. If you can put up something of significant and lasting value to back your loan, your banker will be much more likely to set a date for your closing.

Character

If you are an established member of your community, you have this "C" under control. What constitutes "established" here? Things that connote permanence and stability, like long-term home ownership, family ties, and an already-successful business endeavor. Plus, if you belong to some of the same local clubs and organizations or travel in the same social or professional circles as your banker, even better.

However, not everyone fits neatly into this compartment. Maybe you have just moved to a new community, maybe you don't own your home, maybe you are living in New York but the whole rest of your family lives in Los Angeles. While these may seem like loan-obtaining obstacles, they can be overcome with a little patience and explanation.

Just because you are new to this community does not mean you don't have long-standing ties elsewhere. Renting the same place for ten years can count for as much as owning a home. And even though your extended family lives across the country, that does not mean you don't have strong ties to the community. Let your banker know all of the things that point to your solidity and plans to stick around. Bankers are typically a reasonable bunch, and knowing the reasons that keep you in place will help ease any misgivings.

Credit

There are two sides to the credit equation when you are looking for a business loan: you (and any co-owners) and the business. You have a credit rating, and your company (if it already exists) does as well. A good credit rating—meaning an established pattern of paying back debt on time, as scheduled—can help you secure new loans. A bad credit rating can be a big drawback, but it's an obstacle that can be overcome as long as you are the one to address it.

Before you make even the first overture to any lender, know what your credit picture (and that of your existing business, if applicable) looks like. Even if you think you have nearly perfect credit, check it anyway. Mistakes happen frequently, and if you do not take steps to correct them, they will stay on your credit report, inflicting damage. Plus, your credit report from one source can look different from that of another, since not all companies report to the three main credit bureaus.

Meet the Credit Bureaus

A credit bureau, sometimes called a credit reporting agency, collects information about both consumer and business credit histories. The three main national credit bureaus in the United States are Equifax, Experian, and TransUnion, and you can easily find them on the Internet.

The agencies compile the data, fit it into cookie-cutter reports, and sell those reports to those intending to extend credit. When anyone—an individual or a business—applies for any kind of credit, from a new Visa card to a small business start-up loan, every potential lender orders at least one credit report (and usually all three). The decision whether or not to grant the loan often hinges on the information contained within the report(s).

If there is any erroneous information on any of your credit reports, contact the reporting company immediately and notify them in writing of the error. Most mistakes take at least sixty days to clear up, so the sooner you look at your credit reports (and those of your business), the better.

What if a bad credit rating is not a mistake? There are two important things to do. First, take immediate steps to start improving your record (for example, be scrupulously prompt with every payment you're scheduled to make). Second, be prepared to explain any lapses to the loan officer, how the circumstances affecting the late or skipped payments has changed, and why those past mistakes are not likely to recur. If, however, your unique credit history could present a rather large obstacle, switch your focus to providing top-notch collateral.

Collateral

When it comes to offering collateral to reassure anxious loan officers, it is important to understand the asset hierarchy. While the intrinsic value of the asset is a crucial component to its worth as collateral, its market value combined with its marketability rank even higher. Assets that steadily hold their value are considered better collateral than those that frequently fluctuate. For example, things like real estate, trucks, and production equipment make solid collateral choices. Personal assets (like jewelry, even the really expensive stuff), inventory, and marketable securities come further down on the collateral value scale. Even if they are easily salable, their potential value at the time the bank may need to sell them is very difficult to predict.

In addition to the asset itself, the lender will want reassurance that you have not already promised that same asset as collateral for another loan. If you have, spell out the terms under which that asset can be seized by the other lender, and how much money could be left after they take their share. For example, if you are putting your house up as collateral for your business loan, the lender will need to know the terms of your current mortgage and how much equity you have in that property right now.

The Extra Cs

While the three Cs already discussed are standard checkpoints for most lenders, some may also want to take a close look at one or two other Cs: cash flow and capacity. Typically, these are items applicable to an existing business that is looking for an expansion loan. However, they may also be considered when a business owner is looking to start an entirely new company unrelated to those he already has.

Even more than profitability, a banker about to lend money wants to see evidence of current and sustainable positive cash flow. In the bluntest terms, he wants to see proof that your business has been taking in more cash than it has been sending out—and that the bulk of that cash surplus is generated by ongoing business operations and not external cash infusions. As for projections, he will want comfort that the additional expenditures the company will be taking on (not the least of which will be these loan payments) can be paid from the expected rise in cash inflow provided by the expansion.

In loan lingo, capacity means having enough capability to do what you are proposing. If you are talking about a physical expansion, you must show evidence of the adequate space. If you are going after a new market segment, demonstrate that the market exists, that it has enough space for an extra player, and that you have plans to capture a portion of that market—for example, you'll take on additional sales reps, add a toll-free number, increase your delivery personnel. The bottom line is that you need to back up your expansion goals with solid, reasonable plans to prove that your lofty ideas are based in firm reality.

Getting in the Door

You finally got an interview appointment. You show up a few minutes early, in your most conservative business attire, armed with a full complement of documents. This moment is all about you—you are the crucial factor to your company's eventual success or failure. You have created the business idea and the business plan. You are the one who will get the business going, and you are the one ultimately responsible for making sure the bank gets its money back. This knowledge can be daunting, even a little scary, but keep this important fact in mind: You are the bank's customer, and they need you as much as you need them.

Here are some tips to help get you through your interview with confidence:

- Reread your plan before your meeting and keep the key points in mind.
- Answer any questions with honesty and confidence; avoid taking a defensive position.
- If you don't know the answer to a question, say so, and tell the interviewer that you will get back to him with the answer promptly.
- Ask any questions that you have.
- Don't mask your enthusiasm and innate knowledge; they can tip the scales in your favor.
- At the end of your presentation, ask for your loan; your chances of getting an immediate answer are about fifty/fifty.

Papers You Must Have with You

In addition to your business plan, there are several other documents you must bring with you to any meeting with potential lenders. Having this supporting documentation on hand should anyone ask to see it helps emphasize your reliability, foresight, and preparedness. Not having the requisite paperwork available can, on the other hand, make you seem lax in the eyes of the loan officer.

Below is a list of some commonly requested supporting documentation. Before you pack your briefcase, though, contact the bank and find out if they have a list of required paperwork. If they do, make sure to include everything they particularly request; if not, bring at least the items listed here (you can bring these to supplement their list as well).

1. Organizational documents, like incorporation papers or LLC (or partnership) agreements

2. Significant contracts with customers, suppliers, and leasing companies (for example)

3. Proof of sale, when you have purchased the company in question

4. Personal income tax returns for the last five years

5. Letters of reference, pertaining to both character and credit

6. Proof of ownership for any assets you intend to offer as collateral

Bring copies of these documents, never originals. When you will be meeting with more than one person, make sure to have enough copies for everyone.

Know Which Loan Terms You Want

Once the loan is a pretty sure thing, term negotiations may begin. There are a lot of variables that can be worked into any loan agreement, and the way they are set in the beginning will have a great impact on your business. Yes, getting the money you need is a good thing, but loan terms that will strangle your company's growth potential for years to come are not. Some key issues to put on the negotiating table include the following:

Interest rate: Interest terms come in two main varieties, variable and fixed. Make sure you know which you are signing on for, and whether the rates the banker is suggesting are in line with current norms. Start-up businesses are often subject to higher-than-average rates. Just make sure the rate is not unreasonable and does not result in a payment that your anticipated cash flow can't possibly cover.

Due dates: Do you want to go with a monthly installment plan, or pay one large lump sum two years from now? Maybe a combination will work best for your company—low periodic payments for a couple of years followed by a balloon payment. Whatever you agree to, make sure the payment schedule meshes with your cash projections.

Prepayment terms: Some loans include substantial penalties for prepayment, meaning that you pay off your loan before the ultimate due date (often the result of refinancing). Preferably, you want to be able to pay off your loan at any time, with no negative financial consequences. Look for an agreement that does not impose any charges for early payback (or at least not substantial ones).

Fees: Lenders charge all kinds of fees, such as processing, credit checks, origination, late payment charges, just to name a few. Make sure you know what types of fees are included in your loan up front, and consider them as part of the overall loan package when you compare this bank's offer with any others you receive.

Default definitions: Default usually means failure to make timely payments, but your loan agreement could include other definitions. For example, declaring bankruptcy—even if you continue to make these loan payments on time—could put you in default, as could failure to maintain minimum standards for your business, such as specific cash reserve balances or a predetermined current ratio. At the very least, ask for written notice of any default and a reasonable amount of time to correct it.

Steps to Take After Your Loan Is Approved

Once your loan has been approved, the first thing you will want to do is breath a sigh of relief, then go celebrate. When you've accomplished that, there are a few more administrative steps you will have to take to keep the momentum going.

Before you sign the loan papers, read them thoroughly, making sure you understand absolutely every word they contain. If there is any language you do not understand, consult with your lawyer, accountant, or business advisor. Ask questions, even if you ask different people the same question, until you know exactly what you are signing. If there are any errors in the paperwork (and there very well may be), ask your loan officer how that should be handled. In some cases, they will messenger over a complete new set of papers; other times they will tell you to simply cross out the mistake, write in the correction, and initial the change.

After you have gone through the loan documents with a fine-toothed comb, made any necessary changes, and signed on the line, make sure to get your paperwork in to the bank on time (yes, there will be a document deadline). That also goes for documents that are required even after the loan has closed, as sometimes there will be paperwork that cannot be finalized until after the loan closing. ▸▸ **When the bank makes a request of you (additional information, extra signatures), respond promptly to keep the good impression they have of you going.** It can only help when you apply for your next loan.

Finally, keep in touch with your loan officer. You can give him periodic progress reports, for example. After all, your lenders want your business to succeed as much as you do, and they like to be apprised of what is going on. While it's helpful to keep them informed, it's crucial to let them know about any problems right away. They can advise you on how to handle various issues that crop up, put you in touch with professional problem solvers, and work with you if your loan status may fall into question—but that is only if you tell them about any bad news before it gets out of hand, and before they hear about it some other way.

Alternate Approaches When the Answer's No

When you are asking for a business loan for a start-up or unproven company, expect to hear "No." Don't let that worry you. Lenders can be very subjective, and they each have their own particular expectations and criteria for extending loan offers. What constitutes a "no" at one institution may turn into a "yes" somewhere else, even with the exact same paperwork. Plus, a denial can turn into an acceptance from the same lender if you can make some alterations to your plans.

You can get a lot of mileage out of negative responses, even turn them around. Find out why your application was denied. That information can help you be better prepared with the next lender, or even help you modify your proposal to meet the requirements of a lender who has already turned you down. If a few different lenders have refused your request for the same reason, you will have a specific area to focus on improving before you begin the next round of applications. For example, you may need to clean up your credit rating or consider initially renting space instead of purchasing it outright.

The bottom line here is this: Don't give up. Even if you have been unsuccessful in getting the money you need up until now, or if you haven't been able to get enough money to pay for all of your company's current needs, keep trying. Start with people who have already turned you down—this is not an exercise in futility. In the first place, they may have had a change in circumstance, freeing up previously tied-up cash. Second, your circumstances may have changed. Show them how you have addressed their initial concerns and made appropriate adjustments.

Other Sources for Small Business Loans

Though they are the most common sources, there are places other than banks from which you can get a loan for your business. In addition, there are other ways to get money from the bank besides obtaining a business loan.

Depending on your overall personal financial situation, you may be able to leverage your home for some of your start-up cash. While this is not an ideal solution, it can help a small business jump that first hurdle, giving it a chance to enter the race. If you have substantial equity in your home and a secure source of steady income (not projected income from your business), you can take out a home equity loan or line of credit. These loans typically come with much longer payback terms than business loans (think thirty years compared to three), and that typically means smaller monthly payments. The big disadvantage is that your home is on the line if you can't make payments on time.

Another source of cash that is something of a double-edged sword is your personal credit cards. While they can help you get things started, the risk factor that goes along with maxed-out cards is pretty high. Plus, personal credit card interest is not tax deductible, and for cash advances the rates can be quite high. You may be thinking, "It should be a business deduction if I'm using them for business," but that's not exactly right. In fact, you are using the credit for yourself and contributing additional capital to your business. And, again, it's you—personally—who will be responsible for paying off those credit card balances.

If taking on personal debt to finance your business makes you uneasy, you are not alone. Don't despair—there are still other ways you can finance your business without having to give up ownership shares of your company.

Be Professional When Things Are Personal

Many business loans are made by friends and family members—they can be great sources of small business start-up cash. When not properly structured, though, these financial dealings can cause friction in otherwise solid relationships. The best way to avoid any potential negative fallout is to address the issues from the start, and put it all in writing.

Present your friend or family member with the same type of professional business plan you would provide a loan officer. This helps shift their focus away from the mindset of "helping you out" and plunks it squarely in the "how can I make some money here" column. This loan is a money-making endeavor for them; do not let this critical fact be overlooked.

Treat this loan as if it were from an institutional source. You can buy fill-in-the-blanks loan and note forms at stationery stores or have your lawyer draw up a more formal agreement. Negotiate reasonable terms with your lender, and make sure they are all understood clearly by both parties. In addition to the standards (like interest rate, payment dates, and the like) you may want to include the same types of covenants you would find in a bank loan, like a clear definition of what exactly constitutes default or specific descriptions of any pledged collateral.

Finally, don't take liberties with the payback plan just because you have a close personal relationship with your lender. On top of the fact that it could damage your relationship, it could also wreak havoc on your company's credit rating. Adhere to the loan terms strictly, and make your payments on time. That can help establish your company's good credit and help you secure additional financing in the future.

Consider Leasing Big-Ticket Items

Some of the biggest cash vacuums that a start-up business will face are machinery, equipment, and vehicles. These assets all typically require a large cash deposit and substantial monthly payments when they are financed by debt. Plus, only the interest portion of those payments is deductible for tax purposes, making the cash outlay even tighter. While owning assets makes your balance sheet stronger, which can help you obtain *future* loans, leasing can help you through that initial cash crunch and reduce the amount you need to borrow.

Virtually any physical asset can be leased: computer systems, delivery vans, fax machines, copiers, production equipment, tractors . . . the list goes on and on. Plus, there are some definite advantages to leasing:

- The full payment can be tax deductible.
- Your business won't be stuck holding obsolete equipment.
- It's usually easier to get approved for a lease than a loan.
- Leases require less paperwork than loans.

Keep in mind that (like a loan) the contract terms determine whether it's more beneficial for your company to lease or buy. Pay attention to the length of the lease (which usually closely corresponds to the useful life of the asset), payment requirements (which typically include one large upfront payment and then monthly payments for the remainder), return or termination policies (can you send back problematic equipment with no hassle or terminate a lease if circumstances call for that?), and purchase options (the right to buy the equipment at the end of the lease for a preset price).

For businesses struggling to raise cash and to maintain positive cash flow, leasing makes a very attractive alternative to buying. In the long run, though, leasing usually costs the company more than purchasing the same equipment would have. But without short-term solutions, your business may never make it to the long term, so consider leasing at least some of your major assets at least until you get the business off the ground.

▶▶ TEST DRIVE

Practice your presentation on friends or family before you have your face-to-face with the loan officer. Have them shoot unplanned questions at you, based on information in your business plan. Have them also ask you some chit-chatty questions designed to gauge your level of involvement in the community and personal comfort with all things financial. Ask them to ask questions from every section of the plan and to include some that require numerical answers.

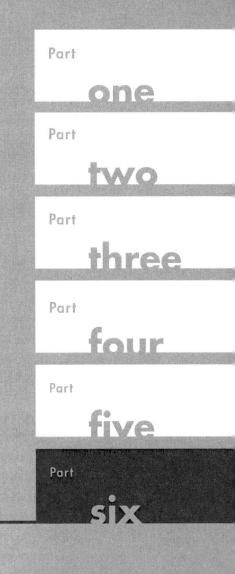

Giving Up a Piece of the Business

Equity investors actually buy a piece of your company, becoming part owners of the business. They will share in your profits when your endeavors succeed, and they suffer losses right along with you while you wait for things to turn around. Depending on your business structure, their losses could be limited to their investment in the company—this is the most common arrangement.

There are two general types of equity investors: those who supply cash and sit back to wait for the profits to roll in, and those who put up funds and expect to have a hand in the way the business is run. The first group will be considered investors for the rest of this section, while the second group will be considered co-owners.

Investors are looking for returns, just like people who buy stocks and mutual funds. They are providing your business with seed money, hoping your company will turn into a veritable money tree. But investors like to see bigger rewards when they are taking bigger risks—and a small business poses a higher risk of loss than an established mutual fund or *Fortune* 500 company stock. That mean your potential investors may be looking for the possibility of higher-than-standard returns to offset their higher-than-average risk of loss. As they read your business plan, their focus will likely be in the forecasts sections, even if your company has enjoyed profitability in the past.

Co-owners share your vision. They typically devote a lot of time to the daily functioning of the business. They expect to share in major business decisions and may even take over particular segments of the day-to-day grind. In the best cases, your company's co-owners will provide experience and skills in areas that you lack, providing talents that are complementary to yours. Make sure to choose your co-owners wisely. You will be making a long-term commitment to working with them, one that may require legal action to get out of if things don't work out quite the way you envisioned. In addition, play it safe and structure your business in a way that limits your personal liability.

Your Business Structure Affects Potential Investors

Certain business structures allow for the easy addition of other investors and owners, on top of simplicity in contributing capital to (or removing it from) your company. Others, though, can put up some roadblocks to those events. Therefore, when you consider the entity that will house your business, think about all the ways you may want to include other people down the line, either as co-owners or investors—not to mention whether or not you will be able to move money into and out of the business (and into your own pockets) with ease. Though these are not the only considerations when contemplating your business structure, they have a definite impact on the way you will interact with your company and how much room there is for growth in the future.

First, here's a brief recap of the basic business structures:

➲ Sole proprietorships are single-owner, unincorporated businesses.
➲ Partnerships are unincorporated companies owned by at least two individuals, and they come in three main varieties: general, limited, and limited liability.
➲ Corporations are fully independent business entities that can have one or more owners, though some varieties may legally limit the number of owners.
➲ Limited liability companies (LLCs) are unincorporated businesses for one or more owners that mix the rules of partnerships and corporations.

Each of these business structures comes with different rules about ownership and money movement. Plus, each can be further limited by agreements among the owners. Finally, certain structures better lend themselves to pure investors than others. If you are looking to attract investors to your company (meaning strictly investors, not co-owners), you will have to create a business entity that allows them.

Get Your Lawyer Involved at the Outset

Business relationships are complicated. While most people like to think they can focus solely on the business side of things, personalities and emotions can take over, making negotiations and contracts seem like personal confrontations. ▸▸ **Anyone who hopes to share ownership of a business with at least one other person should get an experienced small business attorney involved as soon as serious discussions begin.**

In the first place, lawyers know the law—a glaringly obvious point, but one not to be overlooked. Businesses and business structures are constrained by legalities on all sides, whether its federal, state, local, or international. Legal issues hit your company from dozens of directions, from professional licensing concerns to chemical disposal regulations to zoning laws to who can be an owner. Sure, you could try to do the legal research on your own, but you run a fairly high risk of missing some subtle facet of the law. Better to call in a professional and keep yourself covered.

Second, you and your potential co-owners may be emotional, but the lawyer won't be. He will help you wade through all the decisions that need to be made and explain what makes sense and why. He'll let you know what you can do, what you should do, what you can change later on, and what will forever be written in stone. It's much better to settle disagreements now, with a qualified professional handy, than to hash them out in court later.

Here are the most common legal issues that need to be worked out:

- How profits will be shared
- Who can sign the checks
- Who has the final decision-making power
- How decisions will be made
- What happens if one of you wants out
- What each of you could be personally liable for

Keeping It in the Family

Family businesses are everywhere you look, and for good reason. Who's better than family when it comes to sharing the hard work and the resulting profits with you? The way you involve your family in the business, though, has both tax and legal implications, so it requires some thought and planning.

The simplest way to get your family in the picture is to hire them as employees for your existing company. In addition to their salaries constituting legitimate business expenses, you will be able to see who is best suited to take over when you're ready to step down. Even if the kids never want to take over, working for you provides them with job experience and a better understanding of money than their peers may have. As for spouses, your entity choice could in part dictate their role. For example, spouses are typically considered as a single owner of a sole proprietorship when they file joint tax returns, meaning they can't really be considered salaried employees (of course, as with all things business, some exceptions may apply).

Next, you can include your family members as business co-owners. They can be partners, limited partners, LLC members, or corporate shareholders. You can maintain control of the company by means of a contract agreement or by simply holding the largest piece of the equity pie. With some forms (like corporations), it's easier to gradually shift ownership percentages and control to other family members than it is with others (like general partnerships).

To come up with the most beneficial structure for you and your family, consult a family business attorney. They'll help you sort through all the issues, from things like health-insurance coverage to estate-planning strategies.

Bringing in Business Partners

In this context, business partners are people who will both co-own and work the company together rather than the legal business structure of partnerships. These are people who will contribute as much cash, time, or sweat to the enterprise as you will. Even if they have not been involved from the outset, their purpose is to be an integral part of the business, not just an ATM.

Whether you are still in pre-opening mode or have already launched your business, choosing the right business partner involves more than you might think. First, your entity must allow for additional owners, and your co-owner of choice must not be restricted from being an owner (especially critical for S corporations). Second, your prospective partner must be able to contribute something substantial to the company, whether that's experience, capital, or time. Third, you and your business partner must go into the relationship with complete honesty, trust, and a rock-solid business ownership agreement. No matter how close you are, and no matter how well you think you know each other now, preplanned self-protection is a must.

While some business forms offer some personal liability protection from business debts, others don't. If you decide to add a co-owner to your company, don't do it casually and haphazardly. Consider the business entity under which you will house this new enterprise, even if the old one has been working well for you so far. Liability aside, true business partners (in the absence of a clear legal agreement stating otherwise) can have as much authority as you do when it comes to making and implementing major decisions, including to whom they want to sell their share of the business.

Another issue to consider is your prospective partner's personal financial situation. If that person is struggling financially, it could put a big strain on the business. Depending on your set-up, your partner may have unlimited access to the company bank account. Even with a limited liability business structure, using company funds for personal items could result in loss of personal protection for all owners of the company. It may be uncomfortable to ask about finances, but do it anyway. You will need a full set of personal financial statements and tax returns for all owners for the business plan, so use that as your excuse for asking.

Dealing with Venture Capitalists

Venture capitalists are pure investors, though some may insist upon having a say in major decisions affecting the company—especially when that company is a start-up. Basically, these guys are professional investors looking for high-growth business opportunities. They often have stockpiles of cash. Their goal is to find ways to make far higher than market returns on their investments, and they are well aware that that return boost comes with amplified risk.

To that end, venture capitalists are looking for growth–specifically, the promise of significant growth. They usually won't be tempted by companies

How Marc Berger Lost a Lot of Money

Marc Berger was a self-employed electrical contractor. His business was growing steadily each year, and customers often called him to ask for referrals to other tradesmen. He realized that with an in-house plumber, he could make some money from those referrals. So he called his friend, Carl Hamden, and asked if he was interested in going into business together.

Carl and Marc had known each other since high school and had been referring customers back and forth for years. They shook hands, got a tax ID number, opened a joint bank account, and got their new business underway. In the absence of any formal arrangement, their enterprise took the form of a general partnership.

For quite some time, everything sailed along smoothly. Then Carl bought a new van without consulting Marc. Marc was upset, but Carl persuaded him that it was a necessary business decision. A few months later, Marc noticed construction costs on their financial statements. When he asked, Carl said he was putting an addition on his house for an office and storage area for the business. As Marc looked closer at the books, he saw that Carl had been spending a lot of the company's money on things that seemed to benefit him personally more than they did the company. Worse, the company was clearly running out of cash but was piling up bills that needed to be paid.

Collection agencies began calling, but the company didn't have enough money to settle its debts. So the creditors began to look at Marc and Carl. Carl had tons of debt, and negative net worth. Marc had some debt, but he also had a healthy pile of savings and a solid retirement fund. The creditors went where the money was—Marc's personal holdings. Since he was a general partner, he was held personally liable for all the debts of the company.

that are projecting solid, stable, slow-paced growth. They want to get in on the ground floor of businesses that will soar like shooting stars. If your company doesn't meet their growth expectations (and we're talking tens of millions of dollars in sales here), it won't even make it to the consideration pile. If you do fit their profile, get ready to make a lot of money, pretty fast.

What Else Venture Capitalists Can Provide

Since venture capitalists are looking for stellar returns for their extremely sizable investments, they are more than willing to pitch in—in fact, many times they demand it. In addition to supplying wads of cash, venture capitalists also do the following:

⮑ Assist in the business planning stages
⮑ Add inside knowledge of the industry
⮑ Take part in making major decisions
⮑ Guide the business through inception and growth phases
⮑ Oversee contracts and other agreements
⮑ Help companies go public

Where to Find Them

Most venture capitalists specialize in particular industries and specific phases of business development (for example, software design firms on the verge of an initial public offering). As you begin your search to find these sources of funding, look for those whose target customer profiles match your business, both what it does and its current development stage.

You can start your search for a venture capitalist on the Internet, unless you know people who have contacts with these financiers. Some reputable Web sites include vFinance Investments, Inc. *(www.vfinance .com)*, Venture One *(www.ventureone.com)*, and VC Experts *(www .vcexperts.com)*.

Once you've found some good matches, you will set off to woo them. To even get an initial meeting, your prepresentation must stand out and lure them to the table. Once you have them face to face, you will have to impress them—and it takes a lot to impress them. What gets them to come to the party? The promise of substantial swift growth (along the lines of $25 million in projected revenues within five years) that carries sizable gross profit margins.

Other Types of Investors

If giving up some control of your company in exchange for capital doesn't fit into your plans, consider different types of investors, such as these:

Angel investors provide funding to start-ups and infant companies without wresting control. They will, however, provide advice and guidance when asked, and they may increase their level of involvement depending on your needs.

Strategic partners are really other companies with which your business will form a joint venture. In these cases, an established company looking to expand its in-house roster brings a newer, smaller company under its umbrella.

Private placements are one step shy of going public. Stock in your corporation is offered to specific, unrelated individuals as pure investments. These transactions are legally tricky, and they require a high degree of sophistication from all involved parties. If you go this route, use an eminently qualified and experienced attorney.

Public shareholders are members of the general public who each buy relatively small portions of shares in a corporation. With this money-raising method, your company gets a little capital from a lot of people, and power and control can remain concentrated in your hands. There are many legalities involved here, both at state and federal levels, so proceed with caution.

Think Twice Before Going Public

Offering shares of your business to the general public can be a huge and quite complex undertaking; however, it can be the easiest way to allow complete strangers to invest their money in your company. The first rule of going public is to get a competent, experienced attorney to handle all of your paperwork. This is serious business, and the law is the worst possible place to cut corners.

If in raising money for your company you intend to sell shares of stock or other interests (like limited partnership interests) that constitute securities in the eyes of the law, there are certain very strict rules you have to follow. These rules do not apply only to corporate giants, whose shares trade on the major stock exchanges; both federal and state laws can apply to small companies as well. Luckily, though, there are a lot of exemptions designed to help smaller companies, and yours just might fit through one of those loopholes.

These laws exist to protect investors. Unfortunately, they can prove prohibitive for small companies. Federal law requires registration with the Securities and Exchange Commission (SEC), which can be extremely complicated and costly. State laws can vary widely, and companies must know the rules in every state in which their securities will be offered—again, a time-consuming and costly process. That brings us back to the exemptions, one of which probably covers your small business, at least for federal registration purposes. Whether your business will be exempted from state filings depends on the rules of the applicable states.

Many of the available exemptions depend on the legal classification of your investors as either accredited or unaccredited. Accredited investors are described as individuals (or married couples) with net worth of over $1 million, people who earned income greater than $200,000 (or greater than $300,000 for a married couple) for each of the past two years and who will likely earn as much this year, or any business entity (including trusts and charities) that wasn't formed just to invest in the securities and that has total assets exceeding $5 million. Virtually everyone else is an unaccredited investor.

▶▶ TEST DRIVE

Deciding now on the right type of equity investor can save you a lot of headaches down the road. Take this personal style quiz to figure out if you want co-owners or silent partners:

1. Do you prefer to bounce ideas off of someone else or charge right in on your own?

2. Do you make major decisions quickly, or ponder them for days?

3. Do you prefer solo sports or to play on teams?

4. If you play on teams, do you have to be the leader?

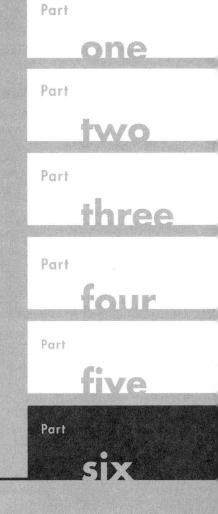

Meet the Small Business Administration

ince it first opened its doors on July 30, 1953, the U.S. Small Business Administration (SBA) has done quite a lot to promote the growth of small business in America. During its first fifty years, it provided nearly 20 million loans and other means of assistance to small businesses throughout the country.

Since its inception, the SBA has delivered over $30 billion to small business owners to finance their start-ups and their continued growth. In the ten-year period covering 1991 to 2000, the agency helped fund nearly 435,000 companies by facilitating almost $95 billion in loans. And in 2001, the SBA helped small business secure over $12.3 billion plus gave them access to at least $40 billion of federal government contracts. No other lender in the nation has done as much for entrepreneurs—especially when it comes to financing—than the SBA.

Fast forward to 2005. For that year, the SBA was authorized to offer over $21 billion in loans to American small businesses through its two main loan programs. That legislation (passed in December 2004) set the agency up with a substantial budget for 2005, nearly $600 billion, and the requisite authorizations to keep all of its programs running.

Small Business Is Big

While the big name corporations on the Fortune 500 are the ones you hear about on the news, it's really the small business that keeps America moving. Part of that is due to their massive numbers: As of 2002 (the latest year of SBA-published statistics), there were nearly 23 million small businesses in the United States. Those businesses supplied about 75 percent of the new jobs added to the American economy, representing over 99 percent of the country's total employers. Small businesses add to our national culture in other ways as well. For example, they hire a much larger percentage of older workers and part-time employees than big companies do.

What the SBA Really Does

The SBA exists to make sure cash flows to small businesses. To reach that end, the agency has a wide variety of programs available to ease the path for small companies that might not otherwise be able to get loans. The SBA works with banks and some other types of lending institutions (like credit unions, for example) to make sure small businesses have access to loans and other means of financing.

Essentially, the SBA guarantees loans made to small businesses; the money itself comes from traditional lending institutions. But the SBA's help doesn't stop when the check is signed over. The agency also provides support and professional development activities for entrepreneurs. They offer advice, training, counseling, and even help prepare business plans. Plus, they can help your small business secure lucrative government contracts. The SBA is there to help your small business come into being, survive, succeed, and grow so big that it won't count as small anymore.

$69 Billion in Contracts

According to an SBA press release of August 25, 2005, American small businesses received a whopping $69.23 billion in federal government contracts for fiscal year 2004. That's nearly 25 percent of all federal prime contracts (which came in at a total of almost $300 billion for private sector companies of all sizes). This is more contract money than small businesses have ever received before from the federal government, and the SBA is confident that the numbers will continue to grow. In fact, SBA Administrator Hector V. Barreto believes that the federal government "still has room to improve in allowing small business to compete for additional contracting dollars."

What Counts as a Small Business?

The exact definition of just what constitutes a small business changes periodically, and it may differ by industry. The SBA, on their Web site at *www.sba.gov*, publishes specific information regarding the criteria that must be met for each of its loan programs. However, there are some simple basic standards that your company has to meet to qualify.

First, your business has to be just that: an enterprise organized for the purpose of earning profits. Second, the company must have an established place of business within the United States. Third, the business must in some way contribute significantly to the U.S. economy, which is easier to achieve than it sounds; contribution methods include things like paying taxes, using American-made products, and hiring American citizens. Finally, the company cannot exceed the stated size standard for its industry.

While there is a distinct SBA size standard for every single NAICS industry sector, the SBA also has its own more generalized guidelines for industry categories. The size standard for each is the absolute largest a company can be and still qualify as a small business for SBA loan program purposes. The size can be expressed either by number of employees or by average annual receipts (which means gross sales).

Here are some size standard examples, taken directly from the SBA Web site.

Some SBA Size Standards

Industry Group	Size Standard
Manufacturing	$6 million
Retail trade	Precise
Wholesale trade	100 employees
Architectural services	$4 million

An Overview of SBA Programs

The SBA offers a lot of different ways for small businesses to get the funds they need. Their specialty is in helping companies that would not otherwise qualify for financing, and they do this by guaranteeing loans made by banks and other private lenders. That means the bank lends you money, you promise to pay it back, and the SBA guarantees that in the event you default, the bank will still get the lion's share of its money. When the bank has less money on the line, less risk, they can be more willing to loosen their guidelines and take more chances on yet-to-be-proven businesses.

Here are some of the general guidelines. There is no limit on the amount of your loan, but there is a limit on the guaranteed portion—that varies by SBA loan program, though the overall maximum is $750,000. The longest available loan term is twenty-five years, and most loans run shorter than that. Interest rates are completely at the discretion of the lender. And the biggest rule of all is that you have to really need the money, meaning you can't get an SBA loan if you have your own (or business) resources available.

Though there are around a dozen general programs small businesses can turn to, the SBA gets the most mileage out of the three most popular forms: their standard 7(a) loan program (guarantees for most small businesses); the 504 loan program (for fixed asset purchases); and the 7(m) Microloan program (for very small loans).

Some of the more focused loan programs include the following:

CAPLines, a bridging-the-gap type program that helps small businesses meet short-term working capital needs.

Export Working Capital (EWCP) Program, which offers short-term solutions with very quick turnaround times to exporters.

Community Express, a pilot program that targets particular "underserved" geographical areas that are just being developed as new markets.

LowDoc, which falls into the 7(a) category, is to provide loans under $150,000 for up to ten years (twenty-five years for asset purchases) with minimal paperwork and thirty-six-hour SBA turnaround time.

SBA Express, another member of the 7(a) family, is similar to LowDoc but with loans up to $350,000 for up to seven years.

Prequalification allows potential borrowers to have their loan packets analyzed and "green-lighted" by the SBA before they take them to the lender.

SBA Loan Guarantees

The SBA backs small business loans made by qualified lenders. They supply loan guarantees to those lenders to eliminate some of the risk they would otherwise face, namely not getting their money back on time (or at all). Although the lenders provide the cash, the SBA sets the guidelines and requirements according to its current federal government mandate. In other words, the rules are subject to change based on new legislation, so ▸▸ **make sure you have the most up-to-date guidelines in hand before you get started in seeking an SBA-backed loan** (you can get current information at *www.sba.gov*).

Under this umbrella, the SBA administers several distinct loan programs, the most commonly used of which is the basic 7(a) loan guaranty. Section 7(a) loans include a world of variations, all with a single unifying theme: they help provide substantial loans to small businesses, including start-ups, with virtually no restrictions on how the proceeds will be used. The SBA's other major program, 504 loans, apply only to money being spent on substantial fixed asset purchases.

To help speed up the process for 7(a) loans, the SBA implemented two quick-fix programs to streamline the flow from lenders to small businesses. These fast-track loan guarantees come into play after the lender has seen that the borrower meets his requirements; it's the SBA guarantee that comes more quickly. For their LowDoc program, the borrow and lender each complete one-page SBA applications, send it in, and can expect a response within thirty-six hours. SBAExpress also speeds up the process for lenders who already have proven SBA track records, though this type comes with some added restrictions on eligibility.

The Basic 7(a) Loan Program

The 7(a) loan is the most commonly used SBA program. Most American banks (and some nonbank lenders) participate in this program along with the agency. The program essentially expands the availability of funds to American small businesses. Each loan is partially guaranteed under SBA program guidelines; that means that the agency shares the risk of loss with the lender if the loan cannot be repaid. Why is this important? Because small businesses, especially start-ups, are risky endeavors for banks, and those who need the money the most often come with the highest default risk. If not for the SBA guaranty program, banks might not be as willing to lend to small businesses, at least not without charging them very high interest rates and subjecting them to very high adherence standards.

This is the SBA's most flexible loan program. The proceeds can be used for most reasonable business purposes, such as working capital, asset purchases, leasehold improvements, and even debt refinancing in some cases. Working-capital type loans usually come with seven-year payback terms (though the maximum is ten years), and those to purchase fixed assets (or refinancing original business acquisition debt) can go for up to twenty-five years. There is one term exception. When the proceeds will be used for construction or significant renovation, the twenty-five year clock doesn't start until construction is completed.

Getting back to loan proceeds, the maximum loan amount (as of December 8, 2004) is $2 million, which comes with maximum SBA exposure of $1.5 million. For lesser amounts, the SBA will guarantee up to 75 percent of the proceeds; and for loans that are for $150,000 or less, the SBA may guarantee up to 85 percent of the proceeds. The percentage exception (and, of course, there is one) is for SBAExpress loans, which are subject to a 50-percent guaranty. When it comes to interest rates, those are typically negotiated between you and your lender; however, they are subject to the stated SBA maximum rates, which are tied to the prime rate. Your rate can be either fixed or variable, and the ultimate rate may depend on both the size of the loan and its payback term.

The Section 504 Loan Program

Section 504 loans come through only SBA-approved companies known as certified development companies (CDCs). The purpose of a CDC is to play a part in the economic development of a region. CDCs, which are not-for-profit private corporations, provide capital for small businesses, but only when the proceeds will be used to invest in fixed assets like land, buildings, and large machinery and equipment. In addition, most of these loans come with the caveat that at least one job must be created (or not eliminated) for each $50,000 spent on the project.

Though these loans are mostly used for small or medium-sized business expansion, there are some instances in which they would be appropriate for start-up companies. For example, when a property ownership (as opposed to leasing) makes more sense financially for a particular start-up company, the 504 program could be tapped into.

As with all SBA-backed loans, these come with set parameters. The loans can come in a wide range of sizes, typically from $500,000 to the cap of $4 million, but the average project cost comes in at about $1 million. (The total project size can be greater than $4 million, but that is the maximum for CDC funding.) These loans are all long-term, with a maximum life of twenty-five years, and they come with fixed interest rates.

What You Have to Do

The SBA is not in the business of just giving money away or guaranteeing loans it does not believe have a chance of being paid back. While the agency may make it easier for untested businesses to obtain loans, there are still a lot of hoops to jump through to qualify—not the least of which is a thorough, solid business plan.

In addition, as with any loan, you will have to demonstrate clearly your expected ability to be able to repay the loan as scheduled. The agency will look at your personal credit history, that of any co-owners, and that of your existing business (where applicable); they want to see that you have been willing and able to pay back debts in the past. They also prefer to see that you have a substantial (for you) stake in the business, and a vested interest in seeing it succeed.

Bottom line: ▸▸ **you have to do at least as much work to get an SBA-backed loan as you do to get one without their assistance.** The main difference is their added willingness to take a chance on your eventual success, but you still have to prove that the potential is there.

The SBA Microloan Program

Does your business need just a little money to get going? Consider an SBA Microloan. The maximum borrowing here is $35,000, and it's available to essentially any small business, including start-ups. These loans work a little differently than the standard guaranty loans. With this program, the SBA makes funds available to lenders (called intermediaries) who then make the loans directly to the small business owners. The loans, however, are not guaranteed by the SBA.

However, some basic SBA guidelines do apply here. For example, the maximum loan term is six years. That timeline does vary, based on a number of factors including the actual loan size, what the funds are expected to be used for, the lender's own guidelines, and the situation of the borrower. Plus, there are also some no-nos when it comes to how you will use the proceeds. For instance, you cannot use them to pay off existing debts or to buy real estate. Other than those use restrictions, you can use the cash for either working capital (meaning to cover everyday expenses) or to purchase things like inventory, supplies, or office furniture—basically anything you need to get or keep your business running.

Even though these loans are considered to be quite small, business owners will still be required to offer up some personal reassurances. For example, many lenders still require the entrepreneur to offer up collateral. Some will even ask the owner(s) to sign a personal guarantee before the bank will hand over the loan proceeds. Plus, MicroLoan applicants may be compelled to receive business-based training or fulfill some specific planning requirements before their loan applications are even considered.

Other SBA Plans

In addition to their general small business loans, the SBA also provides a number of more focused and specialized loan programs. In some cases, these are short-term solutions meant to get your company through a crunch time. In others, the focus falls on attracting new businesses into previously untapped areas.

Squarely in the short-term column comes the CAPLines program, whose primary purpose is to carry existing small businesses through foreseen working capital shortfalls. CAPLines come in five basic flavors, and all but one of them comes with an unlimited cash supply. That one is the Small Asset-Based Line, which is a revolving line of credit with a $200,000 limit. The other CAPLines include the following:

➲ The Standard Asset-Based Line, also a revolving line but with no preset cap; mainly for companies that don't quite hit the standards necessary for obtaining long-term credit.

→ The Seasonal Line, which serves as a cash advance against expected inventory surges and accounts receivable lags.

→ The Contract Line, designed to help small companies finance labor and material costs connected with satisfying existing contracts.

→ The Builder's Line, created specifically to help small contractors and builders complete either commercial or residential projects.

EWCP loans also fill the short-term needs of small businesses, but these loans are only for companies involved in exporting products outside the United States. Sometimes exporters have quick, urgent short-term working capital shortfalls, and this loan program keeps things moving along. Very quickly, too—these loans (provided in a joint effort by the SBA and the Export-Import Bank) require only a single-page application, and they turn around in ten days or less.

Community Express loans exist as part of a pilot program developed by the SBA in conjunction with a parent organization called the National Community Reinvestment Coalition (NCRC). The lenders involved with the program are handpicked by the NCRC, and the loans are only available to businesses starting up in special geographic areas—"traditionally under-served new markets," according to the SBA literature. To find out if your company's location will qualify, surf over to the SBA's Web site at *www.sba.gov.*

Funding Options Closer to Home

Federal agencies are not the only ones that want small businesses to develop, catch on, and take off. Local economies often need the boost of new companies to keep things growing. To that end, most states and many smaller government entities (cities, towns, municipalities, counties) support small business with myriad funding programs to stimulate the home base.

Virtually all states maintain some sort of economic development office that can make funds available to small businesses, whether they offer the money directly or guarantee bank loans in a manner similar to the SBA.

Some offer a type of mix-and-match, where the state government works together with local lenders and provide funding from both sides, allowing small businesses to get every dollar they need to get up and running. Often, the state portion gets folded into the bank loan, allowing the government to deliver much needed funding without the budget-killing administrative expenses that go with processing the loan over its life.

With smaller levels and local agencies, your timing can make all the difference. They typically have less money to offer, more of the miniloan level, and many fledgling companies clamoring for the resources. For this reason, contact your local agencies right away . . . even if you are not yet sure if you will need financing, or how much. Even if funds are not available right now, your company will already be on the list when money does become available. Plus, local municipalities build these pre-requests into their forward budgets. If they get a lot of requests, more than expected, they will build that addition into next year's budget.

One final source of local financing can come from learning institutions such as universities or trade schools. Often, this financing takes the form of a grant, meaning it may not have to be paid back. What's the trade off? The institution may ask you to employ students as interns or apprentices, speak at school functions, or it may even make your business a case study to help future entrepreneurs.

▶▶ TEST DRIVE

Imagine you are a small clothing importer, in a sticky cash flow situation, and you've decided to turn to the government for a loan to tide your company over. The company brings in designer clothing from Paris and sells it to exclusive boutiques throughout the United States. You must pay the French designers before they will ship the clothing, and the boutiques pay you thirty days after they receive the merchandise. Which types of loans could you qualify for? Which would best fit the situation?

APPENDIXES

Appendix One
Glossary

accounting period
A specified time period used to match corresponding revenues and expenses for the purposes of financial measurement.

accounts payable (A/P)
The amount a company owes for credit purchases in the normal course of business.

accounts receivable (A/R)
The amount owed to a company for sales made on a credit basis.

accrual basis accounting
A system of accounting in which expenses are recorded as they are incurred, and revenues are recorded as they are earned, regardless of whether money has yet changed hands.

angel investors
Business financiers known for making investments in start-up companies without wresting control from the owners.

articles of incorporation
A set of formal documents that must be filed in the state where your corporation will be established.

asset
Anything of value owned by a company.

authorized shares
The total number of stock shares allowed to be issued by a corporation, as determined by its founders. For example, if in the original formation papers 5,000 shares are authorized, no more than that may be issued without a formal amendment to the articles of incorporation.

balance sheet
A financial statement detailing the financial position of a company on a particular date. The statement lays out the company's total assets, liabilities, and equity.

board of directors
The governing body of a corporation, the members of which are legally responsible for the corporation.

break-even analysis
A mathematical formula used to determine the total sales (in either dollars or units) necessary for a company to cover its fixed expenses over a specified time period.

capital

Money (and other assets) invested in a business.

cash basis accounting

A system of accounting in which transactions are recorded only when money changes hands.

cash sales

Sales made to a customer in exchange for immediate payment in any form, including money, checks, and credit cards.

cash collections

Money received from customers in payment of sales made during a prior period.

collateral

Assets promised to lenders to guarantee repayment of a loan if scheduled payments are not made.

cost of sales

The complete purchase price of merchandise that is resold to customers.

dba

The acronym for "doing business as," used when a company has both a trade name and a legal name (for example, Joe Smith Corporation dba Joe's Pet Supplies).

debt financing

Funds raised by borrowing which must be paid back, as with a bank loan.

depreciation

An estimate of the inherent loss of value of assets over time, measured for accounting or tax purposes.

disbursement

Money paid out by the company.

distributor

A middleman, either business or individual, that facilitates the sale of merchandise from manufacturers to retailers.

equity

Ownership interest in an asset or a business.

equity financing

Funds raised by selling ownership interests in a company.

expense

Deductible expenditures made in the normal course of business. Examples include rent, insurance, and utilities.

fixed costs

Expenses that are incurred regardless of sales and that typically remain relatively stable over time; also called overhead.

gross margin
Sales less the cost of sales.

inventory
All of the goods a business holds for production (which could include raw materials and work in process) or resale, which may be expressed in both units and dollars.

liability
Any debt incurred by a business, typically divided into long-term and short-term for accounting purposes.

net cash flow
The money left after all the cash disbursements for a specific period are deducted from the cash receipts of the same period.

net profit
The excess of revenues over costs and expenses for a specified time period.

operating expenses
Expenditures incurred in the normal course of business, unrelated to direct product costs.

owner's draw
Payments distributed to business owners (except owners of corporations) instead of salary.

partnership
An unincorporated business legally owned by two or more individuals.

prepaid expenses
An asset consisting of payments made in advance for goods or services to be received in future periods.

prime rate
The interest charged on loans made by banks to their best, biggest, most reliable business customers.

retained earnings
Earnings that are kept inside the company and reinvested in it, rather than distributed to its owners.

secured loans
Debt obligations obtained by pledging specific collateral, which can be sold by the lender if the debt is not repaid as contracted.

sole proprietorship
An unincorporated business owned by one person.

unsecured loans
Debt obligations obtained without any collateral to back them up.

working capital
Funds available to cover the ongoing operating expenses of a company.

Appendix Two
The Elements of a Business Plan

The following is a list of elements that might be included in a business plan. Your own plan will vary from this, depending on what type of business you have, how formal your plan needs to be, how much information you have available, and other factors.

For two samples of complete business plans (which roughly follow the outline below), see the CD-ROM that accompanies this book.

1. Title Page

2. Confidentiality Agreement—includes a place for signing an agreement to keep details confidential; may include instructions on how to handle the copy of the business plan (who to return it to, etc.).

3. Table of Contents

4. Executive Summary—a brief definition of the company, highlighting key points about its market, its plans and objectives, and its strengths.

5. Company Summary—a more detailed explanation of the company's structure and its financial makeup.

6. Services and Products—a description of what the company provides or makes.

7. Market Analysis Summary—a description of the market for the company's products or services, including an analysis of its competitors, its customers, and relevant local and national trends.

8. Strategy Summary—this may include a SWOT analysis and a description of sales and marketing strategies and forecasts.

9. Management Summary—information about the company's partners and management structure, as well as any other current or future personnel.

10. Financial Plan—an analysis of the company's financial picture; this may include documents such as a break-even analysis, a profit and loss statement, a cash flow statement, and a balance sheet.

Appendix Three
Worksheets

Attachments Checklist

If you have existing legal documents or agreements in place, be sure to include them in your business plan. You may also include important items that pertain to your business but are too lengthy to fit in the body of your business plan, such as a customer listing. Peruse the list below, and include any paperwork that applies to your company.

- ☐ Lease agreements
- ☐ Key employee contracts
- ☐ Principal suppliers listing (include name, terms, average annual volume)
- ☐ Major customers (include name, average annual purchases, standing orders)
- ☐ Insurance roster (carriers, policy types, coverage)
- ☐ Maintenance contracts
- ☐ Prior year's annual report
- ☐ Recent publicity clippings
- ☐ Organization papers
- ☐ Site map or location floor plan

Assumptions Worksheet

Plan Name: _____
(the name that will appear as a heading on each page)

Start Month and Year: _____
(the starting month and year of your plan, typically either the launch
date or the beginning of the fiscal year)

Plan Years: _____
(the number of years covered by your business plan and your pro
forma financial statements, typically two or three years)

General Assumptions: _____
(*note:* in the below entries, A/R stands for "accounts receivable"
and A/P stands for "accounts payable")

Cost of sales % _____
Sales commissions % _____
Credit sales % _____
Days of A/R credit _____
Credit purchases % _____
Days of A/P credit _____
Days of inventory _____
Short-term interest rate _____
Long-term interest rate _____
Payroll tax rate _____
Income tax rate _____

Start-Up Expense Worksheet

Common Start-Up Expenses: _____

Legal fees _____
Business cards and stationery _____
Promotional materials _____
Accounting fees _____
Marketing consultant _____
Insurance _____
Rent _____
Other professional fees _____
Entity creation _____
Business licenses _____
Research and development _____
Web-site design _____
Other _____

Total Start-Up Expenses: _____

Start-Up Assets: _____
Immediate cash needs _____
Starting inventory _____
Computer hardware and software _____
Office equipment _____
Office furnishings _____
Other short-term assets _____
Machinery and equipment _____
Vehicles _____
Other long-term assets _____

Total Assets: _____

Total Start-Up Needs: _____
Start-Up Financing

Owner capital contributions: _____

Other investors: _____

Total equity investment: _____

Liabilities:

Short-term loans: _____

Unpaid expenses: _____

Credit cards: _____

Interest-free short-term loans: _____

Long-term loans: _____

Total liabilities: _____

Total Funding: _____

Sales Forecast Worksheet

List each product or service your company sells. Next to each, write down the price you expect to sell that product or service for (the amount your customer will pay).

Product/ Service Name	Unit Price	Cost of Sales %	Expected Unit Sales		
			Year 1	Year 2	Year 3

Index

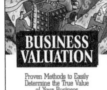

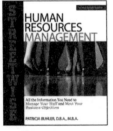

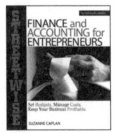

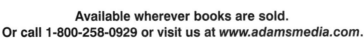

Streetwise® Managing a Nonprofit
John Riddle
$19.95; ISBN 10: 1-58062-698-X

Streetwise® Managing People
Bob Adams, et al.
$19.95; ISBN 10: 1-55850-726-4

Streetwise® Marketing Plan
Don Debelak
$19.95; ISBN 10: 1-58062-268-2

**Streetwise® Maximize
Web Site Traffic**
Nobles and O'Neil
$19.95; ISBN 10: 1-58062-369-7

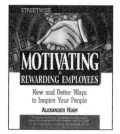

**Streetwise® Motivating
& Rewarding Employees**
Alexander Hiam
$19.95; ISBN 10: 1-58062-130-9

**Streetwise® Project
Management**
Michael Dobson
$19.95; ISBN 10: 1-58062-770-6

**Streetwise® Restaurant
Management**
John James & Dan Baldwin
$19.95; ISBN 10: 1-58062-781-1

**Streetwise® Sales Letters
with CD**
Reynard and Weiss
$29.95; ISBN 10: 1-58062-440-5

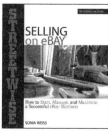

Streetwise® Selling on eBay®
Sonia Weiss
$19.95; ISBN 10: 1-59337-610-3

**Streetwise®
Small Business Book of Lists**
Edited by Gene Marks
$19.95; ISBN 10: 1-59337-684-7

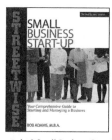

Streetwise® Small Business Start-Up
Bob Adams
$19.95; ISBN 10: 1-55850-581-4

**Streetwise® Start Your Own
Business Workbook**
Gina Marie Mangiamele
$9.95; ISBN 10: 1-58062-506-1

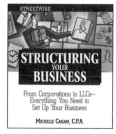

Streetwise® Structuring Your Business
Michele Cagan
$19.95; ISBN 10: 1-59337-177-2

Streetwise® Time Management
Marshall Cook
$19.95; ISBN 10: 1-58062-131-7

Software License Agreement

YOU SHOULD CAREFULLY READ THE FOLLOWING TERMS AND CONDITIONS BEFORE USING THIS SOFTWARE PRODUCT. INSTALLING AND USING THIS PRODUCT INDICATES YOUR ACCEPTANCE OF THESE CONDITIONS. IF YOU DO NOT AGREE WITH THESE TERMS AND CONDITIONS, DO NOT INSTALL THE SOFTWARE AND RETURN THIS PACKAGE PROMPTLY FOR A FULL REFUND.

1. Grant of License
This software package is protected under United States copyright law and international treaty. You are hereby entitled to one copy of the enclosed software and are allowed by law to make one backup copy or to copy the contents of the disks onto a single hard disk and keep the originals as your backup or archival copy. United States copyright law prohibits you from making a copy of this software for use on any computer other than your own computer. United States copyright law also prohibits you from copying any written material included in this software package without first obtaining the permission of F+W Publications, Inc.

2. Restrictions
You, the end-user, are hereby prohibited from the following:
You may not rent or lease the Software or make copies to rent or lease for profit or for any other purpose.
You may not disassemble or reverse compile for the purposes of reverse engineering the Software.
You may not modify or adapt the Software or documentation in whole or in part, including, but not limited to, translating or creating derivative works.

3. Transfer
You may transfer the Software to another person, provided that (a) you transfer all of the Software and documentation to the same transferee; (b) you do not retain any copies; and (c) the transferee is informed of and agrees to the terms and conditions of this Agreement.

4. Termination
This Agreement and your license to use the Software can be terminated without notice if you fail to comply with any of the provisions set forth in this Agreement. Upon termination of this Agreement, you promise to destroy all copies of the software including backup or archival copies as well as any documentation associated with the Software. All disclaimers of warranties and limitation of liability set forth in this Agreement shall survive any termination of this Agreement.

5. Limited Warranty
F+W Publications, Inc. warrants that the Software will perform according to the manual and other written materials accompanying the Software for a period of 30 days from the date of receipt. F+W Publications, Inc. does not accept responsibility for any malfunctioning computer hardware or any incompatibilities with existing or new computer hardware technology.

6. Customer Remedies
F+W Publications, Inc.'s entire liability and your exclusive remedy shall be, at the option of F+W Publications, Inc., either refund of your purchase price or repair and/or replacement of Software that does not meet this Limited Warranty. Proof of purchase shall be required. This Limited Warranty will be voided if Software failure was caused by abuse, neglect, accident, or misapplication. All replacement Software will be warranted based on the remainder of the warranty or the full 30 days, whichever is shorter, and will be subject to the terms of the Agreement.

7. No Other Warranties
F+W PUBLICATIONS, INC., TO THE FULLEST EXTENT OF THE LAW, DISCLAIMS ALL OTHER WARRANTIES, OTHER THAN THE LIMITED WARRANTY IN PARAGRAPH 5, EITHER EXPRESS OR IMPLIED, ASSOCIATED WITH ITS SOFTWARE, INCLUDING BUT NOT LIMITED TO IMPLIED WARRANTIES OF MERCHANTABILITY AND FITNESS FOR A PARTICULAR PURPOSE, WITH REGARD TO THE SOFTWARE AND ITS ACCOMPANYING WRITTEN MATERIALS. THIS LIMITED WARRANTY GIVES YOU SPECIFIC LEGAL RIGHTS. DEPENDING UPON WHERE THIS SOFTWARE WAS PURCHASED, YOU MAY HAVE OTHER RIGHTS.

8. Limitations on Remedies
TO THE MAXIMUM EXTENT PERMITTED BY LAW, F+W PUBLICATIONS, INC. SHALL NOT BE HELD LIABLE FOR ANY DAMAGES WHATSOEVER, INCLUDING WITHOUT LIMITATION, ANY LOSS FROM PERSONAL INJURY, LOSS OF BUSINESS PROFITS, BUSINESS INTERRUPTION, BUSINESS INFORMATION, OR ANY OTHER PECUNIARY LOSS ARISING OUT OF THE USE OF THIS SOFTWARE.
This applies even if F+W Publications, Inc. has been advised of the possibility of such damages. F+W Publications, Inc.'s entire liability under any provision of this agreement shall be limited to the amount actually paid by you for the Software. Because some states may not allow for this type of limitation of liability, the above limitation may not apply to you.
THE WARRANTY AND REMEDIES SET FORTH ABOVE ARE EXCLUSIVE AND IN LIEU OF ALL OTHERS, ORAL OR WRITTEN, EXPRESS OR IMPLIED. No F+W Publications, Inc. dealer, distributor, agent, or employee is authorized to make any modification or addition to the warranty.

9. General
This Agreement shall be governed by the laws of the United States of America and the Commonwealth of Massachusetts. If you have any questions concerning this Agreement, contact F+W Publications, Inc., via Adams Media at 508-427-7100. Or write to us at: Adams Media, an F+W Publications Company, 57 Littlefield Street, Avon, MA 02322.